with Victims of Violence

GOOD PRACTICE SERIES
Good Practice in Social Work
Series Editor: Jacki Pritchard
This series explores topics of current concern to professionals working in social work, health care and the probation service. Contributors are drawn from a wide variety of settings, in both the voluntary and statutory sectors. The editor, Jacki Pritchard, has worked as a practitioner and manager in both fieldwork and hospital settings. She is also an accredited practice teacher and is currently working as a trainer, consultant and researcher focusing on abuse, risk and violence. She is also Co-Chair of the national organisation PAVA (Practitioner Alliance Against Abuse of Vulnerable Adults).

GOOD PRACTICE IN CHILD PROTECTION
A MANUAL FOR PROFESSIONALS
Edited by Hilary Owen and Jacki Pritchard
ISBN 1 85302 205 5

GOOD PRACTICE IN SUPERVISION
STATUTORY AND VOLUNTARY ORGANISATIONS
Edited by Jacki Pritchard
ISBN 1 85302 279 9

GOOD PRACTICE IN RISK ASSESSMENT AND RISK MANAGEMENT I
Edited by Hazel Kemshall and Jacki Pritchard
ISBN 1 85302 338 8

GOOD PRACTICE IN RISK ASSESSMENT 2
KEY THEMES FOR PROTECTION, RIGHTS AND RESPONSIBILITIES
Edited by Hazel Kemshall and Jacki Pritchard
ISBN 1 85302 441 4

GOOD PRACTICE IN WORKING WITH VIOLENCE
Edited by Hazel Kemshall and Jacki Pritchard
ISBN 1 85302 641 7

Good Practice in Working with Victims of Violence

Edited by
Hazel Kemshall and Jacki Pritchard

Jessica Kingsley Publishers
London and Philadelphia

The right of the contributors to be identified as authors of this work has been
asserted by them in accordance with the Copyright, Designs and Patents Act
1988.

First published in the United Kingdom in 2000 by
Jessica Kingsley Publishers Ltd,
116 Pentonville Road, London
N1 9JB, England
and
325 Chestnut Street,
Philadelphia PA 19106, USA.

www.jkp.com

Library of Congress Cataloging in Publication Data
A CIP catalog record for this book is available from the Library of Congress

British Library Cataloguing in Publication Data
Good practice in working with victims of violence. - (Good practice series ; 8)
1. Victims of crimes – Services for 2. Violence – Psychological aspects
3. Violence – Social aspects 4. Victims of crimes – Rehabilitation
I. Kemshall, Hazel II. Pritchard, Jacki III. Working with victims of violence
362.8'8

ISBN 1 85302 768 5

Printed and Bound in Great Britain by
Athenaeum Press, Gateshead, Tyne and Wear

Contents

Introduction

Hazel Kemshall and Jacki Pritchard

In the introduction to *Good Practice in Working with Violence* we acknowledged the low priority given to work with victims, particularly with their long-term care and support. There is a growing recognition of the extent of victimization within society (Wesseley 1999), with victimization ranging from physical violence, sexual abuse and the psychological trauma resulting from fear of, or actual experience of, violence. This can include victimization resulting from the misuse of power, for example, bullying and the systematic demeaning and diminishment of persons in a variety of contexts from schools to workplaces. Bullying or more extreme forms of violence can be the result of discrimination, for example, racial and homophobic attacks (see Tyrer, Chapter 4). Domestic violence can be understood as an abuse of power and control, with its roots within societal gender discrimination and oppression (Dobash and Dobash 1992; Moran and Wilson 1999). The chapters in this volume illustrate changes in both societal and police attitudes to domestic violence. While each focuses on service delivery in their police areas, Woodfield (Chapter 10) places current responses to domestic violence within the legal framework of the Crime and Disorder Act 1998 and highlights the key responsibilities of other agencies in addition to the key role of the domestic violence officer. Fearns (Chapter 11) focuses upon the processes and practicalities of offering victim support both pre and during court proceedings.

Media coverage of victimization tends to focus on extreme events, for example, the murder of high profile celebrities such as Jill Dando. Soap operas have also done much to popularize the role of the victim, for example, domestic violence, child abuse and date rape (Coronation Street, Brookside). Global coverage of conflicts in Bosnia and Kosovo have exposed the public to almost nightly scenes of extreme victimization. However, the general public remains unaware of the more subtle forms of violence and victimization prevalent in daily life. For example, over half of the working population has experienced workplace bullying at some time during their working life (Hoel and Cooper, Chapter 8; Rayner 1997). Other victimization can remain hidden from public view, for example, within institutions. Prison is one such institution and the lack of public awareness is compounded by negative perceptions of inmates. This can leave violence in prisons beyond the public concern. Lack of concern and awareness help to create a climate in which not only is there inmate violence, but staff can also commit acts of violence, aggression and bullying (see Johnson, Chapter 3). Prisons are often environments of fear, threat and intimidation: inmate threats to staff, threats to the orderly running of the institution, staff control of prisoners through threat and fear of violence and the normalization of male violence between inmates (see Webb and Williams, Chapter 13).

The choice of the word victim is deliberate. It reflects the reality that many people continue to live in violent or abusive situations, or continue to live with the long-term effects of such situations. Limited access to appropriate resources and services can severely limit a person's passage from victim to survivor. This book is attempting to provide practical and constructive ways of working with victims and, where possible, to offer concrete strategies for transforming victims into survivors. The book reviews differing methods and services for work with victims, but a key emphasis is upon the skills and knowledge required by practitioners to facilitate positive work with victims.

The book recognizes that this work will be undertaken by a range of practitioners in various settings, and across the voluntary and independent sectors as well as the statutory. It also recognizes that much important and challenging work will be undertaken by unqualified and sometimes inexperienced staff. These workers are often under-resourced and in some organizations receive inadequate supervision. Much work is still conducted by volunteers, often for long periods and in situations in which the healing process for the victim can present serious emotional stress for the worker. In some cases this can leave workers exposed to long-term emotional damage. In these circumstances appropriate support and supervision are crucial, as illustrated in Chapter 15 on social workers working with victims in Northern Ireland.

This book begins deliberately with 'taboo' subjects: male survivors of violence, and homophobic victimization and it closes with those who have been the victims of political violence and conflict. The areas included in this volume are:

- abuse (child and adult)
- discrimination and victimization
- bullying
- domestic violence
- mediation
- institutional victimization
- the effects of political conflict.

We recognize that this does not fully reflect the range of victim types or scenarios. An exhaustive coverage of the topic would exceed one volume. What is important in the present volume is the lessons which can be drawn for practice and service delivery. We have recognized the importance of the victim's voice and Chapter 3 by Johnson provides a powerful account of the personal experience of abuse.

This book is a contribution to the growing literature on victims and to the reprioritization of victims following the implementation of the Crime and

Disorder Act 1998. While abuse, and particularly child abuse, has held centre stage in recent years, there is a growing recognition of the prevalence of violence and its effects upon victims. This book is a step towards assisting practitioners to support victims as they move towards becoming survivors.

REFERENCES

Dobash, R.E. and Dobash, R.P. (1992) *Women, Violence and Social Change*. London: Routledge.

Moran, D. and Wilson, M. (1999) 'Working with men who are violent to partners – striving for good practice.' In H. Kemshall and J. Pritchard (eds) *Good Practice in Working with Violence*. London: Jessica Kingsley Publishers.

Rayner, C. (1997) 'The incidence of workplace bullying.' *Journal of Community and Applied Social Psychology 7*, 249–255.

Wesseley, S. (1999) 'In the culture of counselling, we all risk becoming victims, The Saturday Essay.' *The Independent*, 29 May, 4.

CHAPTER 1

From the Politicization to the Politics of the Crime Victim

Sandra Walklate

INTRODUCTION

Current criminal justice policy and rhetoric would look remarkably unusual if some reference were not made to the victim of crime. The presence of the crime victim in public discourse stands as testimony to the changing balance of concerns within criminal justice policy over the last 50 years; so much so that it would now be difficult to argue that the victim is the 'forgotten party' of the criminal justice system. The question remains, however, as to what underpins this change of emphasis and what are the implications for practitioners working in the criminal justice and related fields. The purpose of this chapter, then, is twofold: first, to offer an overview and a way of understanding this changing emphasis within criminal justice policy; second, to look at the implications of these changes within two substantive areas of practice – domestic violence and families of murder victims. But first it will be of value to offer an understanding of some of the processes which have underpinned the increasing attention which has been paid to the victim of crime over the last 50 years.

REDISCOVERING THE CRIME VICTIM

It would be easy to assume that concern for the victim of crime is a relatively recent phenomenon. However, the presence and role of the victim in the criminal justice process has historically ebbed and flowed. Schafer (1968), for example, refers to the Middle Ages as the 'golden age' of the crime victim. Such historical variations notwithstanding, it is against the backcloth of the emerging welfare state that it is possible to situate the campaigns in the 1950s, led by Margery Fry, for better treatment of both the offender and victim of crime.

In *Arms of the Law* (1951) Margery Fry outlined her ideas on reconciling the victim and the offender in ways which would be both educative for the offender and meaningful for the victim. By the time Margery Fry died, these concerns had crystallized into a campaign for a criminal injuries compensation scheme. This campaign, taken forward in the first instance in legislative form by Reginald Prentice, used the Workmen's Compensation Act as its model. This first attempt at legislation failed, yet the ideas underpinning it solidified. Rock has this observation to make on the process:

> In her [Margery Fry] last formulation of the problem, compensation would represent a collective insurance provided by society. All taxpayers would be regarded as subscribers. All taxpayers were at risk of becoming victims. Since the state forbade citizens arming themselves, it should assume responsibility for its failure to provide protection. (Rock 1990, p.66)

This view of the victim as citizen in need of state protection clearly articulates a continuity of thought between the proposal for compensation for criminal injuries and other moves to establish 'social citizenship' (Marshall 1948) which were embedded within the establishment of the welfare state. When the Criminal Injuries Compensation Board (CICB) took its final form in 1964 it met with little opposition. There were two principles enshrined within it: the principle of insurance and the principle of the innocent victim of violent crime.

While the establishment of this scheme was seen as 'trail-blazing' (Waller 1988), setting an example which other countries have subsequently followed, this all took place without anyone asking what the victim (of violent) crime wanted from the criminal justice process. In this respect it has been argued that the legislation served symbolic political purposes rather than practical ones (Miers 1978). The establishment of this scheme, however, marked the culmination of the logic of the welfare state built on notions of insurance, contract and individual responsibility. In this way the final brick of the welfare state was put in place, cementing both the power and the regulatory potential of the state (see Mawby and Walklate 1994, Chapter 4).

So the establishment of the CICB was embedded within particular notions: that of the innocent victim (perpetuating the distinction between the deserving and the undeserving); that of the distinction between the public and the private (in the legitimacy given in practice to the innocent victim of public interpersonal violence as opposed to the private 'victim' of such violence); and finally that of the principle of insurance. None of these presumptions was considered to be problematic at the time of the inception of the CICB. Indeed, having achieved the aim of compensation for the innocent victim of interpersonal violence, the interest which had been aroused in the victim of crime dissipated. Yet what this process of the early 1960s provided was the means by which the crime victim could be revisited several years later in the way the victim of (violent) crime had become linked to the concept of social citizenship within the welfare state. The nature of these links was both manipulated and subsequently changed during the 1980s.

THE POLITICS OF THE CRIME VICTIM

The development of the CICB in the 1960s laid the groundwork for other initiatives concerned with the crime victim. The first of these was the Bristol Victims Offenders Group, a short-lived organization which paved the way for the foundation of the National Association of Victim Support Schemes – the fastest growing voluntary organization of the 1980s. The second range of initiatives emanated from the feminist movement. The first women's refuge was opened in Chiswick in 1972 and the first rape crisis centre in London in 1976.

Both of these initiatives were to have a different and differential impact on policy and practice responses to the victim of violent crime in the years which followed. A brief comment on each of these developments will be made in turn.

Initiatives emanating from the feminist movement did not have criminal victimization per se at the forefront of their concerns. Their aims were avowedly much more political, concerned to encourage women towards equality and empowerment in all spheres of life. Such idealistic aims notwithstanding, it was clear that much could be achieved, especially when considering the impact of rape and 'domestic' violence, by focusing on the work of the criminal justice system. Consequently feminist informed campaigns and organizations (like Women Against Violence Against Women) directed some of their energies towards changing the law and its practice. It is, however, a moot point as to the extent to which such campaigns were successful in their own right separate from the economic and political processes associated with the 1980s which, in particular, recast the concept of citizenship as consumerism (see, for example, Jefferson, Sim and Walklate 1992). Moreover, at the same time as these feminist campaigns evolved so did Victim Support.

As a voluntary organization, Victim Support grew from one scheme in 1973 to over 300 in England and Wales alone by 1990. Moreover, it was the voluntary organization which secured both Home Office support and funding in the mid-1980s when other groups (like the feminist informed groups) were struggling with much more haphazard sources of funding and support. What is of interest in understanding how policy and practice in relation to the victim of (violent) crime have been formulated is why?

Put simply, Victim Support represented a community voluntary based movement at a time when the government was sounding the 'trumpet voluntary'. It constituted a response to the victim of crime which was intended to reintegrate the victim into the community, not to create dependency. This vision of self-help melded very well with the emergent political discourse of active citizenship. It was a 'cult of the customer' (Edgar 1991) that carried with it a view of the citizen who not only had rights (the view of the 1950s) but also had responsibilities – another theme which melded well with Victim Support philosophy. The presence of Victim Support and its influence within the Home Office (Rock 1990) enabled the government not only to show that it was responding in a meaningful way to the victim of crime, but also providing a mechanism whereby the state co-opted those concerns which had been raised by the feminist movement but in a politically safe way. This was achieved by attaching a condition to the funding of Victim Support that services be developed by them for women who had been raped. In this way the view that Victim Support represented an androgynous victim achieved success (see also Rock 1990).

To summarize, by 1990 Victim Support had gained considerable stature and influence in representing the voice of the crime victim and increasingly the victim of violent crime. Victim Support workers quickly developed the expertise necessary to enable people to make claims on the Criminal Injuries Compensation Board (previously the preserve of solicitors) and was heralded as the expert agency in promoting the interest of the crime victim in general, leading the way in sponsoring projects concerned to extend services to the victim of crime. In the first Victims Charter (Home Office 1990a) this organization was presented as the victim support organization.

So it can be seen that the backcloth to policy responses to the victim of (violent) crime need to be situated within a broad political and economic framework. The changing nature of the welfare state and the concomitant changing understanding of the role and nature of citizenship are key variables in understanding how and why the concern for the victim of (violent) crime emerged in the way that it did. Painting such a broad picture, however, while alerting us to the possible underlying mechanisms that facilitate or inhibit potential policy initiatives, can also gloss some of the tensions and debates which such policy possibilities inevitably generate. Such tensions can be illustrated in a number of different ways. They will be alluded to here in considering responses to two (potentially) different crimes of violence: 'domestic' violence and murder. However, before discussing each of these case studies it will be useful to say something about a broader conceptual and philosophical debate. The debate renders explicit the tensions between organizations like Victim Support and feminist informed groups, that is, should we talk about 'victims' or 'survivors'?

ARE PEOPLE VICTIMS OR SURVIVORS?

The tensions which exist between the concepts of victim and survivor are the classic tensions articulated between the different philosophies that underpin the voluntary groups which have been referred to in this discussion to date; Victim Support and the feminist movement.

Some would argue that feminism and victimology constitute contradictions in terms. Indeed Rock (1986) has argued that victimology has been seen as 'a weapon of ideological oppression' contributing to victim blaming through its acceptance of and adherence to the concept of victim precipitation. This uneasy relationship, however, is more than a matter of semantics; though it is the case that the genealogy the term victim connotes the sacrificiant who was more often than not female. Indeed, when the word is itself gendered, as in French, it is denoted as female. Feminists recognizing the power of linguistics object to the term victim because of its emphasis on passivity and powerlessness, preferring instead to focus on the way in which women actively resist their oppressive personal and structural locations – that is, survive.

But of course, while the terms victim and survivor are presented as oppositional in relation to the ideological purposes they each differently serve, in experiential terms such oppositions are much more difficult to identify. It is possible to think in terms of both active and passive victims and active and passive survivors. Indeed an argument can be mounted that these terms capture different elements of an experiential process (Walklate 1993) and moreover are experienced as such by (not only) women (Kirkwood 1993). Such issues constitute more than just semantics, not only because they tap different ideological and political images of women (and others), but also because those different images can crucially inform the kind of support services which may or may not be developed. Looking to a de-gendered understanding of the process of victimization in this way makes easier an understanding of the impact of victimization on men as well as women. It is with this key tension in mind that more detailed consideration will be made in the context of the two case studies. As appropriate the term victim will be placed in inverted commas to denote its problematic status.

RESPONDING TO 'DOMESTIC' VIOLENCE

As was suggested earlier, much feminist campaigning during the 1970s was focused on male violence towards women. Such campaigns were keen to demonstrate the inadequacy of the general policy response to women as 'victims' of violent crime. Since then, however, there has been, superficially at least, a remarkable change of policy direction on this question. It is difficult to determine the precise influence and impact of the feminist movement per se on the changes which have been observed within the criminal justice system in particular, but certainly the Women's National Commission in the mid-1980s seemed to assert some influence in encouraging government to address some feminist concerns about the criminal justice agency response (Smith 1989). Since that time, and largely following the North American model as developed by the Metropolitan Police, police forces in particular have been involved in developing 'dedicated' domestic violence units and more positive attitudes towards arresting offenders. Indeed both of these formed the basis of the recommendations contained within the *Domestic Violence Circular 60* (Home Office 1990b) which has been telling and potentially far reaching in placing 'domestic' violence squarely on the policing agenda. Indeed, in some respects policy responses on this issue have proceeded apace in the aftermath of the circular. Yet some of the assumptions on which a policy stance such as this have been based remain under-explored. There are a number of issues here from the point of view of the appropriateness of response to the 'victim'. Is arresting the offender the most appropriate course of action? Are the gender relations of the policy implementation process important? Ultimately, what kind of support do women (or anyone else) in a violent relationship actually want?

In the context of 'domestic' violence it has been argued that arresting the perpetrator is likely to have a positive effect: first, in removing the offender from the immediate environment of the scene, thus making it safer for the 'victim'; second, in the longer term the deterrent effect it is argued that such a process is likely to have on the offender. It is hard to dispute the value inherent in the first assertion, should the offender still be present to be arrested. Though as Hoyle (1998) and others have pointed out, this is not necessarily what the 'victim' wants, which may be connected with the problematic assumption that arrest has a deterrent effect. Early empirical evidence from North America seemed to suggest that this was the case (see Berk and Sherman 1984), but later work has failed to substantiate these earlier claims, especially for women from ethnic minorities (Sherman *et al.* 1991). Women in violent relationships may, in fact, know this. Hence the reluctance of some to pursue this as an appropriate strategy, raising a fundamental tension for policy initiatives on this issue. This is a question which will be returned to.

The second question raised here relates to the presumption that in the context of 'domestic' violence (alongside other contexts in which women have experienced violence) women want to be dealt with by other women. The argument that women (in vulnerable circumstances) would prefer to be responded to by another woman is supported by limited though not totally convincing evidence. For example, Heidensohn's (1992) evidence from police-women suggests that certain levels of satisfaction and support are maintained for both the women being supported and the policewomen offering support when involved in 'domestic' violence work. However, Heidensohn's female interviewees pointed out that they could identify policemen equally capable of offering quality support. Of course, one of the problems here is that we have very little gendered knowledge about what it is that people want from service delivery. Radford's (1987) earlier study suggests that 44 per cent of her sample thought that women police officers would be more understanding in relation to violence against women, though 32 per cent thought that they would not. Put alongside other evidence of what is known about the capacity of women to judge and control each other (albeit some would say in the interests of a patriarchal society: see, for example, Kennedy 1992; Lees 1989), then the presumption that women would want to be dealt with by another woman; or that women per se have the appropriate skills to offer the kind of support required, is con-tentious indeed. Yet responses to 'domestic' violence, whether emanating from the police service from feminism or from Victim Support, have proceeded apace, probably quite understandably, without seriously questioning this ass-umption. This issue raises the whole question of what it is that women (or anyone else) in a violent relationship might want in terms of an appropriate policy response.

The answer to this question is neither easy nor straightforward and may very much depend upon the point which the 'victim' has reached in the process of this relationship. Indeed, this highlights one of the most fundamental problems in trying to devise an appropriate policy response at all to people living in the context of a violent relationship. Policy responses tend to be formulated in terms of incidents, that is, what can be done at this moment in time to help, improve, change the circumstances for this particular individual. However, relationships are processes; what worked last week may not work today. So, for example, at the time an individual experiences violence they may want the violence to stop; they may want their partner to change; they may want a listening ear; they may want the person arrested; they may want to leave. The list is potentially endless. It is therefore no wonder that organizations geared towards dealing with one incident to the next become frustrated by what appears to be the reluctant 'victim'.

In some ways the tensions between incident and process which this di-scussion articulates return us to the issue of the false dichotomy which is presumed between the concept of victim and survivor. Experientially, people are likely to be more or less of a victim or more or less of a survivor at different points in time. Whether or not policy and/or practice can be so sensitively formulated to take account of such potential variation is a moot point. The questions raised by the second case study discussed here, responding to families of murder victims, are somewhat different and yet uncannily the same.

RESPONDING TO MURDER

Murder as a crime of violence has its impact not only on the victim (obviously) but also on the family and immediate friends of the victim. Depending upon the nature of the murder, of course, members of the victim's family may, on the one hand, be the prime suspects in any police investigation or, on the other, may at least have to wait until such an investigation has been completed before they can enter into funeral arrangements. Both of these different sets of circumstances may differently interfere with what might be considered to be a 'normal' grieving process and each may require different types and levels of support. However, as Rock (1998) documents, support systems for families grieving in this way have been in place for some considerable time.

The Compassionate Friends was formed in 1969. This organization was intended to help families grieving for the death of a child and out of it developed a group called Parents of Murdered Children (PMC) in the mid-1980s. By 1990 this group had established itself as an autonomous organization. It was formed in recognition of the specific difficulties that parents might have in coming to terms with the death of their murdered child. Also during the mid-1980s Victim Support, particularly at grass-roots level, found itself offering support to families of murder victims. In 1988 Victim Support established a two-year demonstration project in order to evaluate its work with such families and worked alongside PMC. Both of these groups gave evidence to the House of Lords Select Committee on Murder, Manslaughter and Life Imprisonment in 1989 and by 1993 they had formalized their relationships. At this point PMC became Support After Murder and Manslaughter (SAMM) and despite the emergence of a range of different victims groups during the 1990s, SAMM has managed to retain its position as a voice for the families of murder victims.

Offering support for families grieving in this particular way, especially as there may also be a criminal investigation proceeding, demands not only a sensitive and supportive listening ear but also a detailed knowledge of the procedures which may or may not have to be undertaken and why. Given such demands, and of course the recognition that what is underway is a process of gathering evidence, police officers in particular would probably argue that such support is best offered by a family liaison officer rather than an 'outside' volunteer. Such views add a further dimension to work in this area; that of effective, meaningful and sensitive inter-agency working. But what of the families themselves, what kind of support do they want under these circumstances?

In the first instance it is clear that families of murder victims frequently want what victims of crime in general want from the criminal justice system – information. However, murder is not only sudden and unexpected (as is burglary or sexual assault by a stranger), but it is also a final, irrevocable, uncommon yet often purposeful act which people cannot prepare themselves for. There can be no goodbye. Rock (1998, p.41) summarizes the impact: 'There is a pervasive structural disorder that reproduces the chaos within. The loss of another, and especially that of a member of the family, forces unwanted and bewildering changes on the social universe of the survivors.' This structural disorder leads some who have undergone the experience to suggest that they can identify with others who have also experienced it.

The evidence associated with the impact of such events emphasizes its long-term, life-changing nature. Moreover, what families of murder want under these circumstances is frequently not achievable: reconciliation with the dead person, for example. In the event of a criminal trial such needs may turn to punishment, forgiveness or revenge, depending on the development of different coping strategies by the individuals concerned. Overall, however, while there are some very practical issues which can be addressed for families engaged in such experiences, it may be that the impact of such events is so traumatic and so likely to be reliant upon individual family mechanisms that general recommendations of support cannot be made – a problem already commented on in the context of 'domestic' violence. Yet it is also clear that, as with 'domestic' violence, people undergoing such experiences may be at one and the same time or at different points in time active and/or passive victims and/or survivors. Some become active campaigners, other join organizations like SAMM, and yet others may just get on with their lives. Indeed, it is this last group which is the least vociferous and perhaps about whom the least is known, who may comprise the 'normal' response to abnormal circumstances. The question remains whether are there any general recommendations to be offered to those who work in these areas.

CONCLUSION
Treating victims with respect

The purpose of this chapter has been to offer a flavour of the nature and development of victim services, their diversity and some of the questions these developments have and do raise for practice. Indeed, while the diversity of voices claiming to speak for the victim of crime has become increasingly evident during the 1990s, there is a common thread throughout this emergent concern, whether constructed as the innocent victim of violent crime in the 1960s, the consumer of police services in the 1980s or the secondary victim of crime in the 1990s. This thread is the increasing consistency with which the victim has been invoked as the symbolic person for whom we should all care. How that care might be constructed has been differently informed dependent upon the kind of crime under discussion and the impact that such crime is presumed to have. So it would appear that 'domestic' violence requires a differently informed response than murder, for example. Yet arguably the requirement for difference has been exaggerated, at the expense of appreciating the sameness of such experiences. Such a statement is not intended to downgrade the impact that traumatic events may have, but simply to observe that practice may be able to take account of differential impact but policy cannot. The question of sameness can be encapsulated in one term: respect.

It should not be forgotten that victims of (violent) crime are people trying to deal with more or less exceptional circumstances in their lives. They may feel responsible for some of those circumstances. They may feel some are shared with others, while some have just happened to them (Harre 1979). How they deal with such circumstances will be in part dependent upon their own personal resources, the personal resources of those close to them and the kind of support which they may or may not be offered by the various agencies with whom they have contact. Treating people with respect, that is as individuals with personal resources, is a key mechanism for ensuring that, traumatic circumstances notwithstanding, they are enabled to make use of their resources to understand what has happened in their lives. How they might choose to do that is likely to be infinitely variable.

There are a number of implications which can be derived from the position outlined above. One of these implications is that this argument challenges any presumed special status to be assigned to the victim of (violent) crime. This does not mean to say that such crime does not impact upon people. It does. But it does imply that in terms of practice it is useful to remember that 'victims' are people. Arguably the developments over the last 50 years have taken us too far down the road of the 'culture of fear' (Ferudi 1997); too far down the road of the therapeutic society. Remembering that 'victims' are people is no more or less than a plea to remember that victimhood is a condition not necessarily to be recommended.

REFERENCES

Berk, R.A. and Sherman, L.W. (1984) 'The specific deterrent effects of arrest policy for assault.' *American Sociological Review 49*, 261–272.

Edgar, D. (1991) 'Are you being served?' *Marxism Today* May, 28.

Ferudi, F. (1997) *The Culture of Fear*. London: Cassell.

Fry, M. (1951) *Arms of the Law*. London: Gollancz.

Harre, R. (1979) *Social Being*. Oxford: Blackwell.

Heidensohn, F. (1992) *Women in Control? The Role of Women in Law Enforcement*. Oxford: Oxford University Press.

Home Office (1990a) *The Victims Charter*. London: HMSO.

Home Office (1990b) *Domestic Violence Circular 60*. London: HMSO.

Hoyle, C. (1998) *Negotiating Domestic Violence*. Oxford: Oxford University Press.

Jefferson, T., Sim, J. and Walklate, S. (1992) 'Europe, the left and criminology in the 1990s: accountability, control, and the social construction of the consumer.' In D. Farrington and S. Walklate (eds) *Victims and Offenders: Theory and Practice*. London: British Society of Criminology.

Kennedy, H. (1992) *Eve Was Framed*. London: Virago.

Kirkwood, C. (1993) *Leaving Abusive Partners*. London: Sage.

Lees, S. (1989) 'Learning to love.' In M. Cain (ed) *Growing Up Good*. London: Sage.

Marshall, T.H. (1948) *The Rights to Welfare and Other Essays*. London: Heinemann.

Mawby, R. and Walklate, S. (1994) *Critical Victimology*. London: Sage.

Miers, D. (1978) *The Politicisation of the Crime Victim*. Abingdon: Professional Books.

Radford, J. (1987) 'Policing male violence, policing women.' In J. Hamner and M. Maynard (eds) *Women, Policing and Social Control*. London: Macmillam.

Rock, P. (1986) *A View From the Shadows*. Oxford: Oxford University Press.

Rock, P. (1990) *Helping Victims of Crime*. Oxford: Oxford University Press.

Rock, P. (1998) *After Homicide*. Oxford; Oxford University Press.

Schafer, R. (1968) *The Victim and His Criminal*. New York: Random House.

Sherman, L., Schmidt, J., Regan, D., Gartin, P. and Cohn, E. (1991) 'From initial deterrence to long term escalation: short custody arrest for ghetto poverty violence.' *Criminology 29*, 821–849.

Smith, L. (1989) *Domestic Violence*. London: HMSO.

Walklate, S. (1993) 'Policing by women, with women, for women?' *Policing 9*, 109–116.

Waller, I. (1988) 'International standards, national trail blazing, and the next steps.' In M. Maguire and J. Pointing (eds) *Victims of Crime: A New Deal?* Milton Keynes: Open University Press.

CHAPTER 2

When the Victim is Male
Working with Men who were Sexually Abused in Childhood

Kim Etherington

INTRODUCTION

Few men present initially as sexually abused in childhood but rather with some of the symptoms and life problems which have been highlighted elsewhere (Etherington 1995). It is interesting to note that disclosure of male abuse has rapidly accelerated in recent times. Of the 25 men I studied in 1993, one man disclosed in the 1960s and two men in the 1970s; nine men disclosed in the 1980s and thirteen in the 1990s. Bearing in mind that the interviews were conducted in 1993 – only three years into the 1990s, there is therefore a rapid increase in the number of men disclosing as the climate changes from the denial of and ignorance about male sexual abuse.

Since the publication of *Adult Male Survivors of Childhood Sexual Abuse* (Etherington 1995), more men have approached me with their childhood abuse as the presenting problem. One man told me: 'I am identifying strongly with a lot of what I am reading and it is helping me understand. Thank you for writing the book, for recognising and caring about us.' It seems that recognition has made it possible for some men to ask for help.

Recovery from childhood sexual abuse for males is in many respects the same as that for females, although there are some essential differences (Etherington 1995). There is wide range of literature on female recovery issues (Bass and Davis 1988; Briere 1992; Elliot 1993; Hall and Lloyd 1989; Parks 1994; Sanderson 1990) so I will limit myself in this chapter to issues that have been identified through my research as particularly pertinent for males.

DIFFICULTIES IN IDENTIFICATION WITH THE VICTIM ROLE

At a very early age males are taught to become responsible. Socialization messages such as 'Take care of mummy while I'm gone' serve to train boys to believe that being male invests them with power over and responsibility for females. These attitudes are reinforced throughout life, creating a society in which male sexual abuse victims have had to remain invisible if they were to avoid judgement as 'less than a man'.

'Sexual victim' usually conjures up an image of a small, female, powerless creature trapped by a dominant male into a role of submission. The word 'victim' has been rejected by most sexually abused females in preference for the word 'survivor', a more powerful image. If this is how women react against 'victim' it is likely that males will have an even stronger reaction. Recovery cannot begin until he is able to acknowledge the word 'victim' as a human condition which has resulted from a traumatic event and one with which he can identify (Hunter and Gerber 1990). Whereas it may be important to encourage a female to change 'victim' to 'survivor', it is equally important to encourage a man initially to accept his victimization. If there is no 'victim' then there are no adverse effects and no need to engage with what might be overwhelming feelings of powerlessness.

David's first words to me when we met were: 'I don't want to be seen as a victim. I don't want people feeling sorry for me. I've managed up to now and just because I've admitted the abuse, I don't want that to affect the way people treat me.'

David had 'managed' by telling nobody about his abuse until he felt forced by the threat of abandonment by his wife. He had kept the abuse compartmentalized, separate from the rest of his life and in order to do that he had kept part of himself hidden, even from those he most loved. In the end his secret burst out in an uncontrolled manner during an argument about the lack of real intimacy in their relationship.

David felt a threat to his self-concept in letting others know about the abuse. It was only a greater threat (losing his wife) that allowed him to disclose. He had very mixed feelings about having disclosed; a sense of relief that he no longer had to carry the burden alone, but also anger that he had been forced to share something that had belonged only to him; almost like a re-enactment of the abuse when he had also been forced or coerced into giving something of himself unwillingly.

Sexual abuse may not always be violent, but it is always a violation. Sexual abuse often occurs within families where physical violence occurs. O'Hara (1992, p.4) states that although there is little research that focuses on the relationship between sexual abuse of children and sexual and physical violence towards their mothers: 'refuges for battered women were among the first institutions in this country to recognise the prevalence of the sexual abuse of children'.

Men who experience pain or force during their molestation can more easily identify themselves as victims. Those who can connect with the feelings of victim are likely to have sufficient empathy to avoid re-enacting that behaviour on others. However, only 4 of the men in my study (out of 25) experienced any kind of force during sexual abuse. Half the men in the study had experienced physical abuse from one or other of their parents during childhood and virtually all of them had experienced emotional abuse or neglect. When this happens the child is often driven to seek comfort from inappropriate sources – often from unsafe adults who recognize the child's potential for victimization because of their neediness. Needy, vulnerable children are targeted by paedophiles and groomed to become victims under the cloak of giving attention or 'love'. When the victim becomes aroused or when the abuse is part of an otherwise caring relationship, they are less likely to define themselves as abused. Arousal can be wrongly interpreted as pleasure, erection as consent and ejaculation as orgasm. A male's response to sexual stimulation is usually immediate and obvious; the feeling of involvement and responsibility may be all the greater for that. Men need help to understand that arousal during abuse is the outcome of a healthy body's response to unhealthy circumstances; that a child who enjoys sexual stimulation and seeks it out in his relationships with adults is no more responsible for the abuse than a child who felt no arousal, and that it is always the adult's responsibility to hold the taboo.

Violations described by the men in my study and described in detail elsewhere (Etherington 1995) included:

- Intrusive sexualized conversation, e.g. priest asks 'Which way does your penis lie – would you show me?' Teacher's girlfriend asks about size of penis. A male abuser asks 'Do you see your cousin in the bath – what does she look like?'

- Abuse of sexuality, e.g. sexual humiliation: 'My mother's behaviour ranged from hysterical mockery of my sexuality to abject horror of my genitals.'

- Oral sex, e.g. subjects had been made to perform oral sex on both male and female abusers and had oral sex performed on them by both male and female abusers.

- Anal penetration attempted, e.g. boys had been aware of perpetrator trying to push something into them from behind.

- Anal penetration performed, e.g. boys had experienced digital, penile and objects' penetration of their anal passage.

- Vaginal penetration, e.g. subject had performed intercourse on perpetrator; e.g. 'My mother was putting my little hand inside her vagina'.

- Masturbation, e.g. subject had performed masturbation on perpetrator or perpetrator had masturbated boy.

- Fondling, e.g. sexualized touching of perpetrator's breasts, genitals, or of subject's body.

- Frottage, e.g. hugging or rubbing against the body in a sexualized way.

- Deliberate arousal followed by punishment, e.g. 'My mother in some way aroused me to erection and then slapped my penis, telling me I was a naughty boy.'

- Sexualized beating, e.g. headmaster (monk) would beat boy on buttocks with pants down and, before adjusting the trousers, would insist on hugging to show there was no animosity.

- Sexualized kissing.

- Use of pornography, e.g. 'He would put a picture of a nude woman in front of my face while he was coming into me from behind.'

- Exhibitionism, e.g. 'She would make me crouch down and watch as she squatted over a mirror and defecated.'

Some of the boys had been involved in several of these activities and others had experienced a single type of abuse. It can be seen from the above descriptions that many men had been abused by females (n = 13); several of those females had been their mothers (n = 7); several men had been abused by both males and females (n = 5).

COPING MECHANISMS

Males who equate the word 'victim' with 'passive' may reassert their maleness by becoming sexually and physically aggressive or promiscuous. Reaction formation has been identified as a coping mechanism when a person behaves in ways that deny his deep-seated feelings. Robert, who was aggressively abused around the age of 7, describes how at the age of 13 he became a tyrant and in his twenties he engaged in frequent and promiscuous behaviour: 'I had a little black book of conquests ... my wife was the 63rd woman I had slept with. It was how I measured my manhood; notches on my gun.'

IDENTIFICATION WITH THE AGGRESSOR

One of the more gender specific coping mechanisms used by males is 'identification with the aggressor'. When a boy has been socialized to believe that 'real men are powerful' the degree of dissonance created by a sexual assault may cause him to identify himself as the one in control. A young male who is sexually abused, and who has been indoctrinated within a society in which the male is always seen as the sexual predator, might adopt a position of responsibility for the abuse.

Christopher's grandfather abused him over many years and the abuse continued into his late teens. Chris was haunted by the fact that, as a tall, well-built teenager who had been taught that 'proper men were in control', he must have been responsible for the ongoing abuse. Chris was not able to understand that as the abuse had begun when he was a toddler and had been continuous through his adolescence, he was as helpless to stop it at the age of 14 or even 17 as he had been during his earlier childhood. He had been 'traumatically sexualized' (Finkelhor and Browne 1986) while believing that his grandfather, a pillar of society who was a frequent visitor in his home, was a loving and caring person. He coped by believing that he had done something wrong, rather than face the fact that he had been betrayed, overwhelmed and victimized by a man whom he had trusted.

GENDER AND SEX ROLES

When the abuser is a woman the problem may be even more complex. Socialization messages about the nature of females ('sugar and spice and all things nice') perpetuate the myth that females can only be seen as nurturers – thereby negating the reality of females as abusers. The abuse perpetrated by females is often coercive and seductive, rather than aggressive and forceful. This creates additional difficulties in defining the experience as 'abuse', a word which is usually linked with violence. One man said: 'Abuse carries overtones of wickedness and prison: I don't like applying that to my mother.'

A young male who has been abused by a female will frequently identify himself as the one in control. This belief is reinforced by societal attitudes about sex and gender roles in which the male is always seen as the sexual predator. Another man told me of the difficulty defining his mother as an abuser:

> Apart from being my mother, she was a woman. I'd been educated by my fa-
> ther that women were there for the cooking, cleaning and sex. They were put
> on earth for our benefit and every man should have several. They were not
> the abusers; they were to be abused upon. So how could she abuse me when I
> was the man?

A male might acknowledge symptoms but deny their basis in sexual abuse. Paul accepts that his serious medical condition is stress related but cannot connect the stress with his severe, long-term sexual abuse by both parents. He cannot afford to see his mother as his main abuser and because he was actively involved during penetrating her he interpreted that as 'behaving like a man should': 'I didn't feel what was happening was abuse; it was very loving and part of giving affection ... Because it was my mother it was acceptable – if it had been a man then it wouldn't have been.'

The 'you should be so lucky response' often displayed by society when a young boy is sexually abused by an older woman creates confusion and denial for the victim. Societal attitudes educate males to experience any sexual activity with a woman, especially an older woman, as a welcome initiation into manhood. This idea is reinforced by films and the media.

RE-ENACTMENT

When a child has been subjected to an uncontrollable event, he may deal with his anxiety by re-enacting it; he may gain a sense of mastery by becoming the powerful one. Eight men in my study re-enacted their own abuse on other children during childhood and adolescence; two continued to abuse children as adults. When children are being abused they are learning two roles – that of the victim and that of the abuser. Depending on their individual defence mechanisms, they may identify more strongly with either victim or abuser, or may find that in different circumstances they can flip between both roles. Several men in the study re-enacted their victim role in their adult relationships; two men who had been anally raped as adolescents were also raped by men as adults.

Males who are abused by males might identify with the aggressor who shares their gender. George, who went on to become a paedophile, says he felt that 'it was almost as if I was in control' when a stranger molested him at the age of 10. By this means he defends himself from his dissociated feelings of powerlessness. Because he could not perceive himself as the victim, neither could he perceive the 10-year-old girls he abused as victims, but rather that they, like himself as a child, were 'in control' or responsible, or at least equal in status and responsibility. George said of his child neighbour: 'I think she has fallen in love with me. I tell her we just cannot have a relationship.' It was as if he was talking about having an affair with an adult woman.

Robert, who was abused by his mother, abused his daughter and her friends. He refers to his victims as 'precocious' and for this reason it was acceptable to touch them sexually. By identifying himself as the aggressor (at the age of 11 years) and thus avoiding acknowledging his mother as an abuser, he was unable to perceive the children he abused as victims. He will only be able to take full responsibility for his abusing behaviour when he identifies himself as his mother's victim, thereby undoing the defence mechanism which has helped him survive to adulthood.

EXTERNALIZED RESPONSES

Externalized responses seem to be more common in males generally and are therefore more likely among abused men. Men in my study described drug and alcohol abuse, sexual addiction, aggressive, anti-social and sexually abusive behaviour (Etherington 1995). Of the men studied 20 per cent had been convicted of sexual offences; 28 per cent had been convicted of other offences (drunk and disorderly, threatening behaviour, aggressive behaviour which involved throwing a bottle at a passing car and injuring a child, shoplifting, burglary, deception and attempted burglary) making the overall 48 per cent of men with convictions. Home Office figures (1993) describe a cohort study of men born in 1953, which showed that 36 per cent had been convicted of serious offences by the age of 35 (excluding traffic offences). The number convicted of sex offences was 0.6 per cent. This indicates that the sexually abused men in my study had a higher rate of convictions than the average population and particularly for sexual offences (20% vs. 0.6%) which although taken from a smaller sample seems significant.

During the study additional offences were disclosed for which the men had never been charged. Two men admitted to stealing; three men admitted to drug dealing; one of these men had also admitted to gun running after leaving the army. Six had admitted to using drugs (four of whom were addicted) and ten men drank alcohol to excess.

Sexual acting out was common among the men in the study. Most admitted to some degree of compulsivity: masturbation to the level that it interfered with living a normal life and felt self-abusive. Four men had sado-masochistic fantasies while masturbating which caused anxiety and distress. One man described this as 'sick' and another as 'out of balance'. One man felt a compulsion to dress up in his sister's clothes and masturbate. He also engaged in compulsive sexual activity with a dog and fantasized about sex with other animals. Two suffered from premature ejaculation and three from intermittent impotence and difficulty with arousal.

The five men who spoke of being convicted of sexual offences included 'flashing' and masturbating in public places; shouting obscenities in a park (at his dead abuser). One man had been convicted at the age of 15 of 'gross indecency' for having sex with his 14-year-old girl friend on a grave in a public cemetery. One man was charged with 'gross indecency' for picking up men in public lavatories for sex. Another man had been convicted of abusing his daughter and her 11-year-old friend. Another self-identified paedophile had never been charged with any of his offences, but following the study he reoffended and was convicted. He had committed at least seven offences, including abusing his son. Two men reported using prostitutes currently and one admitted abusing them. Six men used pornography.

Two men had become rent boys, one of whom had engaged in this behaviour while absconding from Borstal. The first of these had subsequently become a pimp for his girl friend who had also been sexually abused in childhood. Another one later prostituted himself in a relationship with an older man.

None of the men were directly questioned about these matters but the material arose out of the interviews. It is likely that there would be many more examples of such behaviour if direct questions had been asked. These are sensitive admissions and I imagine some men were not able to acknowledge their problem behaviours.

During recovery men can be helped to face up to these behaviours and acknowledge appropriate guilt and shame, while at the same time developing an understanding that acting out behaviour is a way of coping with unexpressed emotions and may be a way of avoiding dealing with the feelings that are a necessary part of healing. Facing their behaviour within a trusting and accepting therapeutic relationship can provide a healing experience when the men can begin to gain compassion for themselves and others.

However, until the client has new coping mechanisms at his disposal, it is unhelpful to attempt to dismantle the outdated ones. Unfortunately, when men act out in these ways the behaviour is perceived as the problem and they are more likely to end up in the legal system with a focus on punishment rather than on exploring the meaning of the behaviour. In some cases treatment is offered during detention and may be the first opportunity the man has had to obtain help. Men who are causing harm to others or themselves do need containment, but unless this time is used as an opportunity for growth and understanding, it is likely that little will change on release. Indeed the problems may only be compounded as a fresh layer of anger at society is added to the underlying problem.

Damien was in prison when I met him – it was his thirteenth sentence and he was twenty-one. He was abused by all three of his sisters over many years and he had first attempted suicide at the age of six. He had committed arson and burglaries. He used drugs and stole to finance his habit. He had first tried to tell somebody about his abuse when he was 14. His social worker had told him: 'It doesn't happen; women don't abuse blokes.' Damien said:

> That reaction hurt. The social worker didn't want to know about it. It made it hard for me to tell someone else about it; I thought 'if you don't believe me then who is going to?' So I kept it inside myself. I think by the age of 16 I had realised social workers were a load of crap. I'd been beaten up by my step-dad a few times and placed in care overnight but the social workers believed my step-dad and my mum when they said it hadn't happened – they tried to put the family back together again and a few weeks later it would happen all over again. I think that was wrong.

Damien was convicted of indecent assault on his under-age girl friend a year after his attempt at disclosure. During his most recent term of imprisonment he had been offered counselling for the first time:

> My attitude has changed a lot since coming in here, since I've faced up to a lot of things. I used the dope to try and blot out the pain of everything. It's a buzz to live life now, to enjoy life for what I can get out of it. Passing exams, using my brains, which I've never done before; being in love helps a lot.

HOMOPHOBIC CONCERNS

Homophobic concerns can be dealt with by exploration of their internalized attitudes about homosexuality. Family, personal and societal values need to be explored with the client in order to help them to accept their sexual identity. Dissonance may have been created by introjected heterosexist messages about acceptable and unacceptable sexual behaviour.

Clarification that arousal is likely to be the same whatever the gender of the abuser and may not be an indicator of sexual orientation can allow men to reframe what has happened to them in a new light. These issues have been dealt with in greater detail elsewhere (Etherington 1995; Hunter 1990a, 1990b; Sgroi 1989).

Steven felt confused about his sexual orientation, believing himself to be homosexual because a man had chosen to sexually abuse him. He thought he must have been identifiable in some way and that this was the reason for his abuse. He had internalized homophobic attitudes from within his family and his Church and, although he had married and had children, he was still unsure about his sexual orientation. He had married an abusive woman and their sex life was difficult. This reinforced his anxiety about his sexuality, believing that if he did not enjoy sex with a woman he must therefore be homosexual. He had lost sight of the fact that the woman he had chosen had contributed to the problem. Some men who have been abused in childhood are unconsciously attracted into abusive relationships in much the same way as abused women. During therapy it may become necessary for both partners to examine their co-dependency in an unhealthy relationship.

Many men assume that their male abusers were homosexual rather than paedophiliac, or that abuse by a male contributes to development of homosexuality which they may have introjected as societally shameful. Men who were abused by females were more likely to identify themselves as heterosexual than men abused by men or by both men and women. This issue has been dealt with in greater detail elsewhere (Etherington 1995).

THE RECOVERY PROCESS

Once the man has accepted that he has been a victim of childhood sexual abuse, recovery has begun. This realization may initiate a crisis during which there may be flashbacks, intrusive images, thoughts and feelings that need to be 'contained'. The man may fear he is 'going mad' and may need reassurance that this is part of a normal process of healing. Chronic post traumatic stress disorder has been described in detail elsewhere (Mezey and King 1992).

Christopher was suddenly catapulted into facing his abuse when his brother disclosed to his parents. His mother then asked if he had also been abused. Christopher told me:

> I always told myself I would carry my dark secret to my grave to protect my-self and those I love from the pain involved in disclosure. Since events have caught up with me and my secret is out I have been in emotional turmoil to such a degree that it is affecting my family and employment. I either want to cry, or feel very aggressive.

Neither brother had known about the other's abuse, although the same grandfather abused them both. Christopher became overwhelmed by frequent flashbacks, images, dreams and memories that came flooding back, leaving him disorientated, terrified and helpless. It was as if a box had been hidden in the cellar and the lid was suddenly thrown back, allowing blinding daylight to flood the scenes of his past which seemed to be happening in the moment. Christopher thought he was going mad. At this stage clients need to be seen frequently, reassured that they will not be overwhelmed, that they are not mad but perhaps quite the opposite; 'coming to their senses'. Part of themselves that has been kept 'in the box' under extreme pressure is being released and this can only happen when the person is ready and able to accept what is in there. The fact that release is happening now indicates a readiness to reclaim hitherto unintegrated experiences that may have controlled their lives by avoidance of truly intimate relationships or any situations that may trigger off painful feelings.

The degree of the client's fear may cause the counsellor to encourage them to close the box and ignore what is emerging. If the counsellor is confident in the recovery process she can provide a secure base from which the client can begin to explore the distressing memories. Understanding that flashbacks are experi-enced with the full charge of the initial events, and that the client has already survived those events at the time they were happening, will enable the couns-ellor to have courage to guide the client confidently through the process of healing. Once reclaimed and integrated, the memories lose their emotional charge and can then be stored as part of the person's life history.

Rather than encouraging the client to close down, the counsellor can help him capture some of the images through drawing, talking, writing, etc. I believe that 'what we resist will persist', but if we welcome and hold on to the emerging memories and integrate them, the individual will grow strong and whole. If the client is employed he may be too distressed to go to work during this stage and need encouragement to take time off. This is often more difficult for men who are traditionally in the breadwinner role. Men are often less willing to take time off work with stress, preferring to struggle on rather than admitting to what they fear might be perceived as 'weakness'. Or they might be self-employed and without any means of support, other than what they earn by going to work. Men who have been abused are often even more inclined to refuse to give in to ill health or to take time out. Indeed, some cope by becoming addicted to work and use it as a way of avoiding thinking about their abuse.

Stephen, a GP, was horrified at my suggestion that he was should take time off sick, although he recognized that he would make the same suggestion for one of his patients in a similar condition. There is a culture within the medical world of working in the face of major odds. From their student days, trainee doctors are given the message that in some way they should be superhuman, that they are the helpers and not the ones in need of help. Many of the men I have helped through the recovery process have been employed within the helping professions: social workers, nurses, probation officers, etc. It is as if some unconsciously seek a way of vicariously healing themselves through helping others. The 'wounded healer' concept has frequently been identified among helping professionals (Bennet 1987). If we try to help others out of the awareness of our own wound, we can use that awareness as a powerful and enabling tool. When we are unaware of our woundedness, we might be in danger of meeting the needs of others out of the well of our own unmet need. This way leads to burnout and the danger of over-identification.

Stephen imagined that his partners in practice would judge him, reject him and treat him differently if he told them about his childhood abuse. He could not envisage taking time off without telling them the whole story. Clients need to be helped to identify the difference between secrecy and privacy. Stephen had no real need to tell his partners why he needed time off, apart from the fact that he was suffering from stress. Of course he imagined their scorn: 'Aren't we all stressed? Why should you need time off for stress when I continue to work under stress?'

Eventually he decided to tell only the senior partner about the abuse and his therapy. Having at least one person who understood allowed him to take the necessary rest and relieved some of the pressure. Having had a good response from the senior partner, he was then able to tell another colleague and little by little he has risked finding out what really happened when people knew his story. Stephen was able to identify that in fact he was judging and rejecting himself and perceiving it to come from others.

When men have carried stress from childhood abuse within them, they may become addicted to the stress itself and choose very stressful work. Christopher worked in a high security wing of a prison with violent offenders. Never a day passed without serious disruption; staff suffered a punishing amount of stress. During recovery he recognized the unhealthy environment in which he had chosen to spend his working life. Part of recovery may entail major life changes such as retraining for other work – recognizing transferable skills which can be used in less stressful environments.

THERAPEUTIC RELATIONSHIP

Client autonomy is central to the counselling process in general (Bond 1993) and of particular importance in situations where the traumatic experience of the client and their gender role socialization are concerned with power and control. A safe environment will require clearly negotiated and maintained boundaries. In this way the therapist might model for the client how to set personal boundaries in other areas and relationships in their lives. Controlling behaviour, such as the client coming late or staying away, attempts to bully the therapist as a symbol of authority, can be made conscious and explored within the therapeutic relationship, which can become a 'laboratory' for experimenting with new ways of coping.

Trust needs to be earned by the therapist and develops over time. This relationship can provide the client with a testing ground for future relationships and, at best, will heal some of the damage created by the betrayal of trust in the abusive relationship. If the therapist is the same sex as the abuser, this will usually impact on the process. Matthew described his feelings when a male and female member of the community psychiatric team were sent to his home following his rape as an adult. He had been raped previously by a peer at the age of 14:

> They sent me some chap and a female student with him. I responded very well to her but I loathed the chap. I did not want a man there. She had that natural ability and human warmth; he was very analytical and probing, very good – he probably would have made me tackle things but what I needed was some human kindness. On the last meeting she said to me 'the first time I saw you I thought you were going to cry and I could have hugged you' and I thought 'Oh God, I wish you had – that was what I needed' because nobody hugged me and let me cry in their arms.

Having been twice raped by males it is understandable that he did not want to expose his vulnerability to a male. Working with a male might be most useful for both male and female survivors at a later stage, but there is an argument for using female workers at the initial stage of helping. A man may be more comfortable and allow himself to be vulnerable with a female whom he may perceive to be more sensitive to his feelings and less likely to criticize them as unmasculine. Blagg (1989) reports in an NSPCC report a study by Broussard and Wagner (1988) which indicates that male professionals in particular were inclined to hold boy victims responsible for the abuse.

The work with abuse is likely to be long term, although some advocates of brief therapy have developed solution-focused ways of working with survivors (Dolan 1991). Clients come to work at different stages of readiness. If the abuse emerges while working with issues such as alcohol or drug addiction, violent behaviour, depression, anxiety, relationship breakdown or other life problems which may be the outcome of childhood violation that have been highlighted elsewhere (Etherington 1995), it may take additional time for clients to reach the stage of identifying or disclosing their abuse and accepting their victimization. Sometimes clients come for help much further down the line when they are fully aware of the problems caused by their abuse and are ready to find new ways of coping.

Referral to another therapist might be more appropriate if, during the assessment period, it becomes clear that long-term work is required. Sometimes this can occur when sexual abuse is uncovered in another setting such as during detoxification, attendance at a clinic for sexually transmitted diseases or other medical settings, or during marital therapy. The timing of suggestions about referral is crucial. It might be damaging for a therapist to make this suggestion immediately following disclosure when the client might be most vulnerable to feelings of rejection. David spoke of his suicidal feelings when he left his counsellor after naming his abuse for the first time:

> She suggested as I was leaving, that I might need to find somebody else to work with on the abuse. I knew she was only being ethical because she felt out of her depth but all I could hear was the rejection. I thought 'now that I've told her she doesn't want to know me any more'. I drove home thinking about crashing through the motorway bridge. I was devastated.

Some therapists have become anxious about the accusations levelled by those who propound the so-called 'false memory syndrome' and this may create an atmosphere in which both therapist and client avoid working with dreams and flashbacks for fear of being accused of implanting memories. A therapist who avoids leading questions and interpretation and remains tentative has little to fear. Staying with the client in a spirit of shared and supportive exploration will enable clients to discover their truth. Further discussion of the issues raised by false memory lobbyists can be found elsewhere (Accuracy About Abuse; Etherington 1995).

BEING BELIEVED

It is important that the therapist believes the client's 'truth' which might sometimes change over time as it becomes clearer. James, a young man who clearly remembered his abuse by a stranger when he was 12 years old and had vague feelings of having been abused much earlier, described his experiences of working with a psychoanalyst who interpreted his experiences as fantasy:

> I saw an NHS psychoanalyst; he denied my reality and told me I was imagining things. Psychoanalysis goes wrong because its based on a theory that things have to fit; that process devalues the survivors reality and truth; it can be used as a form of denial – used to suppress memories.

He went on to highlight other responses: 'The first person I told was dad; I was 18. He told me to stop making a fuss about nothing. I felt angry at his response but I couldn't tell him.' Some time after the research process was completed James contacted me to say that he had now connected with earlier memories of abuse by his father.

Clients sometimes fear being disbelieved almost more than the abuse. They think they might be judged as 'going mad' because people around them at the time of the abuse told them that everything was fine. William described himself at the age of 11:

> I had 'controlled breakdowns' lasting about an hour during which I would hysterically cry and laugh alternately. At school the teacher asked me if I was OK (obviously aware that I wasn't) and I broke off, looked up and said in a coherent, calm voice that I was fine and then burst out laughing again. She asked me if there was anything wrong at home. I replied (in a coherent pause), that everything was fine at home. I honestly believed what my Dad continually told me – that I was very lucky indeed, very privileged and happy.

Repressed anger can cause depression, suicidal feelings and self-destructive behaviours arising from guilt, feelings of responsibility and badness. Many clients suffered depression and frequently describe suicidal feelings, many having made serious attempts at suicide. I have been struck at the frequency with which men speak of suicide attempts that involve violence: stepping off the pavement in front of lorries, driving recklessly, wrist slashing, holding a gun or knife to the throat, courting danger through being a member of a motorcycle display team, gun running, living dangerously. Very few men I have worked with have used overdosing as a means of suicide. It seems that men choose more aggressive means.

Robert said: 'I wanted to kill myself but I didn't have the balls to do it in cold blood so I tried to drink myself to death, smoke myself to death, fuck myself to death. It was just manic activity to stop myself from thinking about the abuse.'

Men have rarely been taught a language to express feelings. Feelings are sometimes expressed through dreams and can be brought into consciousness by working with the meaning of the dream. If clients are encouraged to write down dreams as soon after waking as possible, they can be encouraged to bring dream material and explore it during counselling. I believe it is important to allow the client to make his own interpretation of the dream rather than to interpret it for him. The following is an example of a client's dream followed by the way he used the material to build his sense of self. I asked him to tell the dream in the present tense, as though he is still in it:

> I am walking on the north coast of Devon or Cornwall. Mum, Dad, Mike, HIM (the abuser – grandfather) and loads of friends are there. I am a young adult. The walk is very long and arduous with very steep hills. The people at the front are going much too fast; they are being a bit silly. I am worried because people are not staying together, but are too far apart, and they may get lost or have an accident. Dad is struggling to keep up as he has a bad knee, which means he is *not* in charge, in control and leading as he usually is.
>
> We get halfway up, to a pub/hotel. Its time to set off again. Dad comes to see and says awkwardly that he can't go any further because mum's *tired*; but I know it's because of his knee. I say okay and dash off through the hotel to catch up with the group before they rush off without me. Then I bump into HIM on the stairs. I tell him he ought to stay behind as he won't be able to keep up. I don't want him to come but I make an excuse that the terrain is too rough, and he won't be able to keep up. I see his face, he wants me to help him keep up; to look after him. He wants me to feel guilty about leaving my old granddad behind.
>
> *Then* I decide not to worry about hurting his feelings. I say *no*, I'm going on, on my *own*, and stride off fast, leaving him *behind* with the others who have dropped out. He looks *upset, hurt but I don't care about him anymore.*
>
> I stride off; there's a very steep hill. I've fallen behind; the others who are near the top are all lost. I know the way. I've done the walk before. *I catch up* and *take control, 'Follow me, I really know the way. It's very dangerous in some parts, you must follow me'.* Then the rest of the group chooses to follow me and we all get back safely.
>
> On the way back we are on an open-top bus, driving very fast, too fast, on winding sharp cliff roads. I'm sat at the front, on the top. Stephen (brother and also a victim) is sat next to me. He looks exhausted, but I don't remember him being on the walk. He is dressed in black and looks sad. I tell him *'You must hold on like me. Look, hold the side of the bus, hold on tight!'* He holds on, we're close together, holding on. It's hard to survive, but we are managing to *stay* on the bus.

Christopher explains his understanding of the dream: It seems to be symbolic of the journey he is on. He is learning to take control of his own life, not allow himself to be manipulated into taking responsibility for his grandfather's needs or allowing himself to be controlled by his father. He recognizes that his father is unable to accept his own weakness and projects it onto others. He is leaving them behind. The journey feels dangerous, difficult and fast. There are feelings of excitement, exhilaration, fear and protectiveness towards his brother, who is on the same journey but not feeling as strong as himself at the time. They have grown close to one another since discovering that they were both victims of their grandfather's abuse.

This dream was an important turning point in the client's therapy. He referred back to it frequently in future sessions. It reinforces his determination to keep going, even when the going gets difficult. It connects him with his power and autonomy.

It is important to help the client connect with the feelings expressed through the dream. Sometimes it will be possible to do so by recounting the dream after having written it down. Sometimes the client will need to draw the dream images and talk through them in the session or even create a clay model or poem about the dream.

Later in his process Christopher began to express himself through poetry – something he had never attempted before. Poetry permits the powerful expression of feelings, images and metaphors that enable the client to pin down their sense of themselves. He used a poem to express his lowest point in therapy:

LEAD

Weighed down
Under a blanket of lead.
Encompassing, all over me
Breathless,
I feel half-dead.
Energy, strength and power
All sapped, drained away.
I don't like it here
Please don't make me stay.
I feel so helpless
Out of control.
Optimism, hope, cheerfulness,
I no longer extol.
Gone away,
Replaced by fear.
Unemployment, debt, homelessness,
All feel so near.

As the client lets go of his familiar ways of coping, he may begin to wish he had never started the process of recovery – the newly felt emotions are threatening to the client's security. At this point the client may become angry with the therapist as the one who has brought him closer to his pain. The therapist may feel like an abuser. Strong counter-transferences can be hard to handle and good supervision is essential if the therapist is to hold the client through the pain without too much anxiety.

The client may feel affection for the abuser and need to protect them. Positive feelings towards the abuser need to be accepted by the therapist, especially when the abuser has been a close family member. Clients may have coped by idealization of the abuser and have internalized all the 'bad'. They can be helped to understand that conflicting feelings can exist within and towards the same person. This might also give them permission to both love and hate their abuser.

As this process develops the client may feel his fear. Validation of fear contributes to the understanding of the event as abuse, even though coercion rather than force was used and he may see himself as a willing participant. Fear is an appropriate response to being violated and if he has been socialized not to acknowledge fear it might feel overwhelming. During this phase the client might respond by extreme acting out as he thrashes about trying to find ways of avoiding the pain. He might feel suicidal, drink too much or fall back into old, unhelpful familiar patterns of avoidance. The right to confront or challenge this behaviour needs to be earned. Inappropriate or untimely confrontation can reflect the original abuse of power.

During this stage the client might prematurely wish to forgive the abuser to avoid the painful feelings or the pressure from family or Church. Matthew describes his need to forgive his rapist: 'To not forgive is to twist yourself up with hate and I don't think it does you any good; it might for a while, but forgiveness is part of having compassion and letting go and forgiveness isn't words, it's doing something.'

His need to 'do something' was satisfied when he unexpectedly met up with his rapist one night in a pub:

> I bought him a drink and felt really proud of myself. He didn't notice but I was gripping the bar and my knuckles were white 'cos if I took my hand off the bar they would have been shaking. I didn't accuse him because I don't think he would have understood. To be fair he has got an argument; as an adult you are responsible for your own actions to some extent. It was up to me to make sure that I didn't make myself so vulnerable.

Matthew was still avoiding his fear and anger and was caught up with a sense of having some responsibility for his rape because he had drunk too much. Anger may create fear and shame.

The client may fantasize violent revenge. Jeremy says:

> I would have just got my mates to have battered him to hell, then taken all his money and burnt his house down. I don't care if I go to prison for it. It would give me the satisfaction of really hurting him. Maybe I'll do something really horrible like cutting his knob off and chuck it in his mouth and say 'suck that! Look what you made me do – you can do it yourself now.

Such strong feelings might frighten the client who may judge himself to be as bad as the abuser, triggering shame and self-loathing. Most of us have been indoctrinated to believe we have no right to anger; we may have been punished for anger. Violence is not the same as anger. The two have often become confused and part of the work of therapy is to help men to separate out the emotion of anger from the acting out on others through violence. As children we have rarely been taught how to express anger in a healthy way and people fear that any expression of anger will be destructive.

When a man begins to connect with his angry feelings towards his abuser or those who failed to protect him from the abuse, he can be helped to find ways to discharge the accumulated anger from the past. Using a thick felt pen (red or black) on a large piece of paper (flip chart or reverse side of old wallpaper), he can write letters (not to be posted). These letters can be directed at whoever has caused the pain (Etherington 2000). Additionally men have drawn life-sized figures of their abuser and then screwed up, torn or burnt the paper as a ritual discharge of old stored up feelings. The physical activity can create an opportunity for release pent-up feelings in a managed and contained way that will hurt nobody.

The client may grieve for the loss of childhood innocence. 'Big boys don't cry' is a phrase that still echoes in homes and institutions today. Jeremy internalized these messages:

> I never cry in front of anyone. I've felt like committing suicide loads of times. My friend found me once when I'd taken some paracetamol. I have fantasies about killing myself to get rid of the pain. I suffer from a lot of pain about my life, in my mind and in my heart. No one knows the way I feel. I tried to tell a girlfriend once and she said 'pick yourself up and get on with it'. And that's when I started thinking I was damaged goods; I go to sleep crying and I wake up crying.

Eventually the client begins to shift attention from the abuse to ways he can live an enjoyable life. The abuse becomes a memory of an experience that has affected his life but no longer dominates it. Men can find some meaning in the experience and feel strengthened by dealing with the abuse.

A gentle, helpful and skilful way of working with a man who needs to accept, feel and work through his victimization, hurt and anger is demonstrated on video by Carl Rogers (see references). It is particularly helpful as a tool for learning about working with issues concerned with gender and race in a person-centred way.

SUMMARY

Presenting recovery in the above way may seem to oversimplify what is a complex, lengthy, painful and usually non-linear process of healing. The client may go in and out of stages and return at times to previous ones. I do not wish to underestimate the difficulties, but recognizing a process might enable the helper and client to avoid feeling overwhelmed. Knowledge of the process can be shared with the client as a tool for self-empowerment, particularly when the going seems rough and clients are tempted to retreat. It is therefore important for clients to find out about the different approaches to counselling and therapy. If the counsellor is humanistic they will work in a way that is transparent and empowering and will believe in the importance of the 'working alliance' that is exemplified by being fully present and in 'contact' with the client. It is not enough to be empathic, understanding and respectful if the client is not made aware of that. This requires that the counsellor communicates those ways of being with the client verbally or non-verbally and does not withhold information about themselves that might be useful for the client; that questions are given answers and that transference (i.e. when the counsellor becomes aware that the client might be feeling something towards them which may belong in a previous relationship) should be brought out into the open and talked about. Clients should be encouraged to 'interview' prospective therapist/counsellors and to ask questions that will enable them to know if they feel comfortable with that person. The relationship is crucial to healing and if the counsellor is not prepared to be fully present in the work, the client will not feel sufficiently held.

There is no way of knowing how long individuals will need to heal from their childhood experiences of violation and abuse. If the client comes for counselling immediately after disclosure, they may have been catapulted into a state of crisis and need frequent holding without necessarily 'doing the work'. For others they will find meeting even once a week too threatening and may need less frequent contact until the trust has built. Sometimes clients will come regularly for a short time and then leave counselling for a while, returning when their current life events raise awareness of their need to work further with their abuse issues.

Careful assessment of client needs must be made and a qualified counsellor who listens, observes and learns from the client will be best able to negotiate how those needs might be met. The individual's experience is unique and cannot be compared to anybody else's. It is probably the worst thing that has happened to them, although clients have sometimes acknowledged that the way their abuse was dealt with has sometimes been as abusive or more abusive than the original experience. Perhaps they have tried to tell someone who has not believed them, blamed them or dismissed their feelings. I have sometimes spent many hours undoing the client's experience of feeling abused in previous therapy, especially if the therapist has worked in a way that has felt disempowering for the client and thereby mirrored the original abuse of power.

It is essential for counsellors and helpers who are working with survivors of sexual abuse to ensure they have good supervision. The work can be long and difficult as well as rewarding. The complexities of the transference and counter-transference within the relationship need careful identification and management. Workers can become enmeshed in the unconscious victim-perpetrator dynamic as the client attempts to find their way through the painful process of telling their story, developing trust, expressing their feelings and connecting with their own sense of power. Without good supervision we run the risk of missing some of the unconscious communications that might help us move our clients through their painful past to the present.

Having read through this chapter I can see that I may have over-emphasized the difficulties and problems involved for the client. I think because I am so familiar with the journey, both my own and that of people with whom I have worked as a counsellor, I did not want to give the impression that the work is easy or painless. In doing so, maybe I have not adequately communicated the positive aspects of doing this work, both as a client and a counsellor.

My own journey as a client has been life changing. I think it was Epicticus, in the first century, who said: 'Men are disturbed not by things but by the views which they take of them.' We cannot go back and undo the events that have happened to our clients or ourselves but we can change how we feel about them and respond to them. To do that we have to know them, consciously, feel them and understand the effect they have had on our lives. The freedom created by consciousness allows us to reclaim ourselves and in that freedom we can create new ways of using the rest of our lives – given the resources we discover within ourselves.

As a counsellor I have received so much from my clients. They have taught me, challenged me, stimulated me, loved me and hated me, probably in equal amounts to all that I have taught, challenged, stimulated, loved and at times hated them. I have felt alive, useful, creative and honoured by their company. I shall never forget any one of them. Christopher told me recently:

> It's been a long journey – lots of things have happened. Although I wish the abuse hadn't happened, going through the healing process has changed me dramatically. I think I'm more alive, more feeling and understanding – more of a whole person – a lot more tolerant of other people, less rigid, less staid. Life's better in lots of ways but it is also more difficult in some ways because changing so drastically has coloured relationships. I still feel I'm on the journey – I'm not at the end of it and I think I probably never will be. It's going to be with me all the time – but I've learned how to deal with it now. I'm glad that I came to the point of seeking help. I don't know what would have happened to me if I hadn't. I think without question I've benefited from it – I think it has made me a stronger person for sure. It's good that from the terrible things that happened to me, something good and positive should come from it. And looking back now, although I said before that I'd never forget what happened, it does seem to have gone a little bit into the distance – it seems longer ago now – seeing you seems longer ago and what happened to me as a child seems a lifetime away now; whereas before it always seemed right there – but in the back ground.

In conclusion I would like to use a quote from Alice Miller (1990) by way of recommending that helpers in this field need to have dealt with their own childhood traumas before embarking on the process of helping others:

> Only therapists (helpers) who have had the opportunity to experience and work through their own traumatic past will be able to accompany patients (clients) on the path to truth about themselves and not hinder them on their way ... for they no longer have to fear the eruption in themselves of feelings that were stifled long ago, and they know from their own experience the healing power of these feelings. (Miller 1990, p.316)

REFERENCES

'Accuracy About Abuse.' PO Box 3125, London NW3 5QB. Contact Marjorie Orr.

Bass, E. and Davis, L. (1988) *The Courage to Heal*. New York: Harper and Row.

Blagg, H. (1989) 'Fighting the stereotype – "ideal" victims in the inquiry.' In C. Wattam, J. Hughes and H. Blagg (eds) *In Child Sexual Abuse: Listening, Hearing and Validating the Experiences of Children*. Harlow: NSPCC/Longman.

Bolton, F.G., Morris, L. and Mac Eachron, A. (1989) *Males at Risk: The Other Side of Sexual Abuse*. Newbury Park CA: Sage.

Bond, T. (1993) *Standards and Ethics in Counselling in Action*. London: Sage.

Bradshaw, J. (1988) *Healing the Shame that Binds You*. Deerfield Beach FL: Health Communications.

Broussard, S. and Wagner, W. (1988) 'Child sexual abuse: Who is to blame?' *Child Abuse and Neglect, 12*, 4, 563–569.

Briere, J. (1992) *Child Abuse Trauma*. New York: Sage.

Dolan, Y. (1991) *Resolving Sexual Abuse*. New York: Norton.

Egan, G. (1986) *The Skilled Helper*, 3rd edn. Monterey CA: Brooks/Cole.

Elliot, M. (ed) (1993) *Female Sexual Abuse of Children: The Ultimate Taboo*. Harlow: Longman.

Etherington, K. (1995) *Adult Male Survivors of Childhood Sexual Abuse*. London: Pavilion Publishers.

Etherington, K. (1996) 'Therapeutic issues for sexually abused males.' *Counselling, 7*, 3, 224–228.

Etherington, K. (forthcoming) *Narrative Approaches to Working with Adult Male Survivors: The Client's, the Counsellor's and the Researcher's Story*. London: Jessica Kingsley Publishers.

Finkelhor, D. and Browne, A. (1986) 'Initial and long term effects: a conceptual framework.' In D. Finkelhor *A Sourcebook on Child Sexual Abuse*. Beverly Hills CA: Sage.

Hall, L. and Lloyd, S. (1989) *Surviving Child Sexual Abuse*. London: Falmer Press.

Home Office (1993) *The Offender's Tale: Janus Studies*. London: HMSO.

Hunter, M. (1990a) *The Sexually Abused Male*, vol.1. Lexington MA: Lexington Books.

Hunter, M. (1990b) *The Sexually Abused Male*, vol. 2. Lexington MA: Lexington Books.

Hunter, M. and Gerber, P.N. (1990) 'Use of terms "victim" and "survivor" in grief stages commonly seen during recovery from child sexual abuse.' In M. Hunter *The Sexually Abused Male*, vol. 2. Lexington: Lexington Books.

Mezey, G.C. and King, M.B. (eds) (1992) *Male Victims of Sexual Assault*. Oxford: Oxford Medical Press.

Miller, A. (1990) *Thou Shalt not be Aware: Society's Betrayal of the Child*, 2nd edn. London: Pluto.

O'Hara, M. (1992) 'Domestic violence and child abuse – making the links.' *Childright 88*, 4–5.

Parks, P. (1994) *The Counsellor's Guide to Parks Inner Child Therapy*. London: Souvenir Press.

Rogers, Carl. Videotape of session on 'Hurt and Anger'. Available from Concord Videos, 201 Felixtowe Road, Ipswich, IP3 9BJ. Tel: 01473 726012.

Sanderson, C. (1990) *Counselling Adult Survivors of Child Sexual Abuse*. London: Jessica Kingsley Publishers.

Sgroi, S. (1989) *Vulnerable Populations*, vol. 2. Lexington MA: Lexington Books.

ACKNOWLEDGEMENT

The author wishes to acknowledge that permission has been given to use some material that was originally referred to in the article 'Therapeutic issues for sexually abused males' which was published in *Counselling*, **August 1996, 224–228.**

CHAPTER 3

A Personal Account

Robert Johnson

I was born on 3 September 1945 but it was not until October 1994 that I learned of the full circumstances surrounding my mother's pregnancy, my entry into this world and my earliest days as an infant. My mother, I discovered, had explained to my wife how during her pregnancy she had been beaten by my father and that his actions had led to a life or death situation for both of us. When we talk about violence, therefore, I guess you can say that I was an early starter. I was born apparently black and blue with the bruises from my father's blows. Forceps needed to be used in order to bring me into this world and even this life-saving act can later have adverse effects as force, however well intended, cannot ever be understood by an infant. I am certain to this day that my earliest recollections of fear and danger were from within a womb which was so obviously unsafe.

One of the most appropriate therapies I feel I did use to its full potential later on in my recovery involved me getting in touch with events around my birth. This meant being prepared to explore the scenario around my birth, the images that were conjured up: labour ward, doctors, nurses, my mother in labour. Rather than a joyful occasion for either doctors, nurses or my mother, the scene was likely to be more tragedy and despair. It must have been certain to all those present that if violence was evident immediately prior to my birth, then violence would return when my mother and I left hospital.

Re-birth therapy enabled me to express my anger at my father. It explained too my ambiguity around my mother's role. Why did she not protect me? She of course did what she could, yet I almost felt abandoned during therapy. Could this be how I had felt as an infant? While painful, it was nonetheless extremely beneficial.

I have since learned from my mother herself that almost throughout her entire pregnancy violence toward her was a regular occurrence. There were in fact few occasions when violence was not part of her married life. I was conceived in this environment, born and brought up in it. I fully understand how events such as those I experienced at that time and later throughout my formative years can and do have an influence on the here and now.

What I learned from my wife, while enormously painful at that time, later became a validation of my efforts in recovery from life as a child in a violent home. It also helped me further come to terms with the pain, sadness and confusion around my life as a young adult who later on in life came actually to enjoy meting out violence to others. It also made lots of sense about my suspicions and reasoning around my slide into oblivion as an addict in my early twenties up until my late thirties. My mother's disclosure was to provide me with the last few pieces of a jigsaw that it had taken me since birth to assemble. It is now complete.

Fear and violence go hand in hand. The impact, especially on a child, is I feel lifelong. Memory can help retain that impact and bring to the fore almost as brutally on recollection, the suffering one felt in the first instance. Yet such is the ability of not just myself but many others to overcome whatever we may have faced in our lives. Ultimately we need not retain anything that impairs us and stops us leading the life we choose. It does mean of course that in order to be free from the archaic shackles and burden of the past that appropriate therapy is sought and carried out. As a survivor I can truly say that the effort needed to do this is well worth it.

I have not only survived my dubious beginnings but have since gone on to work in an environment that means I meet many people who are starting out on the long, hard road to recovery. Without doubt it can be argued that I do this perhaps to satisfy unmet needs that lie within me. Maybe so. Meanwhile I will carry on in the hope that if this is indeed the case then I can think of no better and more appropriate reason for continuing.

As much as I have worked on the issues from my past and what they have thrown up for me – sadness, grief, anger, rage, joy, despair, guilt, laughter, hurt and the like – I feel that perhaps these feelings and many others no doubt will forever be part of my present. Such is the threat that it can hover over me even to this day, although with nowhere near the same intensity. Writing about violent episodes in my life can still evoke the feelings of fear and anxiety within me. Nowadays, however, my understanding of the past, its subsequent effects and my emancipation is probably as complete as I would like. The fear comes of course from my past. It is but a memory.

My memory, especially that of my past, is at times crystal clear and it can present me with constant challenges. I remember the first time I sat down to try to write my life story as part of an essay for a diploma in counselling skills some years ago. I could almost feel the eyes of my deceased father boring into me and the powerful physical presence of my mother, who is very much still alive today. My hand just would not move to write. For to condemn the actions of my parents was taboo – especially as a child and even later as an adult: 'You never ever let anyone know what you are feeling. You never show you are hurt, you just hurt them back even more. You never cry or I will give you something to cry for.' Such was the message. I did know that I would eventually put pen to paper and overcome the enormously debilitating situation, but it took some time and therapeutic support before I actually did complete my task.

The satisfaction I get from being prepared to face the issues which almost destroyed me makes all the effort worthwhile. No longer do I have to wake in total fear from nightmares. No longer do I isolate myself and hide behind curtains. I do not need to take powerful drugs to suppress my fears, neither do I need alcohol to wash down the pills. I do not expect to have to undergo any more surgery to cut out my pain as was the case when, by the time I was 20, I needed an operation to remove duodenal ulcers that were threatening to burst within my stomach: a stomach that was the carrier of all my fears. My memories of this and of other equally painful episodes are now, in fact, almost a blessing. For from them I have been able to extract the useful and discard with pleasure those bits that I never wanted in the first place.

Memory can be an asset and equally it can be the provider of rather more unwelcome times. It has meant of course that I am able to use it now, without fear, while I sit and write this chapter. One of my earliest recollections is of the time when as a child I was ordered to play my part in the running of the home.

I am sat on the front doorstep; it is 1950. My fingers are growing hot and I squirm uncomfortably on the concrete doorstep, conscious of the noise, the abrasive scrape as my hand moves left-right, left-right, left-right. I lift my hand and examine the coin I hold. Still a long way to go yet I think. In an effort to cool both coin and fingers I dip them into the saucer of water placed at my side. How I hated this chore. How, even at my age, I could feel the embarrassment. The reason I was doing this, 'filing down the halfpennies', was not really understood by me at that time. I didn't really know that because of the poverty and deprivation and need for survival a filed down halfpenny would take the place of a shilling piece in the gas meter. I just knew that if my efforts were not good enough I would get a hiding. If this were not a sound enough reason I had the extra incentive that if I did not reshape the coin to fit the meter we would all go cold and have no cooked meal. No gas, no food, as simple as that really.

At five years of age I guess most things are simple, especially if the yardstick is plain survival. But at five years of age, rubbing away with the coin burning my fingers, paranoid with fear of ridicule and criticism looking over my shoulders threatening me, survival and simplicity were life itself.

Therapy which can show the impossible situation for the child and his powerlessness in these circumstances is so useful. Prescriptive interventions such as highlighting the power of the adult over the child can be so helpful. For example, do you feel a child under threat of violence is likely to say no to an abusive adult when that adult wants the child to comply? I feel this helps redress a sense of imbalance. It also importantly helps to validate the sense of helplessness which of course can play a major role in adult life.

My mind is the only true record I have of my life as a child for there are few photographic reminders – even of the type which might show a life other than one of survival. Only one or two photographs of me aged between five and eight years stare back at me as a reminder of the young life I endured. A young life that was fear itself, that led to an ulcerated gut in adolescence and that often knew fear as its only medium. Gestalt therapy around working with photographs is therefore a medium through which issues can be explained.

I guess it is always easier to recall pain. To recall bad times and forget the joy and happiness that ordinarily is the right of us all. But that was it. That was the way the toilet rolls as my late brother so eloquently put it.

He found his own way out. He never came to find a way in which he could truly come to terms and live with his past. It was too painful for him: mid-forties, head shot away through 30 years of alcohol pickling, straight from the jar, down the throat, forget yesterday, forget today; don't even think about tomorrow. If it comes it will hurt, hurt more than yesterday with tomorrow as the constant reminder of more pain to come. See you again, my brother, no more 'asshole to breakfast time' – that threat, that awful threat from a tortured mother, whose own fear and pain drove her to total despair. Release for her included use of the boiler stick while encouraging us to 'behave or I'll fucking beat you from asshole to breakfast time'. Goodbye, my brother, God bless.

Therapy helped ensure that if ever I was going to write it was always going to be as near to the truth as I could recall, though it was always going to be lacking in some detail. Violence distorts the truth for in saying no just to save ourselves from a beating, we create confusion and can, I feel, lose track of what is right and wrong. There was no way as a child, where if the truth meant a hiding or worse still isolation, I would be truthful. Instead I learned to cheat, to lie, to comply. It was so much safer to do things that way.

Maybe one day, my own continuing development as an emancipated person permitting, the full story of my life may be told. For now though, my emancipation as a capable adult, accompanied by 'Little Mickey Dripping', my child within, continues on its way. Unlike my deceased brother, I do have a future. A future that I look forward to and one which I deserve. For I have earned it. I am a proud survivor of abuse – sexual, physical, emotional – whatever form you care to name. I am a survivor of addiction and a survivor of humanity. This is the business. This chapter is now my medium.

Fear still plays a part. But so does love, joy and happiness. No more rubbing of coins; only now and again when they jangle in my pocket. My strength is my conscience and my conscience is perfectly clear around those formative years, subsequent growth into adulthood and my later years. It may be that now, in the relative autumn of my life, transitions and their often debilitating effects are less taxing. I am glad to be the father of two children who have helped to confirm I was right to battle and not to succumb. I was right to go on and on until I felt I could go no further. Then I went twice as far. I was right to get the ink on paper, to reverse the script that was my life. I was right to marry Carol and to have remained with her for over 30 years. 'Don't marry her,' my father said. What the fuck did he know about relationships? What the fuck was he thinking of every time he battered and bruised my mother? What the fuck was he thinking of when he battered her pregnant bulge, battered me inside her womb and swore that when she nearly died he would swing for me if she did? Oh yes, I swallowed that all right. Most of my life believing it was my fault she nearly didn't make it. It was me all right. Not my father. Never him. I worshipped him always trying to gain his love, always looking for his approval.

It never came.

Maybe this is why paedophiles can find the easy meat. Maybe this is why I liked the kind man with his tin leg, soft manner and sweets. Yeah, maybe. He showed affection to me far more than my dad and, yes, I liked him, felt drawn to him. My father on the other hand represented fear. A no go – danger. Even the light that swung from the ceiling upstairs was dark red, coloured so that negatives could be processed and pictures he had taken of 'punters' could be sold to them. I hated that light, hated my father but loved him. Confusion too was my life. His photography business was one way I suppose he did try to earn some money. It didn't matter really. What it did manage to do was to frighten me.

Whenever he did make enough money it would go not to the upkeep of the home but on drink. My mother would rear up, they would fight, me and my brothers and sister would get hurt. No one asked how we felt though. No one asked at all. They would fight, we would get hurt. Simple really.

Violence is not just the blow – being physically attacked. It is much more than that. Of greater impact to me was being witness to violence. It was especially difficult to hear my parents fighting. First there would be shouting, then lots of swearing. Almost like a crescendo, becoming louder and louder until the dull 'thwack' of the blows and then silence. That was the worst of all – silence. Then in the morning I would see the bruises, see, hear and feel the tears. I would then bottle up my own feelings so that my mother would not see the tears. I then became the rescuer.

It was little wonder of course how my young stomach became ulcerated. I held in my pain, my grief, my sadness, my anger. Not until I began to get relief from this internal suffering, first through drink and drugs, then finally through therapy, did I ever feel a true integration; between the hurt in my stomach, through to my brain as it tried to make sense of everything.

My journey to becoming healed began when I finally decided that the drugs, the pills and booze combination was not what I really wanted. They had stopped working anyway. I had reached the bottom, there was nowhere else to go. Total despair and isolation were coupled with the increasingly alarming thoughts that I might even harm my family through violence.

I was fortunate that my local GP whom I had depended on for so many years – he was my supplier of prescribed tranquillizers – finally decided that he would help me stop taking the pills. When I approached him on one particular occasion he could see I was at the end of my tether. During the horrendous two years or so of my withdrawal from the drugs I met with him on a regular basis and also with a psychologist.

While this was obviously successful in part – I did give up the drugs – I was never asked about my past or my life as a child. Neither was there any investigation into any underlying factors. Counselling or therapy was not offered as an option.

On reflection perhaps this was appropriate as getting off the stuff was more than enough to cope with at the time. It would have been useful though for it to be acknowledged that perhaps my past was having its effects on my present. At one time the GP did however suggest I read a book about transactional analysis and this made some sense, especially where it referred to the possibility of the 'child' being healed and the 'adult' becoming free.

It was not until I trained as a counsellor, however, when the criteria for selection included students having counselling themselves that I really began to get down to it and begin to talk of those events in my life which I feel led me into addiction.

Counselling was good for me. Without doubt the strength I gained through taking risks and sharing my fears with a counsellor provided me with a springboard into what I finally felt was what I needed. During my road to recovery I had been introduced to Kim Etherington. Through Kim I met Sarasi Rogers and it was Sarasi's techniques and skills that finally helped me meet my unmet challenges. With Sarasi I learned about body work through massage, anger work through expression, including beating the hell out of a cushion with a tennis bat, the use of images, hypnosis, neuro-linguistic programming (NLP) and plain listening. All these techniques I found to be ultimately most beneficial.

I am now healed, there is no more fear, I can and I do live my life free from my past.

It is still there of course, but it no longer dictates my future. I have come to terms with violence through my determination to be free, my courage and my faith. I can truly honour myself. My healing is a testament to my efforts and also to all those people who have helped me along the way. For this I sincerely thank them.

CHAPTER 4

Changing the Contexts of Fear
Responding to Homophobic Violence

Paul Tyrer

INTRODUCTION

This chapter focuses on issues relating to violence against lesbians and gay men and asks questions about developing effective work with those who experience it. I begin by considering how we can define homophobic violence appropriately, with reference to the scale of the problem as established by recent British studies. I then move on to explore who is at risk and in what circumstances and look at the impact of such violence on the individual and on the wider community. I close by exploring via case studies some of the particular concerns of lesbians and gay men about violence, with 'dos and 'don'ts' and a range of questions so that readers can develop their own ideas for practice.

From time to time I have contextualized my discussion with quotations from interview and focus group transcripts prepared as part of the Violence, Sexuality and Space (VSS) project, based at the University of Manchester.[1] This is a two-year study looking at the relationships between safer public spaces and homophobic violence. This chapter is not based on our research findings, but certain insights by research participants have helped in the development of my argument.

BACKGROUND
Definitions and research findings

It would be easy to equate homophobic violence with a physical assault of some kind, since research suggests that such attacks are a relatively common experience for lesbians and gay men. For instance, in the 1994 Stonewall national survey, the most extensive British study to date, one in three men and one in

---

1   The Violence, Sexuality and Space project is based at the Department of Sociology at the University of Manchester. This is one of 20 projects operating under the auspices of the Violence Research Programme at the Economic and Social Research Council (ESRC).

four women said that they had been assaulted at least once in the previous five years because of their sexuality (Mason and Palmer 1996). In British research of cities with large lesbian and gay populations, the figure for assault was still higher: 45 per cent to 47 per cent of respondents (Lewisham Gay Alliance 1992; Truman *et al.* 1994). Assault would appear to be an even greater problem for young lesbians and gay men, with one in two respondents under eighteen reporting being queerbashed (Mason and Palmer 1996).

Despite the frequency with which such assaults are reported, however, classifying only physical attacks as homophobic violence is problematic, although some anti-violence projects do classify in precisely this way (Stanko and Curry 1997). Such a limited classification system serves to minimize the real pervasiveness of homophobia and decreases pressure on the police and other agencies to act. Many in the field would therefore propose a wider definition, like the one recently developed by the ESRC's Violence Research Programme[2]: 'Broadly speaking, violence involves the infliction of emotional, psychological, sexual, physical and/or material damage to people and their wider communities' (Stanko *et al.* 1998). Such a definition would then make space for experiences of verbal abuse, which are still more pervasive than assault, with 73 per cent of the Stonewall sample and 80 per cent of young lesbians and gay men in schools reporting homophobic taunting, teasing or name calling (Mason and Palmer 1996; Rivers 1996). Moreover, a wider definition would enable the range of experiences reported by lesbian and gay men to be taken into account. For example, although some of the experiences listed below by Stonewall respondents might not be classed as physical attacks, they demonstrate the real breadth of homophobic experience:

> 'Threats' (45 responses), 'spat at' (23), 'rape' (9), 'attacked and robbed' (6), 'brick through window' (3), 'sexual assault' (3), 'pushed' (2), 'threatened with knife' (2), 'stoned' (2), 'jostled and tripped', 'bottle smashed over head', 'stabbed three times', 'pushed around', 'held at gunpoint', 'mental torture', 'indecent exposure', 'indecent assault', 'police assault', 'sexual abuse', 'shirt set on fire', 'shot above head with air rifle', 'bullied, pushed, intimidated', 'eviction', 'abusive mail', 'sexual harassment', 'shot in the back', 'shit thrown into house', 'held at knifepoint', 'front door kicked in', 'tear gas', 'pissed on from flats', 'mental abuse', 'attacker tried to pull me out of taxi', 'shot at', and 'run over'. (Mason and Palmer 1996, p.8)

A broader definition that can take in all these experiences is not intended to minimize the impact of a specifically physical assault upon the person, but rather to emphasize the extent to which a wide range of behaviours are experienced as violence, as attacks upon the person that cause harm. Indeed, it is incumbent on researchers (and care workers) to frame questions about violence in such a broad way that research participants (and clients of care services) feel able to report every and any homophobic incident. All too often, victims of non-physical forms of violence feel that such incidents are not

---

2   The Violence Research programme is an initiative by the Economic and Social Research Council (ESRC), featuring 20 research studies across Britain looking at different aspects of violence. Violence, Sexuality and Space is one of these.

significant enough to be reported, even when they are aware of their own immense personal suffering as a result of the experience (Kelly 1988).

The evidence cited here suggests that most lesbians and gay men will experience some form of homophobic violence – experiences which they may deal with on their own, with the help of friends and partners, or by getting in touch with care agencies of various kinds (Herek 1992). In the second half of the chapter, I consider how carers and care agencies can respond positively to the issues raised. But before that, I would like to look a little more at particular issues to do with homophobic violence that may be raised during care interventions.

Contexts of 'recognition'

One way of making sense of the detailed evidence about homophobic violence is to argue that perpetrators use particular 'contexts of recognition' in order to be in a position to act on their prejudice. By contexts of recognition I mean the frames of reference by which a perpetrator can deduce, rightly or wrongly, that someone is lesbian or gay. I have picked three particular contexts to look at here: gender presentation, space occupied, and whether one is alone or in a pair in public space. These would appear to be the most important contexts from the research evidence.

Although gender (the way people present masculinity and femininity) and sex (whether one is born male or female) are not necessarily linked, the idea that men are essentially masculine and women essentially feminine has been widely promoted in society. Men and women may of course be more or less masculine and feminine and can show this – consciously or unconsciously – by how they present themselves, their attitudes and behaviours. Particular examples that have emerged from our research include clothes, hairstyles, footwear, choice and size of alcoholic drink, general demeanour, level of self-confidence and self-assertion, ways of sitting, standing, walking, and so on. Such norms of gender presentation are, I would argue, so ingrained – we all know them so well – that it is often immediately apparent to others when we step outside them. Thus departing from these norms provides someone who has a fear or intense dislike of lesbians and gay men with a 'context of recognition': that is, he may 'recognize' from gender which is presented differently from the norm that someone is 'queer' (Harry 1982, 1990; Namaste 1996; Von Schultess 1992). The perpetrators's recognition may of course be wrong – the 'masculine woman' may not be a lesbian and the 'feminine man' may not be gay. But as Namaste notes, 'bashers do not characteristically inquire as to the sexuality of their potential victims, but rather make this assumption on their own' (1996, p.225). Some victims of 'homophobic' violence, then, may not be lesbian or gay at all, but transgendered, bisexual or straight[3]. Namaste cites studies suggesting that men and women appearing to contravene societal gender norms are more than twice as likely to be assaulted as those who are seen to conform.

3   This is not to argue that there is not specific violence enacted against transgendered people because they are seen as transgendered. See Namaste (1996) for more on this.

A second 'context' concerns whether one is alone or in a same-sex pair or group. Research by Comstock (1991) suggests that lesbians are more likely to be attacked when walking with another woman (48%) than when walking alone (28%). This has been borne out to some extent by lesbians in our focus groups who pinpoint one explanation for this context of conflict:

> Bev: I often find that if I am with someone that the men will interfere ... They will give a bit of banter to my partner – I think they see me as a bit of a threat, they'll start giving a bit of banter to my partner and start going 'Oh come on lass I'll give you a better time than any of this' and all this and getting really tight and it is just like 'What are you doing?'

> Keri: I have experienced crap from men and it wasn't even with my partner it was with a friend of mine. They just gathered around her and started groping her and invading her space ... When I am with her, because I am her best friend it is like the dynamics are different, they have a go at her and I'm stepping in even though we are not in a partnership together. (VSS focus group)

Clearly, for these women, being seen in a pair brings unwanted heterosexual attention, with men perhaps sensing a particular kind of threat to their 'right' to control and possess women. This puts lesbians in the difficult position of either tolerating this behaviour or rebelling against it. In either case, violence of some sort (as in the examples above) may result.

Being in a pair or group may be more risky for lesbians, but gay men are more likely to be attacked when they are alone (66%) than when they are with another man (14%; Comstock 1991).[4] Gay men are also more likely than lesbians to be outnumbered by their attackers. It would seem from these findings that gay men are victims of a particular brand of group masculinity that singles out those who are felt not to fit in. Evidence on this comes from Weissman (1992), who interviewed a number of homophobic perpetrators, all but one of whom identified gay bashing as a form of normative group behaviour. They describe their attacks as variously: 'a rite of passage', 'a symbol of prestige', 'really a joke' – a joke being something you share with friends, of course. One man even described the attack as an intimate bonding experience: 'After ... there was also a strong close feeling. That we were all in something together.' This bonding is possible, it seems, because of the widely shared negative views of young heterosexual men about gay men. For Weissman's young men, to be gay is 'disgusting and immoral', 'not right' and 'not natural' (Weissman 1992, pp.170–178).

A third 'context of recognition' is that individuals may be targeted when they are seen in what are perceived or commonly designated as 'gay spaces'. These may be lesbian or gay bars, lesbian or gay parts of town or gay cruising areas. As Myslick (1996) and Comstock (1991) have shown, gay men are more likely to experience violence in and around these gay spaces than anywhere else – a decidedly ironic finding since these are often hailed as 'safer spaces' and much

---

4   It is notable that the figure for violence against both gay men and lesbians drops significantly when a person is accompanied by a member of the opposite sex (Comstock 1991).

has been done to shore them up as such.[5] Myslick notes on this that 'queer spaces are generally perceived as safe havens from this discrimination and violence, but they often serve as 'destinations of choice' for bashers' (Myslick 1996, p.157). As one of our focus group members noted, merely to be in gay space can confer the sign of queer upon you:

> Fred: I found that when I was in Glasgow, I never once got hassled, whereas down here, the amount of times I've been hassled personally just down the village [Manchester's gay area] – and I look straight – 'cos people think that just because you're walking through the village, you're gay. Instantly don't they? I mean, come on.

[General agreement]

> Sam: I'd definitely agree with that. (VSS focus group)

Fred's comment here – 'people think that just because you're walking through [gay space], you're gay' – implies that those who are not lesbian and gay may also be at risk if they socialize in or walk through gay areas. This has been demonstrated in a most graphic way by the 1999 Soho nail bombing, where two of the three people killed inside the gay pub the Admiral Duncan were heterosexual.

Although lesbians are also at risk in lesbian and gay space, they are as likely to be vulnerable around 'straight-identified, domestic, and higher educational settings' (Comstock 1991, p.49; see also Brett 1999). Thus lesbians are likely to experience violence as a much more pervasive threat than gay men, as they are at risk both on the street and in gay areas. This difference seems to relate to the fact that lesbians have to deal not only with society's homophobia but with its sexism as well. They experience violence both because they are lesbians and because they are women. Lesbian research participants and service users have commented that they sometimes find it difficult to tell whether the harassment they experience is motivated by perpetrators' views of lesbians or of women in general (Herek 1992; Mason 1996). With this in mind, it is particularly worrying that lesbians continue to be marginalized in discourses of homophobic violence. Although they often get 'name checked' in the debate, their detailed concerns about safety and violence are ignored and ideas of 'homophobic violence' tend to be referenced around the needs, concerns and experiences of gay men. Stanko and Curry (1997) note the tendency of community and police meetings to focus on men's concerns about, for instance, the insensitive policing of public sex settings rather than on more general fears about safety in the streets, in one's own neighbourhood or at home. This tendency effectively removes many lesbian concerns from debates about

---

5   For example, Health Gay Manchester launched a major 'Safe in the Streets' campaign, which aimed to 'reclaim' Manchester's gay area from the threat of homophobia and the perceived lack of respect for gay space from heterosexuals. The campaign featured huge banners celebrating 'the Lesbian and Gay Village', as well as pennants from every lamp-post and posters in most bars. Other initiatives, like the Manchester Lesbian and Gay Mardi Gras, have also promoted the concept of specifically lesbian and gay space in which heterosexuals are welcome so long as they remain respectful of lesbian and gay interests.

homophobic violence, yet it also obscures gay men's own need to debate the range of issues relating to day-to-day safety and risk.

Contexts of fear

These contexts through which homophobia finds shape and form necessarily have some kind of impact on lesbian and gay behaviour. Arguably, contexts of recognition can become effective contexts of fear, since lesbians and gay men may feel compelled to behave in self-restricting ways owing to the perceived homophobic threats just described. Mason has argued that lesbians are 'disciplined into believing and acting as if they should not be there, into regulating their own behaviour so that they become unseeable' (Mason 1996, p.99). Valentine agrees, noting that lesbians (like women in general) have to 'exercise constant self-vigilance, policing their own dress, behaviour and desires to avoid confrontation' (Valentine 1996, p.149). In a similar way, Myslick has pointed to the 'editing of behaviour' that many gay men feel is necessary to avoid violence. Most gay men, he argues, see this as 'the norm' (Myslick 1996, p.165).

A number of examples of this behaviour editing have emerged from our research. One of our lesbian informants told us how for a long period she could not leave her house for fear of verbal and/or physical abuse from neighbours and others on the estate where she was living. This is clearly an extreme example of what is felt necessary to avoid violence. At the other extreme, comments by a gay respondent reveal that behaviour editing can be very subtle indeed:

> Steve: I do find if I'm walking by a group of lads, I'll hold my cigarette different ... I'm normally just like that [*freely waves imaginary cigarette in his hand*] and I'll change it round and smoke like that [*holds cigarette still in front of his mouth*] ...
>
> Paul: So is there anything else apart from your cigarette that changes that you're aware of?
>
> Steve: Probably my walk really ... My friends do tell me that I walk really, really camply. I don't know, I have tried, but I obviously don't do it very well, 'cos they all laugh at me. (VSS focus group)

Comments like these indicate the extent to which the threat of violence encourages the internalization of repressive behaviour. They also suggest how difficult it must be to resist such internalization when even one's gay friends are complicit in the policing of behaviour. Indeed, research would seem to suggest that the impact of contexts of fear is significant for lesbians and gay men, whether or not they experience violence as a significant factor in their lives (Garnets, Herek and Levy 1992; Mason 1996; Myslick 1996; Valentine 1996; Wertheimer 1992).

Positive responses to homophobic violence

This is not to argue that contexts of fear are always successful in repressing lesbians and gay men. Clearly, events like Pride or Lesbian and Gay Mardi Gras are evidence of the spirit of resistance in today's lesbian and gay communities. We have been documenting many other examples of resistance, both institutionally and individually, during our research. Institutions such as

Manchester City Council and the police have recently supported large-scale, anti-homophobic violence campaigns. Equally, Healthy Gay Manchester (HGM), a gay men's voluntary organization, mounted a successful poster and banner campaign in 1998, reclaiming Manchester's lesbian and gay space after a series of hate-attacks and muggings. Individuals have also made a difference, speaking out against heterosexist oppression, despite threats to their own safety. Danielle's intervention here is an attempt to reclaim the gayness of the village streets:

> Danielle: There were six [straight] men walking down behind me, coming towards the Rembrandt which is very much a gay men's bar, you often see lots of gay men standing outside. And one started pushing the other one towards the door of the bar and he said 'Don't put me near there! Don't let me go near them. Urgh, I'm not going in there!', you know. And I just turned round to him, stopped and ... I know I put myself in danger here because they were very drunk ... and I said 'Well don't come into the village then if you don't like it.' I said 'This is a lesbian and gay village and don't you forget it!' (VSS interview)

There are also more radical forms of campaigning, as another of our key informants points out:

> Lynn: Other smaller initiatives ... you'll get ones where this drag artist will go round in a limousine, you know, up tall, with a megaphone, shouting to people in the streets 'You are now entering a lesbian and gay zone.' ... He did it for two nights just round the perimeter of the Village just shouting out of this megaphone before the police turned up and told him to shut up. He'd go away for a bit and then come back.
>
> Lindsay: Did he do that off his own back?
>
> Lynn: There was a group of them, about half a dozen of them that did it. (VSS interview)

It is clear from these examples that lesbians and gay men are not sitting idly by when faced by the contexts of fear I have described, but are involved in resistance of all kinds.

Some lesbians and gay men who experience violence first hand, however, may find it difficult to live healthy and happy lives without some kind of help from others. Some, particularly lesbians (Herek 1992), will turn to lovers and friendship networks for support. Others, most likely to be gay men (Herek 1992), will seek professional care and support from a range of agencies, either generic or lesbian and gay specific. In the following section, I will develop upon many of the issues likely to be raised through two case studies. Both of these provide some guidance on important issues relating to each story, but questions are also posed so that the reader can reflect on her own individual practice.

WORKING WITH VICTIMS OF VIOLENCE
Case study: John's story

> ## Case Study
>
> John, 25, has only recently decided to come out. He has made a start on this by telling his parents, but neither of them has been in any way supportive, something that has left John feeling distressed. He had planned to tell other people, but as his parents have been so negative he has decided not to just at the moment. John feels lonely – although he has some friends at work none of them are gay, or at least none of them have come out to him. There is a gay pub in town, but someone might see him going in and put two and two together … so instead he just goes out to pubs with his mates or from time to time will go cruising in the park. Late one evening, John decides to visit the park. He might meet someone nice and even if his friends see him – well, he's just out walking, isn't he. He does meet someone there, quite a good-looking man in maybe his early thirties. They talk and then move into a darker part of the park and start having sex. Suddenly a group of young men appear. The man John has met runs off and the gang sets on John. They call him queer, punch him to the ground and kick him repeatedly. After the attack, John manages somehow to get to casualty and is treated for a couple of broken ribs and some minor injuries. The staff ask if he wants to report the attack to the police and John agrees that he should (though he has only told the staff the sketchiest of details about what happened). He'll do it later. When he gets home. The nurses have a conversation about John. None of them feel convinced that he is going to be able to report the crime. He seems withdrawn and emotionless.

This case study raises many issues for any care practitioner. One of the most immediate is whether and how John should report the violence he has experienced. The particular circumstances of the violence in John's case – being attacked while having sex in a well-known cruising area – mean that John is likely to feel worried in case it is he rather than the perpetrators who becomes the focus of police investigations. What is most worrying in general terms is that, historically speaking, John's reluctance to report his experience to the police is understandable. A 1994 study of lesbians and gay men found that 47 per cent of respondents had experienced homophobic comments from police officers, while 42 per cent felt that the police had been overly intrusive when taking personal details after a crime had been reported (Truman *et al.* 1994). Nevertheless, reporting crime can 'offer a constructive channel for anger, increase feelings of efficacy and provide the satisfaction of helping to protect other members of the community from the sort of violence one has experienced' (Garnets *et al.* 1992, p.220). In other words, reporting may be one way of beginning the therapeutic process for John.

A possible solution to John's difficulty here might be to call a Hate Crime Hotline (HCHs) or any similar joint venture between the police and lesbians and gay men. These are now being set up in a number of British towns and cities, or are being introduced into existing services like lesbian and gay counselling and information helplines. HCHs enable people in John's situation to report the range of homophobic incidents to a volunteer (another lesbian or gay man) in a confidential setting, without having to report to the police direct. Following John's call, the police will be given a description of the incident and perpetrator(s) and can then take action, while John retains his anonymity. Equally, if John chooses to report the crime to the police direct, he may be able to take any subsequent complaints about police behaviour to the force lesbian and gay liaison officer, many of whom are now in post. The HCH could then help John in a variety of ways – in practical terms (for example, information about rights or police procedures) or by telephone counselling. HCHs could also refer him on to agencies better equipped to deal with other specific needs or problems. The main difficulty for John is that he is not likely to know about HCHs or similar services because he is not socialized into gay circles and is not necessarily going to tell any generic care worker, who might be aware of the service, about his sexuality.

There are clearly other issues to work on aside from reporting the crime. First, John may need help in coming to terms with what victims of any kind of violence have to face. Common reactions include 'sleep disturbances and nightmares, headaches, diarrhoea, uncontrollable crying, agitation and rest-lessness, increased use of drugs, and deterioration in personal relationships' (Garnets et al. 1992, p.208). These physical symptoms may be accompanied by feelings such as self-doubt, loss of trust during day-to-day encounters and interactions, questioning his own worth, isolation, disillusionment, shock, guilt and self-blame, all of which may be experienced on a short- or long-term basis (Garnets et al. 1992; Herek 1992; Wertheimer 1992).

Second, John may feel less able to deal with these reactions because he is in the closet about his sexuality. Many victims of violence get invaluable support from family and friends, but John may decide to keep quiet about his experience because of the possible negative reactions if anyone finds out the context of the attack and then deduces that John is gay. This is effectively a dual form of isolation for John: first the violence, then the inability to talk about it. As Stanko and Curry point out, 'the closet can be an especially lonely place to deal with the effects of homophobic violence for it reduces the emotional support often available through friendship networks within the gay, lesbian and transsexual communities' (Stanko and Curry 1997, p.527).

Third, John's experience of violence is likely to make coming out still more of a crisis for him than it might otherwise have been (Garnets et al. 1992). John will therefore need help with developing his self-esteem, particularly around issues of sexual identity and hope for the future. If not, he may fuse together in his mind an association between being attacked and enjoying sex with men and come to see the attack as some kind of punishment for his sexuality (Garnets et al. 1992). What John does not need to hear is that he can avoid violence if he behaves differently – if he stops going cruising, if he avoids certain areas of town when his is on his own, if he dresses in particular ways. Placing the responsibility for avoiding violence upon the victim of crime makes closeted behaviour – self-invisibilization and behaviour editing – normative and therefore more difficult to overcome.

Although he may not know it, John probably has several options in terms of where to access care. He might be lucky enough to be referred to a local agency with a good reputation for working with lesbian and gay clients, or with practitioners who are themselves lesbian or gay. Of course, John may not come out at first in any care setting, nor indeed for some time afterwards, and the practitioner may have no idea from what John has said that sexuality is even an issue for him. Therefore it is important for all care agencies to ensure that the care environment feels safe, comfortable and affirming, so that John can come out at his own pace. Generic care organizations may also need to think about whether and how they can provide longer term therapeutic interventions for John should he need them on the range of issues that concern him. If not, they should consider carefully where they can refer John on to, so that his longer term needs can be addressed.

An alternative to generic care, of course, is a locally based gay organization and indeed such an agency may be best placed to provide many aspects of the support John is likely to need. He would probably benefit from peer support, for instance – talking with other gay men – in tackling his personal isolation and his lack of self-confidence in his sexuality. However, where there is no such organization locally, John might consider travelling to the nearest city. Alternatively he could ring the nearest helpline from which immediate help, support and advice should be available.

Case Study

Lubna, 30, and Sylvia, 42, share a house in the inner city. Although they have lived peacefully together there for almost ten years now, recently things have started to change. A group of girls from the local school have started harassing them, although at the moment the harassment seems to be fairly minor – at least that is Lubna's view. Some girls followed her home from the station and kept making what seemed like abusive comments from a distance, although she wasn't sure whether the comments were about her lesbianism or her ethnicity. At one point a stone landed close to Lubna's feet, but again she wasn't sure if it was thrown or kicked accidentally. Sylvia though is more worried. Two girls from the school called out to her as she was opening the front door. They called her a 'lezzie' and a 'Paki lover'. Sylvia feels extremely upset about this, though Lubna is still shrugging it off. However, the problem has recently become worse. A small group of girls now occasionally hangs around outside the house. They say nothing at all when they see the two women, but their presence intimidates Sylvia particularly. Lubna is worried about Sylvia.

As with the case study of John, this case study throws up a range of issues. Let us begin by highlighting some of the assumptions that care practitioners might make when working with Lubna and Sylvia on the information given above. We might assume that a reported act of violence against a lesbian or gay client has been perpetrated by a heterosexual male stranger but, as with some other forms of violence, this is not necessarily the case.[6] On the one hand, perpetrators may be known to the victim. They might be fellow students, relatives or neighbours (Brett 1999; Comstock 1991), or they might be in a relationship with the victim. Domestic violence can, of course, occur within same-sex partnerships as a number of research studies have documented (Hickson *et al.* 1994; Landolt and Dutton 1997; Lockhart *et al.* 1994). Practitioners should be aware that for some of their women clients making out that a violent female partner is actually a male partner might seem easier in all kinds of ways. Perpetrators may also be strangers but female, as in this case study. Incidents where a female perpetrator is involved are unfortunately not unknown: in American studies, heterosexual women are responsible for 15 per cent of reported cases of violence against lesbians (Comstock 1991).[7] Practitioners will therefore need to start with an open mind about who the perpetrators of any homophobic act might be.

Other possible assumptions relate to the care options that are open to Lubna and Sylvia. It would be wrong to assume that the women will want their needs to be met by a lesbian and gay organization. Locally based organizations may have no lesbian-specific services, even in the larger cities, or such services may have a poor reputation in the community. Another difficulty might be that such services are staffed by people they know, especially in smaller communities – in which case anonymity and confidentiality become problematic. For these reasons, Sylvia and Lubna may prefer to access care and support from women-only organizations like Rape Crisis (Herek 1992). Lubna, however, might not be happy with either of the previous options. As an Asian woman, she may prefer to seek help from a black/Asian support group, although it will be important to check that the agency in question has a track record of successful working with lesbian clients and their issues in order to avoid possible further homophobic victimization for Lubna. This checking is important when referring lesbian clients to any non-lesbian organization. Of course, in an ideal world Lubna would be able to contact a black lesbian and gay or black women's organization. However these may not be available locally.[8] As in John's case, a trip to a big city may be required to access such services.

6   US studies suggest that homophobic perpetrators are extremely likely to be heterosexual men (96%) under 22 years old, white and in groups (Comstock 1991; Myslick 1996).

7   This compares to the US finding that only 1 per cent of incidents against gay men are committed by heterosexual women (Comstock 1991).

8   However, having a sense of what black lesbian and gay organizations there are appears especially important since violence is experienced more frequently by lesbian and gay respondents from minority ethnic groups than by their white peers. This is particularly the case in relation to certain violent behaviours: being chased or followed (43% minority ethnic groups compared to 29% white) or having objects thrown (31%–18%) (Comstock 1991). Another study has suggested that lesbians from minority ethnic groups are consistently more likely to report physical attacks, threats, vandalism and rape than white lesbians (Von Schultess 1992).

The women may of course rely on friends or each other for support and counselling, but if they do seek outside help there are certainly some difficult care issues for them to raise. The couple's very different reactions to the verbal abuse they have experienced, for example, may cause conflict between them: while Sylvia is extremely upset, Lubna shrugs it off. It may be that Lubna is underestimating the damage that can be inflicted by verbal abuse. She has certainly shown herself to be less concerned than Sylvia about the verbal abuse, but perhaps this is the role she always takes at the expense of voicing her own fears and worries. Garnets points out that the psychological effects of verbal abuse 'may be as severe as those following physical assaults and possibly more insidious because victims of verbal abuse may find its "psychic scars" more difficult to identify than physical wounds' (Garnets *et al.* 1992, p.215). As a result, some victims of verbal abuse minimize the pain and upset they are experiencing, because they cannot bring themselves to believe that verbal abuse is a serious crime (Garnets *et al.* 1992). For Lubna, there is an additional problem in that she is confused about whether the abuse is motivated primarily by homophobia, racism or, as seems likely, a combination of both. Sylvia for her part may become frustrated if she feels that Lubna is not taking the problem seriously. This may exacerbate her feelings of anxiety and cause her to withdraw from Lubna, a very important source of support. Both women may need help in understanding and working through the reactions and feelings of the other.

Another problem the women face is the fact that the girls have started hanging round outside the home – an extremely important place for any couple. For lesbian and gay couples the home is particularly important and is likely to be seen as a refuge from the homophobia of society. The home, in other words, may be the only lesbian or gay space to which they have access. With this in mind, practitioners should consider how they can help the women through not only the emotional but also the practical aspects of this problem. An effective 'care' role may thus involve liaising on the women's behalf with local housing agencies, the council, community police and the school. Alternatively, the practitioner can help by ascertaining whether any of these agencies has done work on or has policies on anti-homophobic action before the women themselves take this further.

Finally, it will be important for any practitioners to consider how such an experience of woman-on-woman violence may affect those like Lubna and Sylvia, who are very likely to feel strong political and personal kinship with women. A significant crisis of trust may occur, which could affect friendships, work and family relationships and issues to do with identity.

All the points made here, of course, are indicators of possible feelings which the women may have. In a sense, this case study, like the last one, is attempting to indicate some of the possible conflicts and difficulties, rather than suggesting that these will inevitably arise. Indeed, it is important that practitioners are able to see Lubna and Sylvia and others like them as potential survivors of homophobic abuse. As Garnets points out, these women are potentially 'active, problem-solving individuals, capable of coping with the attack and using the experience as an opportunity for growth' (Garnets *et al.* 1992, p.207).

DOS AND DON'TS

- Do provide opportunities for clients to speak positively about being lesbian or gay. Be prepared to do this yourself if clients find it difficult.
- Don't underestimate the potential impact of homophobic verbal abuse.
- Don't assume that perpetrators of anti-lesbian or gay violence will be heterosexual male strangers.
- Do encourage clients to report incidents of homophobic violence if possible, even if anonymously – it can help the therapeutic process significantly. Find out about the anonymous reporting services offered by some lesbian and gay switchboards/hate crime hotlines.
- Do be prepared for a vast range of reactions to an experience of homophobic violence, ranging from positive defiance to complete withdrawal and suicidal thoughts.
- Do ask for/seek out training on sexuality issues. Even if you feel fairly confident about the issues, it is always useful to find a forum where you can talk with others about practice and you may even find yourself challenged by people with very different care experiences.
- Do press for all staff from your agency/organization to receive training on sexuality matters. If there is resistance, you might ask: how will lesbian and gay clients react to staff members who are clearly not comfortable with lesbian and gay issues? What happens when a lesbian or gay client does not disclose their sexuality at the outset of care inventerventions with such staff? All the staff where you work will have had clients who will not have disclosed that they were lesbian or gay.
- Do think about what you and your colleagues can do to promote a culture of valuing lesbians and gay men and their experience within your workplace. How does your organization make sure it has a climate where clients can either disclose their sexuality if they want or choose not to? What are the essential ingredients of such a climate?
- Do find out whether there are any relevant policy documents that cover lesbian and gay issues within your agency. If so, do they need updating? Have all staff discussed and agreed any recommendations made?
- Do make contact and keep in touch with local lesbian and gay agencies. Who are the key contacts? What services do they provide? Do you have information on these services easily to hand?
- Do make enquiries of your local police force to find out whether there is a lesbian and gay liaison officer. In some forces (e.g. Lancashire) there will be a named officer in each division.
- Do make sure that when you refer clients on to other agencies, these agencies have a positive outlook on lesbian and gay issues. They may say they do. How can you be sure?

CONCLUSION

In this chapter I have identified behavioural and emotional issues related to homophobic violence, including behaviour editing and dealing with contexts of fear. Such issues have relevance for all lesbians and gay men, regardless of whether they have significant experience of homophobic violence (or indeed actively seek out care and support services) because of the pervasiveness and normalization of heterosexist values within society. Those who do have direct experience of homophobic violence, however, may require particular support on issues such as isolation, fear, self-esteem, making relationships work, coming out and developing trust. The case studies here and the recommended readings and organizations listed at the end of the chapter should help practitioners to develop their own models of effective working on these issues. Crucially, this is the duty of any agency that sees itself as having a caring role, not just lesbian and gay organizations.

However, ending homophobic violence requires not merely change for individuals, but change at institutional and state levels as well. General negative attitudes towards lesbians and gay men effectively provide the backdrop for the kinds of homophobic violence described in this chapter. State legislation that creates lesbians and gay men as inferior citizens with fewer rights than their heterosexual peers gives credence and validity to homophobic values and attitudes. While institutions like schools and the police force have recently begun to tackle their own homophobic cultures, some would argue that so far this change has been inadequate (Douglas *et al.* 1997). Unless this broader kind of homophobia can be excised, work with victims of homophobic violence will inevitably be fraught, because society will continue to give out the conflicting message: that homophobia is unacceptable and yet, at the same time, tolerable. Institutions and individuals should consider carefully how they might contribute to a changing climate; one where lesbians and gay men are able to access excellent, non-judgemental and anti-homophobic care services as a matter of course.

RESOURCES

Groups can come and go quite quickly, so if the numbers and addresses here do not connect you with the group you want, check either the listings section in *Gay Times* or phone the switchboard service nearest you.

Birmingham Contact Project, anonymous reporting of homophobic crime, 0121–622 5322.

Birmingham Lesbian and Gay Policing Group, 0121–622 5322.

Bristol Black Lesbian and Gay Group, SAFAR, Box 43, 82 Colston Street, Bristol BS1 5BB.

Bristol Lesbian and Gay Switchboard, 0117–942 0842.

Belfast Cara-Friend, helpline, 01232–322 023.

GALOP, help for those dealing with homophobic violence and the police. General number 0171–704 6767. Helpline 0171–704 2040. Write to: 2G Leroy House, 436 Essex Road, London N1 3QP.

Glasgow Gay and Lesbian Centre, 11 Dixon St, Glasgow G1 4AL. 0141–221 7203.

Greater Manchester Lesbian and Gay Policing Initiative, PO Box 100, Manchester M22 4GZ.

Leeds Lesbian Line/Gay Switchboard, 0113–245 3588.

London Black Gay and Bisexual Group, support and social meetings for black gay men, 0181–675 6001.

London Lesbian and Gay Switchboard, 0171–837 7324 (24 hours).

Lothian Switchboard, 0131–556 4049.

Manchester Action on Hate Crime/Switchboard, anonymous reporting of homophobic crime, 0161–274 3999.

Pink Therapy, network for lesbian and gay counsellors. ACAPS, 34 Electric Lane, London SW9 8LZ.

Preston Lesbian and Gay Policing Initiative/Action against Hate Crime, 01772–209115.

Shakti, South Asian Lesbian and Gay Network. Write c/o 86 Caledonian Road, London N1 9DN.

Sola, for lesbians in abused relationships, Thursdays 7pm–9pm, 0171–328 7389.

Spyce, Birmingham's black lesbian and gay group, 0121–622 3956.

Strathclyde Switchboard, 0141–332 8372.

Stonewall, campaigning group that works on homophobic violence, 0171–363 68860.

REFERENCES

Brett, R. (1999) *Report of the Findings from the Survey of Lesbian Experiences of Crime and Harassment: Manchester 1998.* Manchester: Greater Manchester Lesbian and Gay Policing Initiative.

Comstock, G.D. (1991) *Violence against Lesbians and Gay Men.* New York and Oxford: Columbia University Press.

Garnets, L., Herek, G.M. and Levy, B. (1992) 'Violence and victimization of lesbians and gay men: mental health consequences.' In G.M. Herek and K.T. Berrill (eds) *Hate Crimes: Confronting Violence against Lesbians and Gay Men.* London: Sage.

Harry, J. (1982) 'Derivative deviance: the cases of extortion, fag-bashing and the shakedown of gay men.' *Criminology 19*, 546–563.

Harry, J. (1990) 'Conceptualizing anti-gay violence.' *Journal of Interpersonal Violence 5*, 330–358.

Herek, G.M. (1992) 'The community response to violence in San Francisco: an interview with Wendy Kusuma, Lester Olmstead-Rose and Jill Tregor.' In G.M.

Herek and K.T. Berrill (eds) *Hate Crimes: Confronting Violence against Lesbians and Gay Men*. London: Sage.

Herek, G.M. and Berrill K.T. (eds) (1992) *Hate Crimes: Confronting Violence against Lesbians and Gay Men*. London: Sage.

Hickson, F., Davies, P.M., Hunt, A.J., Weatherburn, P., McManus, T.J. and Coxon, A.P.M. (1994) 'Gay men as victims of nonconsensual sex.' *Archives of Sexual Behaviour 23*, 3, 281–294.

Kelly, L. (1988) *Surviving Sexual Violence*. Cambridge: Polity Press.

Landolt, M.A. and Dutton, D.G. (1997) 'Power and personality: an analysis of gay male intimate abuse.' *Sex Roles 37*, 5/6, 335–359.

Lewisham Gay Alliance (1992) *Violence against Gay Men in Lewisham*. London: Safe Neighbourhoods Unit.

Lockhart, L.L., White, B.W., Causby, V. and Issac, A. (1994) 'Letting out the secret: violence in lesbian relationships.' *Journal of Interpersonal Violence 9*, 4, 469–492.

Mason, G. (1996) 'Are you a boy or a girl?: (hetero)sexism and verbal hostility.' *International Victimology 27*, 91–10.

Mason, A. and Palmer A. (1996) *Queer Bashing: A National Survey of Hate Crime against Lesbians and Gays*. London: Stonewall.

Myslick, W. (1996) 'Renegotiating the social/sexual identities of places: gay communities as safe havens or sites of resistance.' In N. Duncan (ed) *Body Space*. London: Routledge.

Namaste, K. (1996) 'Genderbashing: sexuality, gender, and the regulation of public space.' *Environment and Planning D: Society and Space 14*, 221–240.

Rivers, I. (1996) 'The victimization of gay teenagers in schools: homophobia in education.' *Pastoral Care*, March, 35–41.

Stanko, E. and Curry, P. (1997) 'Homophobic violence and the self "at risk": interrogating the boundaries.' *Social and Legal Studies 6*, 4, 513–532.

Stanko, E., Marian, L., Crisp, D., Manning, R., Smith, J. and Cowan, S. (1998) *Taking Stock: What Do We Know about Violence?* Uxbridge: ESRC Violence Research Programme, Brunel University.

Truman, C., Bewley, B., Hayes, C. and Boulton, D. (1994) *Lesbians' and Gay Men's Experiences of Crime and Policing: An Exploratory Study*. Manchester: Manchester Metropolitan University.

Valentine, G. (1996) '(Re)negotiating the "heterosexual street"': lesbian production of space.' In N. Duncan (ed) *Body Space*. London: Routledge.

Von Schultess, B. (1992) 'Violence in the streets: anti-lesbian assault and harassment in San Francisco.' In G.M. Herek and K.T. Berrill (eds) *Hate Crimes: Confronting Violence against Lesbians and Gay Men*. London: Sage.

Weissman, E. (1992) 'Kids who attack gays.' In G.M. Herek and K.T. Berrill (eds) *Hate Crimes: Confronting Violence against Lesbians and Gay Men*. London: Sage.

Wertheimer, D.M. (1992) 'Treatment and service interventions for lesbian and gay male crime victims.' In G.M. Herek and K.T. Berrill (eds) *Hate Crimes: Confronting Violence against Lesbians and Gay Men*. London: Sage.

FURTHER READING

Appleby, G.A. and Anastas, J.W. (1998) 'Violence in the lives of lesbians and gay men.' *Not Just a Passing Phase: Social Work with Gay, Lesbian, and Bisexual People*. New York: Columbia University Press.

Davies, D. and Neal, C. (eds) (1996) *Pink Therapy: A Guide for Counsellors and Therapists Working with Lesbian, Gay and Bisexual Clients*. Buckingham: Open University Press.

Douglas, N., Warwick, I., Kemp, S. and Whitty, G. (1997) *Playing it Safe: Responses of Secondary School Teachers to Lesbian, Gay and Bisexual Pupils, Bullying, HIV and AIDS Education and Section 28*. London: Health and Education Research Unit, Institute of Education.

Elliot, M. and Kilpatrick, J. (1994) *How to Stop Bullying: A KIDSCAPE Guide to Training*. London: KIDSCAPE.

Herek, G.M. and Berrill, K.T. (eds) (1992) *Hate Crimes: Confronting Violence against Lesbians and Gay Men*. London: Sage.

Mason, A. and Palmer A. (1996) *Queer Bashing: A National Survey of Hate Crime against Lesbians and Gays*. London: Stonewall.

ACKNOWLEDGEMENT

I would like to thank Stephen Hicks of the University of Central Lancashire for his invaluable help during the writing of this chapter.

CHAPTER 5

Working with Children who have been Subjected to Violence

Ann Cattanach

> Jack and Guy
> Went out in the Rye
> And they found a little boy
> With one black eye
> Come says Jack let's knock him
> On the head
> No says Guy
> Let's buy him some bread
> You buy one loaf
> And I'll buy two
> And we'll bring him up
> As other folks do.

VIOLENCE THROUGH ABUSE

The nursery rhyme of Jack and Guy describes the plight of an abused child as the adults decide whether to hit him or feed him. The decision does seem somewhat arbitrary with the child as an object for attention, good or bad, rather than a person with thoughts, feelings and rights.

My work as a play therapist is with children who have experienced violence through abuse by adults or older children. They might be familiar with the discourse in the nursery rhyme and probably received a knock round the head rather than a loaf of bread.

I work in child and family psychiatry and as an independent consultant for social services departments. The referrals for therapy come mainly from social services but some through GPs or paediatricians. Some of the interventions are short term, helping children to make sense of a particular violent episode. This may be from three to eight sessions with the child and meetings with family and other carers. Long-term work can be to help a 'looked after' child cope with past experiences of violence and to move on to a more permanent placement. Some of these interventions can go on for a considerable time as a new placement is found. I normally see children once a fortnight, but circumstances can vary and meetings are negotiated to coincide with the needs of the client.

Much but not all violence experienced by the children with whom I work is family violence, some of which is directed against the children. But some children are exposed to violence as witnesses of adult aggression, often by their parents or carers attacking each other, but always with the threat or menace that the children may be next in line. In these settings roles become blurred and the child witnessing violence may take responsibility for protecting the abused partner and become the adult with feelings of guilt and powerlessness if s/he is unable to protect the vulnerable one. If the violence is overwhelming then the child's sense of self disappears in the terror of watching.

Many years after witnessing violence between his mother and her many partners, John still felt numb with the pain of it all. He did a drawing and described it as follows:

> There was once a drawing and it had a name and the name was Nothing.
> There was an arrow pointing to Nowhere and scribbles, which were nothing.
> The scribbles begin then they fade.
> In order to become Something the Nothings need nothing
> So they will always be Nothing.
> Nobody knows what it is like to be Nothing.
> It is horrible being Nothing.

DEFINITIONS OF VIOLENCE

Definitions of family violence must be within the context of a general definition of interpersonal violence. This includes both fatal and non-fatal violence where physical force or the threat of force is used by one person with the intent of causing harm, injury or death to another.

Family violence refers to the intentional intimidation, physical and/or sexual abuse, or battering of children, adults or elders by a family member, intimate partner or caretaker. The term 'family violence' is inclusive and encompasses child maltreatment (physical abuse, sexual abuse and neglect), adult intimate partner violence (the abuse of adult women or men by married or unmarried partners) and elder mistreatment (elder abuse and neglect).

Abuse is described as a pattern of behaviours organized around the intentional use of power, including but not requiring physical violence, by one person for the purpose of controlling another. Child maltreatment always involves the abrogation of adult responsibilities for the care and protection of children. The forms of maltreatment of children include physical abuse, sexual abuse, emotional abuse and neglect.

Any of these behaviours can be witnessed, frequently repeatedly by a child. Debilitating psychological effects are noted among children who witness all forms of interpersonal violence.

EFFECTS OF VIOLENCE ON CHILDREN

Lieberman and Van Horn (1993) state that children who have experienced violence in families are both fearful of adult aggression but come to accept it as part of everyday life. Children who witness domestic violence approve of it as a way of resolving conflict and have higher levels of aggression than comparison groups of children. They also suffer from higher anxiety, more behavioural problems and lower self-esteem.

However, Yates (1996) states that children who are reared in violent homes do not necessarily become violent parents later on. There is little evidence to support the claim that abuse begets abuse. One-third will grow up to follow a pattern of inept, abusive or neglectful parenting and one-third will not. The remaining third could go either way, depending on circumstance and social stress. However, more than half of children reared in violent homes demonstrate severe behaviour problems and below average social competence.

Knapp (1998) states that many studies demonstrate that witnessing the battering of their mothers may be as traumatic to children as being direct victims of abuse. She states that many studies demonstrate that violence observed by children increases the risk that they will react violently later in life. Sons who observe their fathers' violence against their mothers have a 1000 per cent greater risk of repeating this abuse with their own future spouses.

In a review of effects on children of witnessing violence Attala et al. (1995) state that across the studies children from families with domestic violence tend to have more difficulties than those from non-violent families. Most difficulties encompassed emotional and behavioural problems. Manifestations of children's difficulties consisted of preoccupation with physical aggression, externalizing and internalizing behavioural problems, adjustment complications, academic problems, developmental delays, lower levels of social competence ratings, depressive symptoms and being subject to abuse themselves.

Yates (1996) states that children reared in violent households tend to identify with either the victim or aggressor. Children who identify with the victim may become self-punitive. They often think they caused the fight and should have been able to stop it. Those who identify with the aggressor express violent themes in play wiping out less powerful figures.

This is the story of a boy who was physically and emotionally abused by his parents. This abuse took place over a period of two years and started when James was 6 years old. The abuse ended when James (aged 8) was taken into care. His father went to prison and his mother for treatment in a psychiatric hospital. He felt responsible for the abuse and his coping mechanism was to be passive and take everything that happened to him without response:

> There was once a whirlwind with no name.
> It blew around and ate humans.
> He sucked up humans.
> They didn't die but got spotted with the whirlwind.
> They didn't mind being sucked up
> Because they knew they would be thrown back again.

Sarah (aged 11) is angry living with her aggressive mother and has taken the role of aggressor for herself. Her mother has outbursts of temper when she hits Sarah and is verbally abusive, swearing and name calling. Sarah's mother finds it very difficult to praise her daughter although she fights for her and her rights.

> Once upon a nightmare a space ship flew across earth planning to take over
> the world so they could breed their own species and live there.
> So out of the space ship came Homer, Marge, Bart and Lisa.
> Bart is the alien's son and Lisa the alien's daughter.
> Then suddenly the evil Homer grabbed hold of an earth boy and sucked his
> blood.
> The boy dies because he has no blood.
> The evil Homer grabs hold of Marge and says
> 'I've come to take over the world.'
> He pushes Marge over a cliff
> She shrieks 'AAAAAArgh'
> But it's only a small cliff and she survives.
> This big evil monster came from hell.
> Then Homer turned into Moby Dick.
> And the alien space ship came and surrounded the monster.
> Then Lisa and Bart scream 'ha ha ha'.
> Just like Sarah when she feels angry.
> The End.

Alpert, Cohen and Sege (1997) state that a child who witnesses violence may show signs and symptoms of post traumatic stress disorder (PTSD), particularly if the child is younger, if the violence is frequent and if it occurs in close proximity to the child. Many children who come for therapy have symptoms of PTSD.

The majority of sexually abused children have recurrent nightmares, not usually about the perpetrator but about some fearful monster who chases them. The complexity of penetration of the child's body, in whatever form, in sexual abuse, can create an extreme fear of the perpetrator, which is qualitatively different from physical violence. There is a sense of enslavement to the other which is hard to separate from the self. The image children often use is of being eaten.

John (aged 8) described the feeling in his story:

> There was a big, slimy good guy,
> And he got ate with a big monster.
> The monster took him out of his mouth,
> And put him on his horns on the top of his head.
> The rest of the good guy came out of the monster's mouth.
> The End.

Children from violent families are preoccupied with violence. They often fear places familiar to the perpetrator. Their imagery in storymaking is full of violence with power struggles between fearful monsters and their victims. There is constant repetition in stories and play as the children try to gain mastery of events in their past.

Peter (aged 10) had lived with a violent stepmother for three years between the ages of 3 and 6. He was taken into care and there have been many attempts to rehabilitate him back home with his father and stepmother. Peter and his brother Alan are still 'looked after'. He constantly repeated stories about witch women. He wanted to be sure that she was contained and this was a theme in all his play:

Once there was a witch called Ugly and Harry buried her because he was angry with her.
She swore at him and hit him and was very nasty to him in all sorts of ways.
She shouted a lot and died.
She stayed dead.
Everybody in the whole world was glad she was dead all because of Harry.
Her spells were buried with her so nobody could do her bad magic.
The good dragon came.
He flew into the country and sat on top of the witch's grave.
The End.

By the time many children come to therapy these fears and terrors have become debilitating. It is important to decide whether a diagnosis of PTSD is appropriate.

POST TRAUMATIC STRESS DISORDER (PTSD)

The diagnostic criteria for post traumatic stress disorder involve the following:

1. The person has been exposed to a traumatic event in which both of the following are present:

    a) The person experienced or witnessed an event that involved actual or threatened death or serious injury or a threat to the physical integrity of self or others.

    b) The person's response involved intense fear, helplessness, or horror.

In children, this may be expressed instead by disorganized or agitated behaviour.

2. The traumatic event is persistently reexperienced in one (or more) of the following ways:

    a) Recurrent and intrusive recollections of the event. In younger children, repetitive play may occur in which themes or aspects of the trauma are expressed.

    b) Recurrent distressing dreams of the event. In children there may be frightening dreams without recognizable content.

    c) Acting or feeling as if the traumatic event were recurring (includes flashbacks) In young children trauma specific re-enactment may occur.

    d) Intense psychological distress at exposure to internal or external cues to the trauma.

    e) Physiological reactivity on exposure to internal or external cues to the trauma.

3. Persistent avoidance of stimuli associated with the trauma and numbing of responsiveness as indicated by three (or more) of the following:

    a) Efforts to avoid thoughts associated with the trauma.

    b) Efforts to avoid activities, places or people that arouse recollections of the trauma.

    c) Inability to recall an important aspect of the trauma.

    d) Markedly diminished interest or participation in significant activities.

    e) Feeling of detachment or estrangement from others.

    f) Restricted range of affect (e.g. unable to have loving feelings).

    g) Sense of forshortened future.

4. Persistent symptoms of increased arousal, as indicated by two (or more) of the following:

    a) Difficulty falling or staying asleep.

    b) Irritability or outbursts of anger.

    c) Difficulty concentrating.

    d) Hypervigilance.

    e) Exaggerated startle response.

5. Duration of the disturbance for more than one month.

6. The disturbance causes clinically significant distress or impairment in social, occupational or other areas of functioning (adapted from American Psychiatric Association 1994).

ACCOMMODATION TO VIOLENCE

If children live in an atmosphere where violence and threat are considered normal then they learn to accommodate to that environment. Children develop a variety of strategies to survive according to the way the violence is expressed. Three common strategies are:

- frozen watchfulness
- cutting off and blanking out the experience by imagining they are elsewhere
- hyperactivity and incitement to violence to 'get it over'.

These are excellent survival strategies but can become dysfunctional in other circumstances and environments.

Frozen Watchfulness

The child who is frozen often misses learning opportunities as they disappear into the walls of their school but at playtime may be bullied and hurt by other children who sense their vulnerability. Their physical frailty and aura of neglect make them a clear target for other adult perpetrators of hurt and violence and the strategy of being 'nice' can lead to further violent abuse. Being 'nice' usually means being 'nothing' because the child is still involved in coping with fear to such an extent that there is little time or space which does not contain anxiety.

There seems no 'safe' place for such a child. This is Janet's story at the beginning of our time together:

> There was once a house, which was smashed because of the tree and the aeroplane.
> The people were not in the house because they were moving to another house.
> There are builders digging a hole just because they got nothing to do.
> They were told to make the cars go up and down again.
> The builders had a green car.
> They forgot about it.
> The buried it because they forgot about it.
> The builders were moaning because they were being silly.
> Everyone is in such a hurry there is a big crash.
> One lorry had tomato ketchup and it all fell out.
> The crash got bigger and bigger.
> They are never going to get home.
> It got bigger, bigger, bigger.
> They are not going to get home in time for dinner.
> 1,000 cars crashed together.
> There is only one car in the world that is not in the crash.
> Strange isn't it.
> The End.

These non-specific fears about disaster striking down on the powerless are constantly repeated. There are no solutions; the terror is arbitrary and over-whelming in size. But at least in this story there is one car that is not in the crash and we can build on the hope presented as the story ends.

Many of these stories sound like those folk tales told round the fire at night. Some children are aware of this and tell their tales in that mode. Alan (aged 12) starts his with:

> Once upon a time there was a big fat monster with 800 legs.
> He ate little tiny boys one year old.
> He had to eat 100 a day or else he would be sick and die ...

These stories are symbolic representations of the life experiences of children who live in daily fear and threat of violence. Threat is all consuming.

Cutting Off

Some children who experience the trauma of violence switch off when it is happening around them. They often fill their thoughts with imaginary stories to block off the violence. Such children run through films in their thoughts or imagine they are a character in a story. Peter Pan, Superman, Supergirl, the Power Rangers are popular characters described to me by children. Perhaps the fact that many of these characters can fly or have other magic power is important when the child feels helpless and without any control. The desire to flee the situation is strong and to fly away is the perfect solution.

When her father was angry Jane (aged 9) imagined a family who were moving house. Jane's father often drank too much and in this state stormed and raged around the house threatening to beat up her mother and anyone else who got in his way.

> This story is about a family moving house because they don't like their old house.
> The old house is dirty and they don't like it anyway.
> The dad is called Andrew.
> The mum is called Daisy
> And the Nan is … Nan
> The children are called Chloe and Tom.
> There is a gran and granddad called Michael and Rosie.
> They all live together.
> They get packing away first.
> They pack away toys, clothes.
> Dog food, ornaments, the telly.
> They are getting sorted for the move.
> The dogs go in front of the car.
> They all eat before they go.
> The pram has to go out the back.
> They don't want to get into muddles.

When there were violent scenes at home, Jane would go through the house moving in her head, imagining the move and how she would pack all her stuff. This helped her cope with her anxiety. At school she is called a dreamer and the teacher is cross because she does not pay attention. When the teacher challenges her, Jane becomes more distant. The teacher thinks Jane is indifferent and so the situation escalates.

Getting it over

Some children seem to push angry parents to acts of violence by confronting and demanding attention in what often seems a dangerous way. These children seem to invade the personal space of others and lack awareness of the impact of their social interactions. In the violent environment there is an excitement about aggressive scenes between family members and a sense that the group is building up to such a scene. In these situations some children push the adults into confrontation to relieve the tension of the build-up to aggression. The children feel that they are 'bad' so a tirade from an angry parent simply reinforces what they think about themselves.

Jamie was such a boy. His grandparents who cared for him often got angry and shouted at each other. Other family members joined the row and Jamie ran from one person to another, physically pushing himself forward until all turned on him. He felt worthless and all the family reinforced this. Then the anger was diffused and Jamie left the room in disgrace.

For such families there is the paradox for the children of fearing the violence yet finding the excitement of scenes and drama an addictive process. Jamie was always the scapegoat in his family dramas. His stories were all about 'slobs' and 'slimeheads'.

> There was once a greedy monster called Sammy Pammy and he was a greedy slime head.
> He ate and ate and ate until he was full up.
> And he did a big fatty poo poo.
> He did a burp.

After he was eating people.
He knocked houses down
And he farted.
This monster is a greedy pig.
He eats two men.
He farts and farts and slobs over his eyes.
In the end he ate himself and died.
But he came alive again.
The End.

HOW THE BODY ACCOMMODATES

If children are subjected to attack they shut down on sensitivity; all the senses except sight become dulled to accommodate pain. Children are often noisy, boisterous and clumsy with little sensitivity to heat, cold or pain. Jamie had no awareness of his body in space when he began to be fearful and he pushed and stumbled about, always standing too close to others.

Janet felt frozen as though her body did not exist but she was very observant using her sight, always watching to avoid violence. She could tell you the route from home to school, from family centre to home, family centre to school. But she could not say if she was hot or cold, if she felt pain or hurt.

HELP THROUGH PLAY THERAPY

It is important that children should be safe from further violence before treatment begins. If children are still living in a violent environment then help should be given to find activities and time out of the home so the child can develop skills and enhance self-esteem. If the child is removed from the violence then it is appropriate to offer therapy so the child can make sense of these experiences.

In play therapy when child and therapist meet and form a therapeutic alliance, the therapist is helping the child construct a narrative of identity. We use toys and other play materials to make stories and narratives about past and present. We co-construct together. There is a storyteller and a listener and the story acts in the middle as a way to negotiate a shared meaning between therapist and child. Children tell stories as containers for their experiences, constructed into the fictional narration of a story. I have described this play therapy process with abused children in previous writing (Cattanach 1993, 1997)

John (aged 10) begins his stories, then always remarks that it is fiction. He is clearly aware that he can explore his life experience through storymaking but his life is embedded in the fiction, which helps him to feel safe.

Beginning

It is important in the initial interview with the child and carer to find out what images about violence are dominating the child's cognitions. Terr (1981) identified four characteristics common to childhood trauma. These are: intrusive images, repetitive play, trauma-specific and mundane fears and changes in attitudes about people, life and the future.

The majority of young children who come to therapy have disturbing nightmares and intrusive thoughts about violence they have experienced or witnessed as common symptoms. It is important to work with these images and find narratives, which alleviate the sense of helplessness.

We often begin with nightmares. The child describes the nightmare which usually ends with the child left trapped and helpless as the 'monster' approaches. We think of a more powerful ending together. Perhaps we imagine changing ourselves into a TV character like Superman or Bart Simpson and flying away from the 'monster' like Superman or jumping on the skateboard and escaping like Bart Simpson. I suggest that the child might think of the whole narrative of the dream before they go to sleep that night. Then they will be able to incorporate our new ending into the dream. These new narratives also give the child the idea that problems can be solved and we can even change aspects of our dreams.

Playing

The play therapist offers the child the opportunity for imaginative play. There should be materials for sensory play to help the child develop body awareness. Then toys and other small objects for storymaking and puppets and costumes for dramatic play. The therapist is audience, listener or participant in the play according to the demands of the relationship.

Children who have experienced violence tell stories about monsters and scary places. Often there are no endings but violence and no solutions except more violence because this is clearly the lived experience of the child. As the therapy develops and the child and therapist co-construct their relationship the child is helped to develop and expand the repertoire of imaginative ideas. The therapist might suggest or ask if there are other ways for heroes to win than through violence and hurt. Can the hero get out of the situation by negotiating? I might tell a story to the child:

Two Close Calls

One day a he-goat was browsing on the mountainside. It was very hot and when he came to the mouth of a cave he decided to go inside to escape from the sun. But when he stepped into the cave he found himself face to face with a lion. He was terrified. 'How can I save myself?' he thought 'This lion will surely eat me.' 'What do you want?' growled the lion who was licking his lips hoping for a good meal.

The goat stared at the lion looking at him very hard. Then he said, 'I am one of the angels of heaven. The Lord of Creation has sent me to kill seven lions and seven hyenas and seven jackals. I was checking to see if your markings fit the description of any of those animals I must destroy. No, you are not one of them. You will live long. Rest here in your cave while I continue my search.'

And the goat walked out of the cave. The lion was shocked by what had happened. When he met a jackal some time later, the jackal asked him what was wrong.

'I have just seen a creature sent by the Lord of Creation to devour seven lions, seven jackals and seven hyenas. Luckily I was spared. But you had better beware.'

'What was this creature like?' asked the jackal.

'Black, ' said the lion, 'with a long beard and thick hair.'

'It sounds like a goat, ' laughed the jackal. 'Let's go and find him.'

Off they went and soon they saw the goat in the distance.

'This time there is no escape,' thought the goat. He began to tremble in fear.

When the lion and the jackal came up behind him, the goat bellowed to the jackal, 'You stupid cur why are you bringing me this lion? I have already examined him and he is not the right one. That's not the lion I asked you to bring me.'

When the lion heard the goat he turned on the jackal and the goat managed to escape and went back to the safety of the herd. (Morocco)

John (aged 10) who was clear about fiction also liked to be told stories like 'Two Close Calls'. He didn't want to talk about the violence in his family but his fiction was what it felt like to him. He made his stories in the containment of the sand tray with borders, boundaries and edges:

Nasty Land

This is a country called Nasty Land.

It is nasty because there are lots of snakes and the snakes bite people and put venom in them.

There is a dragon that is bad.

There were lots of trees but not now because the snakes and the dragon eat the trees.

The snakes have babies and the grownups teach them to be bad because the grownups think that bad is good.

There are two mermaids who are scared of the snakes

But they live there so they have to put up with it.

There are lots of baby snakes all learning to be bad.

There is a dog who is scared and another dog and a cat and an evil troll.

The witch is the queen and the dragon is the king.

The mermaids are scared because it is the dragon's place.

But they can jump into the water.

They have a car as well but it is half covered up because the island tried rolling on it.

There is a baby, which is going to die.

The snake put venom in her and the poor baby dies.

The mum has got another son called Superman.

The mum was very scared when the baby died.

She couldn't do anything.

The earth is rolling over the car.

Everyone is saying 'Oh no' because the earth cover is breaking and tearing.

When the earth came back it was all nice and clean.

Although the baby died it became a God and everyone prayed to him.

They prayed: 'Please God make the snakes go away.'

A caterpillar came who could kill everything.

The snake poo is very smelly poo and they eat it.

The country is very crowded.

Another caterpillar comes alive.

It is too dangerous.

Nearly everyone in the country dies of starving.
Everybody is crying and sad and miserable.
The End.

There is a sense that the mother cannot protect the children and this is also the theme of Mary's story. Mary is 12 and she is now in foster care. He father beat her mother who wanted to care for the children, but in the end was unable to do so and requested that all of her nine children be taken into care. Mary has been in foster care for a year and feels safe now.

The Snake from Hell

He is called Smellybot and this is his kingdom.
He has a wife who is angry with Smellybot because he keeps beating his children.
She is trying to stop it but she can't.
The snake is guarding his kingdom so the children can't escape with their mother.
The children are called Brownhat, Fluffly, Musket, Gromit, Dopey, Lucky, Fidget and Patch.
The youngest don't really understand but all the others are really angry and will do anything to get out of there.
They have to do what they are told by the snake.
At the end all the snakes get drowned in slime.
Smellybot gets thrown out and the rest get taken out of the country.

These fictional stories contain some of the feelings the children have about their families but expressed in the safety of the story.

RESOLUTIONS

The therapist and child explore the past, present and perhaps a more hopeful future. Alan (aged 8) told me this story. He is the brother of Peter and he too was afraid of his stepmother and the possibility of living with her again:

There was once a boy who had a lump of slime on his fingers and realised it was for life.
At first he didn't mind the slime because he could play with it all day.
But soon he got fed up
And went to the doctor,
And the doctor got it off.
The End.

It is difficult for children who have experienced violence to feel good about themselves. They take responsibility for the abuse and feel blamed. Alan wanted to leave his past and find his own talents. He wanted another narrative about himself as a person with skills and qualities not bound up with the slime of the past. It was nice to play with it for a time but not for ever. He had to move on.

I told him a story about an apache boy:

The Lazy Boy who became a Great Runner

There was once a boy whom everyone thought was lazy.
He was too lazy to eat even.

He would lie down all day long.
In the day when the other boys were out playing, he stayed inside.
He wet his bed all the time because he was too lazy to get up.
Finally they began to wonder about him.
He was never around at night and seemed to sleep all day long.
Nobody knew where he went or what he did.
One day his family was hungry.
They had no food left.
The boy had no weapons, nothing to kill deer with, but he went out and ran down a deer on foot.
This was in the daytime.
After that he went out often and chased after deer on foot.
Then the family found out what he had been doing at night.
He had been practising running.
He got to be a great runner. (Chiricahua Apache Indian)

CONCLUSION.

Children who have experienced violence or witnessed violence may sometimes need therapy to help cope with their fears. In play therapy children can use the medium of play and storymaking to express these fears. They can reframe their own life experiences through stories about imaginary violence. The imaginary world of play gives the children distance from their own terrors and fears. These can be mediated through the play and stories, which make up a play therapy intervention. As they emerge from the terror, the therapist can help express other aspects of self and other ways of solving disputes and conflicts so that violence is not endlessly repeated.

REFERENCES

Alpert, E., Cohen, S. and Sege, R. (1997) 'Family violence: an overview.' *Academic Medicine* (Supplement) *72*, 1, S3–S5.

American Psychiatric Association (1994) *Diagnostic and Statistical Manual of Mental Disorders*, 4th edn. Washington DC: American Psychiatric Association, 209–211.

Attala, M., Bauza, K., Pratt, H. and Viera, D. (1995) 'Integrative review of effects on children of witnessing domestic violence.' *Issues in Comprehensive Pediatric Nursing* *18*, 163–172.

Cattanach, A. (1993) *Play Therapy with Abused Children*. London: Jessica Kingsley Publishers.

Cattanach, A. (1997) *Children's Stories in Play Therapy*. London: Jessica Kingsley Publishers.

Knapp, J. (1998) 'The impact of children witnessing violence.' *Pediatric Clinics of North America 45*, 2, 355–365.

Lieberman, A. and Van Horn, P. (1993) 'Attachment, trauma, and domestic violence.' *Child and Adolescent Psychiatric Clinics of North America 7*, 2, 423–443.

Terr, L. (1981) 'Forbidden games: Posttraumatic child's play.' *Journal American Academic Child Psychiatry 20*, 741–760.

Yates, A. (1996) 'When children witness domestic violence.' *Hawaii Medical Journal* *55*, 162–163.

CHAPTER 6

Child Victims of Bullying

Andrew Mellor

Anyone of any age can become a victim of bullying – all it takes is to be in the wrong place at the wrong time. Research studies into bullying at school have found that the population divides itself into two parts. About half of the children questioned say that they have been bullied at some time; the other half cannot understand what all the fuss is about.

THE EFFECTS OF BULLYING

Some people who experience a brief spell of bullying survive the experience relatively unscathed. Some are affected in subtle but significant ways. Others are driven to the edge of despair and beyond by their experiences. A handful take the ultimate step of ending their own lives as a means of escape.

Bullying damages schooling: it is impossible to concentrate on lessons when your thoughts are dominated by worry about what is going to happen at playtime. Bullying harms self-confidence, possibly in a subtle way that victims will not even acknowledge to themselves, but this can have long-term effects that shape the whole course of their adult lives. How many people have failed to apply for a position which they are more than capable of fulfilling because their fragile self-confidence makes them unable to take risks? This is a needless waste of potential which has consequences for the whole community.

At its worst, bullying may kill. One night in February 1996 in a small town on the remote Scottish Isle of Lewis a 16-year-old girl went to her bedroom, swallowed a handful of painkillers and never woke up. Katherine Jane Morrison left a note for her parents that read: 'I want to get away from the messed-up girls that are making my life hell.' Seven weeks before she died, Katherine Jane was attacked in the street by a group of girls, including some who were described as her friends. The attack (or fight, as some people have called it), though serious, did not leave any permanent physical injury. For the next seven weeks Katherine Jane got on with her life. She went to school, went out at night and did not tell her parents that she was being bullied. But deep inside her mind was a worry, which became real when a girl's voice over the phone threatened that her head would be shaved if she did well in her forthcoming examinations. It was shortly after this that Katherine made her final escape from her tormentors.

At Christmas time eight years earlier, two happy little girls had been photographed sitting on Santa's knee. One, Katherine Jane, would never reach adulthood; the other, Michelle, was to be sentenced to three months in prison for taking part in the street assault on Katherine. This image graphically confirms that the victims of bullying often suffer at the hands of their friends, or people with whom they would like to be friends.

Many lives have been touched by this tragedy. Katherine Jane's family, friends and teachers wonder why she did not confide in them. Michelle and another girl were convicted of assaulting her and given three-month prison sentences. They, their families and friends have had to bear accusations that Katherine Jane was driven to her death by evil bullying.

Some good has resulted. Communities throughout Scotland have been forced to confront the uncomfortable truths that bullying happens everywhere. It is not just 'part of growing up'; it is not just 'something you have to put up with' and it can have terrible consequences. Katherine Jane's school was subjected to a critical examination by government inspectors and their report has set the standards of care and welfare which schools are expected to provide for their pupils.

Suicides ascribed to bullying are mercifully rare. A handful of cases hit the press each year, but we can never know all the reasons behind such events and it seems likely that a number of factors are involved. These might include the victim's age, state of health and the support structures available from family, school and the community. The incident which apparently triggers such a suicide can be very minor. It may be a short telephone call or an ill-considered remark. But the consequences are usually out of all proportion to the harmful intentions of the bully.

In a study which I completed in Scottish Secondary schools (Mellor 1990) 44 per cent of the youngsters involved said that they had bullied someone else at some time. The vast majority of them will have grown up to be responsible caring adults who would be horrified to think that their actions might have caused any real harm, but statements from victims suggest that the damage runs deep:

> When I was at primary school I got picked on non-stop for two years. No one talked to me. I hadn't done anything to get blamed for, and I still don't know the reason I got picked on. I wasn't any wealthier or poorer or a different race.
>
> I used to cry myself to sleep every night. I was miserable. My parents knew and they talked to the headmaster but he wasn't interested and said he couldn't do anything about it. My parents knew all the bullies' parents. One girl even lived in the same street and we had been friends since we were two. Like a sheep she dumped me because no one else talked to me. This all happened in primary 6 and I have lost nearly all my self-confidence and hate being on my own. I'd hate to think this was happening to anyone else. I have a fear that if one girl doesn't talk to me they will all start again and it will never stop. I don't want it to go on for the rest of my school life. I couldn't cope. (14-year-old girl)

That girl is now an adult and I sometimes wonder what has become of her. The penalty of conducting a confidential questionnaire survey is that a 'cri de coeur' such as this may be heard but cannot be answered.

Other people have described how being the victim of bullying has changed their lives, but not always in a predictable way. One mother told me about her daughter who had been bullied repeatedly at school. When she was moved to another school she continued to be bullied, although the children responsible had no knowledge of her previous troubles. It seemed that she had in some way adopted the role of a victim and this was transmitted through her demeanour to the children in her new school. Even as an adult she continued to suffer. She had a series of relationships with men, each of which ended with her being physically abused.

A newspaper reporter told me how she had been similarly subjected to long term bullying but her response was to develop a resolve to do something to help other victims. She persuaded her editor to publish stories, which helped to raise awareness of the issue and of the strategies that schools could implement to deal with it. She said that this positive action helped her to cope with recurring memories such as that of blood starting to flow from the back of her hand as she watched the blackened fingernails of one particularly persistent bully slowly dig into her flesh.

WORDS MATTER

> Bullying mentally I think is the worst kind of bullying, because anyone can take a good kicking. Bruises go away but anything anyone says does not. (15-year-old boy)

Words are the most powerful weapons in the armoury of bullies. They know how difficult it can be for adults to intervene if there is no physical evidence of wrongdoing. They also know that the threat of violence, quietly and menacingly repeated over a period, can be far more terrifying than a physical assault.

The words that well-meaning people use can also cause problems. Through-out this chapter the words *bully* and *victim* are used as a succinct way of describing children who bully others or who experience bullying. But in our dealings with individuals we should never attach these words to them because there is a real danger that they will start to live up to the labels. Bullied children need to be told that anyone can be bullied, that it is not their fault and that they have a right to attend school without being in fear. They must be encouraged to believe that the abuse they are suffering is not inevitable and can be ended.

The actions of children who bully others should be challenged and con-demned, but if we want to change their behaviour we have to believe that they are capable of redemption. Labelling individual children as bullies may make it more difficult for the very small number who habitually bully others to change their behaviour. Adults working with such young people must remember that they often have low self-esteem and that bullying may be the only way they have of raising their perceived status. If we are so outraged at the cruelty which they have inflicted on their victims that we write them off as being incurable bullies, the task of rehabilitation may become impossible.

Words such as 'grass', 'tell-tale' and (in Scotland) 'clype' must be avoided. Teachers and parents must work to counter the youth sub-culture that discourages openness and must try to set a good example. They must not admonish children for being 'tell-tales' and they must be more open in their dealings with them. This does not mean that we should burden young people with our personal problems but rather that we should be prepared to acknowledge our mistakes and not pretend to be able to solve all problems.

Even using the word 'tell' can cause problems. In children's minds it may imply a promise that if they tell a teacher that they are being bullied the teacher will take over the situation and make everything better. But children know that this is often a false promise. One of the reasons why they do not tell adults that they are being bullied is that they do not trust them to act wisely. Why 'tell' if the adult is only going to do something which makes the bullying worse? Why 'tell' if you have done so in the past and the bullying did not stop? Why 'tell' if there is a taboo within your peer group against doing just that? It is much better to encourage children to 'talk' to someone if they are being bullied, rather than to 'tell'. This is not just semantics but can be a clear signalling that the victim will play a full part in discussions about any possible action.

WHAT IS BULLYING?

The word 'bullying' covers a spectrum of behaviour that has at one extreme the sort of systematic physical and mental brutality that can drive a victim to despair. At the other extreme it is the kind of name-calling that may be hard to distinguish from the mild teasing which is a normal part of a humorous social interaction between friends. A number of points can help to define bullying:

- it is an abuse of power
- it may be physical or psychological
- an episode of bullying may include a variety of different actions, each of which contributes to the victim's state of mind
- there may be one individual bully or a group
- if it is repeated the effects may become cumulatively more serious.

Some definitions of bullying include a statement about intent, such as this one from *Action Against Bullying* (Johnstone, Munn and Edwards 1992, p.3): 'Bullying is the wilful, conscious desire to hurt or threaten or frighten someone else.'

Such definitions can be helpful if we want to emphasize a bully's responsibility for the effect that his or her actions can have. However, it is vital to remember that bullies are not always aware of just how much damage they have done. Some bullying is deliberate and the bullies may enjoy seeing the pain which they have caused, but much bullying is simply thoughtless. Bullies may genuinely believe that they are engaged in a 'bit of fun' which has no serious consequences. This is especially true of name-calling. Even some victims choose not to describe this as bullying: 'There is this boy in my class, he keeps calling me names but I don't think this is bullying. When he calls me names I get very hurt and then others start but I just ignore them' (12-year-old girl).

In many communities a nickname can be a sign of belonging. Children can hardly be criticized if someone is given a nickname that does not cause offence, but they must be challenged if they saddle an individual with a name which causes pain each time it is used. Unfortunately, distinguishing between the two is not always simple. When one boy in my school started to be called 'Frog', I tackled his peers about this. It seemed to me that this nickname was drawing attention to a speech defect which was the result of the boy's profound deafness. His classmates and the boy himself assured me that he did not mind. Many years later, as an adult, he continues to be called the same name. Was this bullying? Maybe not, but a similar case in which a boy with severe eczema was called 'Spud' (because his skin peeled) certainly was – the difference being the reaction of the boy concerned.

A consistent feature of all types of bullying is that the victim is unable, at that time and in that situation, to prevent it happening. The victim is also hurt in a significant way. If these conditions are not present then whatever is going on is not bullying, no matter how much onlookers disapprove or are shocked. Of course it may be necessary for other reasons to challenge behaviour which falls outside this narrow definition of bullying. For example, a fight between two individuals of approximately the same strength is not bullying, but it is potentially dangerous to them and to others. It could also contribute to an ethos of violence which is prejudicial to all members of a school community.

TYPES OF BULLYING

There are many different ways in which bullying can be classified. A typical list might include the following:

- rejection or exclusion
- extortion
- name calling
- hitting and kicking
- spreading rumours
- threatening
- racist bullying
- sexual harassment.

Such a classification serves to emphasize the scope of the problem. It also helps to highlight inconsistencies in the way in which we respond. For example, extortion and physical assault are crimes which, if committed by adults, would be reported to the police, but which schools often deal with through their own discipline procedures.

Understanding that bullying is not one thing but many should help us to realize that it is impossible to respond in the same way every time bullying is alleged or observed. A distinction must be made between group bullying (mobbing) and bullying by an individual, where that behaviour is only one manifestation of serious underlying personal and social difficulties.

MOBBING

Konrad Lorenz (1974) described how animals sometimes mob an individual that is different in some way. (People who have kept poultry will probably have seen a moulting bird, or one that has been newly introduced to the flock, repeatedly pecked by its companions.) In borrowing the English word 'mobbing' to describe bullying among children, the Scandinavians originally stuck very closely to Lorenz's meaning of the word: mobbing is uncontrolled and undirected violence by a group against an individual. More recently, most Scandinavian educationalists (Olweus 1993) have come to accept a definition of bullying which also incorporates attacks by individuals, but the term mobbing is still used. In Britain, however, the words bullying and mobbing are not synonymous. All mobbing is bullying, but not all bullying is mobbing.

Perhaps the most exasperating thing about mobbing is the way a perfectly normal and affable group of children can turn on one of their number without warning. The victim may have some distinguishing physical or behavioural feature that might explain why that child has been singled out. But quite often there is little, if anything, to distinguish victims from their attackers.

Even if some children take no active part in the mobbing, their role as bystanders is important. Some will act like a crowd at a boxing match, cheering the victor and ignoring the distress of the vanquished. Others will disapprove but will be too frightened to intervene: 'I feel sorry for people who get bullied but if we say something to the people who are bullying them they might start bullying you' (12-year-old girl).

Sometimes a child is bullied for no better reason than that it is his or her turn. I have described this as *rotational mobbing*. It is most common among teenage girls, but the complexity of the situation makes intervention difficult. There may be a key individual who is controlling things but who may not appear to do much overt bullying. Sometimes there is no apparent instigator, just a group of 'friends' which is strengthened by ensuring that someone is always outside the group. This type of bullying is often indistinguishable from a relationship problem and poses a particular challenge to teachers who may wish to help a victim whose distress is real but possibly temporary. Even if his or her problems are solved, there is a chance that a new victim will be singled out and the old victim may, either actively or as a bystander, start to contribute to the mobbing.

Mobbing tends to be episodic: it starts without warning, continues for a while, then dies out. Sometimes this is because adults have effectively intervened. Sometimes the children find their own solutions:

> I have bullied and I have been bullied. I could not handle being bullied. Luckily the people I got bullied from are friends with me now. But there is one of them which I am still very afraid of. If this girl told me to do something I would do it.
>
> I feel a lot of people are above me and if they picked on me I would not be able to do anything about it. Myself and my best friend now hang about with a group of girls which are very popular. We feel protected. These girls are very nice. They never really bully anybody, maybe just a little laugh at someone now and then but nothing really all that serious. (14-year-old girl)

INDIVIDUAL BULLYING

> I can only remember one case of bullying in recent years. It involved two second year girls. One was making the other carry her books and extorting money from her. It was discovered by a teacher. (Principal Guidance Teacher)

Stereotypical bullies are individuals, like the fictional Flashman, who use their physical strength and strong personalities to boost their own self-esteem, to raise their perceived status or to gain advantage. They may act alone but more commonly they dominate and lead a small group of acolytes. It is, of course, wrong and unhelpful to imagine that all bullies conform to such a stereotype. It is also wrong to imagine that the actions of such a person can be easily explained. Usually, their bullying is one manifestation of a complex set of personal and social problems. Understanding this may help to explain their behaviour, although it cannot excuse it.

Individuals may bully others in a variety of ways, ranging from subtle psychological mind games to brutal physical attacks and extortion. Because teachers are likely to take stern action if extortionists are discovered, culprits take care to cover their tracks. Victims are carefully chosen. They must have something worth stealing and they must be capable of being so terrorized that they will keep silent. Just how effective these threats can be was brought home to me when I discovered that a former pupil had been terrorized for over six months. Every day the boy had handed over his dinner money to the bully. He and the few classmates who knew about it were too frightened to tell an adult. It was three months after he had left school before the boy finally plucked up enough courage to tell his mother. The story eventually came back to the school, but by then there was little that could be done. I felt a profound sense of failure that we had not been able to create the conditions which would have allowed the victim to talk to someone about what had happened. We were well aware that the bully had serious emotional, social and behavioural problems but his peers were too frightened of him to talk and his teachers felt unable to respond effectively without proof.

NAME-CALLING

Pupils, teachers, parents and even educational researchers all agree that name-calling can be a form of bullying. However, these groups would have great difficulty in agreeing a distinction between harmless and harmful name-calling. So much depends upon the individuals concerned and the context in which the event happens. If like this girl you live in an area where actual physical violence is common, then what does a little name-calling matter? 'It is very cruel to bully someone and I wish it would all stop but most people are too scared to tell anyone. Also someone who is just getting called names doesn't always feel that this is bullying and so they just ignore it' (16-year-old girl).

Although it may be difficult to measure the seriousness of name-calling, one thing is certain, it is extensive. In my 1990 survey 13.8 per cent of boys and 17.8 per cent of girls said that they had been 'picked on or called names' recently. This was higher than the total number of children who said that they had been bullied recently, perhaps because some did not consider this type of behaviour to be bullying. Sometimes it is known as 'slagging': 'Slagging means verbally pulling someone to pieces. This normally involves two or three people and starts off good-naturedly but soon focuses on one person' (Principal Guidance Teacher).

Slagging seems to be seen by children as a kind of game, the object of which is to carry out a destructive character analysis, the winner being the person who finds the most flaws in his or her opponent's psyche. An assistant head teacher told me that his pupils often went in for 'wee slagging sessions' but it can get out of hand:

> I have been picked on. People think I am nothing and say anything they want to me. Every day I feel rejected. It's not that people use violence much but I feel as if I am treated as a dustbin. I do want to come forward about this but as I am leaving in a few months I don't see any reason to do so. Nor have I the courage. (16-year-old boy)

THREATENING

There is a distinction between threats and other types of verbal bullying. Intimidation which stops short of actual physical violence is difficult to detect and even more difficult for teachers to prove. But if the victim believes that the threat is real, the effect can be just as devastating as being hit or kicked.

A common threat made to children in the last year of primary school is that when they go to secondary school their heads will be flushed down the toilet. The threat is often made by older friends or siblings who have no intention of carrying out the action themselves – although they may well enjoy the reaction that their 'teasing' produces. Teachers know that 'flushing' or 'bog-washing' (there are various terms used to describe the practice) is extremely rare. They reassure the primary school children of this and usually treat the matter fairly lightly. After all, if there is virtually no chance of the threat being carried out it can hardly be described as bullying, can it? However, some youngsters do believe the threat and, as a result, the weeks before they go to their new school are filled with worry rather than the pleasant anticipation which adults would want to encourage.

INITIATION CEREMONIES

There is a kind of perverse logic to initiation ceremonies: 'We have all been through it so you will have to as well if you want to be one of us.' It is a type of bullying that adults have tolerated, and sometimes even sanctioned. Very few adults can have gone through life without coming across such a ceremony. We know that it goes on in the armed forces and can be brutal in the extreme. A violent assault against a new recruit to the King's Own Scottish Borderers took place in 1987. Private James Guthrie alleged that his testicles had been burnt by a makeshift flame-thrower; he had been sexually assaulted with a broomstick; dropped out of a window and forced to march on the spot with a length of string tied to his testicles and ankles. The army has since responded to such incidents with severity and fewer have been reported in recent years, but initiation ceremonies can still be found in some schools. Victims may even agree to take part. Private Guthrie said that he was 'keen to get it over with and become accepted'.

A Principal Guidance Teacher told me about an initiation ceremony at his school:

> Just after the war, I was a pupil at this school and a tradition known as 'O'er the Wa' was started. It still continues 40 years later.
>
> When it started, first-year boys were thrown over a nine-foot wall into the girls' toilets by older pupils. If you were really unlucky you could end up being belted by the teachers for being in the girls' toilets.
>
> After these were demolished the ceremony switched to a six-foot wall separating the school playing field from a teacher's garden. Nowadays they use a four-foot wall within the school grounds. As far as I know, no one has ever been seriously injured, but it is the first thing that Primary Seven pupils ask about when we talk to them. We tell new pupils to hang about the windows of the staffroom. They can easily avoid the older ones if they do that. We ask them to come and tell us if it happens – but they never do. I can still remember it happening to me but I think that those children who want to avoid it can.

An initiation ceremony like this is a tradition which demeans the institution which tolerates it. It should and could be stopped. Providing a safe haven (under the staff room windows) for frightened youngsters is hardly an adequate response. How long are they expected to stay there – a few days, a few weeks or a few months? One can only hope that in the few years since this example was described all teachers have realized the dangers of allowing such practices to continue.

PREVENTING BULLYING: THE BENEFITS TO SCHOOLS

The most effective way to reduce the level of bullying in schools is to develop a whole school policy to which all members of the school community have contributed. Schools that adopt such positive anti-bullying policies become better schools. They are better not just for those pupils who are bullied, but for all pupils and teachers. A school board chairman described the immediate benefits: 'An already happy and vibrant school now has a much greater awareness of the potential problems and is able to meet them head on before they become major.'

In the longer term, links with learning become more apparent. The creation of a non-bullying ethos in schools demonstrates to young people the effectiveness of such a positive working environment. In the classroom, teachers are increasingly seeking to encourage children to consider the skills and values that will help them to tackle bullying at school and in their adult lives. These include assertiveness, empathizing, openness, self-respect and a respect for others.

A WHOLE SCHOOL POLICY

There are three prerequisites for the successful development of a whole school anti-bullying policy:

- *Recognition*: schools must be honest about admitting that bullying exists (after all we know that it happens in every single school in the country).
- *Openness*: opportunities must be provided for people to talk about bullying without fear of rebuff or retribution.
- *Ownership*: if parents, teachers and pupils are involved in formulating an anti-bullying policy they will have a vested interest in making sure that it succeeds.

Young people who have been the victims of bullying in the past and their parents can help others by contributing to the development of policies. They have two advantages over those who have not been victims: they are highly motivated and they can use their experiences to bring home to others the damage which bullying can do. One mother became involved in anti-bullying work after her daughter had been bullied so severely that she had been forced to change schools and, eventually, to seek medical help. She asked me to put a series of questions to anyone connected with education. 'Could you,' she asked, 'watch your child bite or scratch herself? Could you do nothing if you found her rolled up in a ball under the quilt saying "Don't put me through it any more"? Could you watch as she becomes a prisoner in her own home because she is too afraid to go out, or watch her open her birthday presents through tears of fear and depression? Could you listen to her saying "Let me die, please let me die, then it will be all over"?'

Schools are changing all the time. Many are trying out new ways to cope with bullying. Where this is happening it shows that the problem is being treated seriously. But no school has the answer to every problem and no single method can be used to deal with all bullying incidents. More traditional responses will also continue to be used. Punishments such as suspension or expulsion can mark the seriousness with which an episode of bullying is viewed and can also help to provide a safer environment for victims, at least until the excluded bullies return to school. But the great majority of bullying goes unpunished so some new ways of helping the thousands of hidden victims of bullying are needed. We also need strategies that will help children who bully others to change their behaviour in the long term. Exclusion from school rarely does that. The real work starts when the excluded child returns. Here are examples of some new ideas with a brief comment on each:

- Assertive discipline: a method developed the USA (Canteraul Carter 1976) which involves a rigid system of rewards and sanctions consistently applied by all teachers in a school. It is claimed that this method helps to motivate learning and to reduce the level of classroom indiscipline, but its effectiveness in coping with bullying is not clear.
- Bully boxes: a simple method whereby youngsters can put their concerns on paper and post them in a 'bully box'. What happens to these notes is the key to the success or failure of this technique. Can genuine comments be distinguished from frivolous or malicious ones? How can victims be reassured that their concerns will be tackled appropriately?

- Bully courts: the idea that young people should play a part in making school rules and in deciding what should happen to those who break them is not new. Some progressive schools introduced councils to do this over fifty years ago. More recently a few schools have tried to establish courts or councils solely to deal with cases of bullying. These could provide victims with an opportunity to have their concerns aired in a formal setting. However, the principle that young people should sit in judgement on their peers and punish wrongdoers remains controversial. What is clear is that adults must play an active and guiding role in such proceedings in order to protect the welfare of all the young people involved. They must ensure that the actions of the council do not rebound on the victim and that the council members do not bully those accused of bullying.

- Counselling: a teacher or another adult may have the skills and time to offer support to young people involved in bullying. Both bullies and victims can benefit from this process. The main problems are that it is time consuming, the youngsters must take part voluntarily and there is a lack of trained counsellors in schools. However, even busy teachers can use simple counselling techniques in their efforts to support victims.

- Mediation: some schools have introduced schemes where two parties to a relationship problem agree that a third person, who may be either an adult or another young person, help to negotiate a solution to a problem. This seems to be helpful in many situations, especially where there is not too large an imbalance of power between the protagonists – but not in all cases of bullying. A bully may refuse to take part because s/he has no interest in ending the bullying. A victim may feel that a negotiated solution is not appropriate when it is the other person who is entirely in the wrong.

- Peer counselling: a small number of schools have used older pupils as peer counsellors. Good training and continuing support is vital if these young volunteers are to be able to help victims who may be quite seriously distressed. Peer counsellors who have experienced bullying themselves have reported that they find these schemes particularly rewarding.

- The 'no blame' approach: a step-by-step technique which allows early intervention because it does not require that anyone should be proved to be at fault. A group of young people, which includes bystanders as well as possible bullies, is made aware of a victim's distress and is asked to suggest solutions. This approach is particularly useful in dealing with group bullying and name-calling, when it may be difficult to use more traditional remedies. Adults who use this method must be sensitive to the fact that the victim's feelings are exposed and, if things go wrong, this could make him or her feel more vulnerable.

> • The 'shared concern' method: a Swedish technique (Pikas 1989) which has much in common with the 'no blame' approach, although it has not been widely used in Britain, perhaps because it is more elaborate and time consuming. Both of these methods have been criticized for failing to allocate blame. However, both aim to encourage bullies to accept responsibility for their actions as well as providing a means of bringing bullying to an end.

Some of these techniques are still experimental and will not be suitable for dealing with all those things which we call bullying. But teachers, pupils and their families now have the opportunity to work together to develop new ideas like these. We can make schools change for the better so that fewer young people are forced to change schools to escape from bullying.

ANTI-BULLYING AND CHILD PROTECTION

The actions which schools take to protect children from bullying are linked to other concerns such as child abuse. Encouraging children to talk about bullying can make it easier for them to talk about other forms of abuse and harassment. Some educationalists view the development of anti-bullying policies as a benevolent Trojan horse that allows new ideas about personal and social education to be smuggled into those schools which are resistant to a more direct approach.

Another linked concern is the danger from adult intruders. After the massacre at Dunblane primary school in 1996, stricter controls on movement in and out of schools were introduced. These can help to protect the bullied child, as well as reducing the risk of unwanted adult intruders.

A TRUE STORY

A senior education official gave me a copy of an essay written by a 15-year-old girl. He invited me to quote from it but not to reveal the name of the school that the girl had attended:

> People would steal my money, they would batter me after school ... The people who bullied me were ... my friends. Well at least I thought they were ... then all of a sudden they turned on me.
>
> I was very scared and didn't know what to do. I would sit in school and cry to myself. Eventually I went and told my guidance teacher ... but all she did was tell the kids to be nice to me. Then they not only made fun of me but her.
>
> It went on and on ... It was so terrifying and it was something that was never spoken about at school so I did not know what to do ... One time I got slapped on the face with books in the class and the teacher did not do anything.
>
> I would lie awake at night and worry about going to school the next day ... Going to bed was the only time I ever got a rest from the bullies ...

> I decided to go back to my guidance teacher ... All she said was just to ignore it ...
>
> I was left to struggle on my own ... I would come to school and walk along the dark corridor ... all those kids pushing, kicking and shouting things ... People say 'sticks and stones will break your bones but names will never hurt you', well that's not true ... it can hurt a lot.

Despite repeatedly asking for help at school, things eventually came to a head at home:

> I felt really safe at home with my family but there was a time my mum and dad went out and the bullies came round to my house ... Realising that my parents were not in they decided to try get inside ... I had to lock my doors and windows ... I was so scared. I hadn't a clue what to do. I sat at the back of the door hoping they would go away.

It is difficult to imagine the ordeal of this child as the one place she thought was safe was violated. When her parents came home she broke down and told them for the first time what had been going on. The police were called and the girl was removed from school. Her story reminds us that we cannot yet be confident that all schools will respond compassionately and effectively to this insidious form of abuse. However, we have come a long way in the past ten years.

In 1995, towards the end of my spell as Scottish Anti-Bullying Development Officer, I concluded that the challenge for the future was to find a manageable way for schools to continue to develop their policies. It had become clear that there is unlikely ever to be a single all-purpose strategy against bullying and that effective action necessarily involves an examination of many themes and issues within a school – ethos, values, child protection, special needs, relationships, parental partnerships, guidance, and so on. However, the very fact that bullying interfaces with so many other issues can create problems. How can a parent tell the difference between a school which genuinely believes that bullying should be tackled within the context of, say, discipline and is doing so effectively, and another which says the same but is using this as an excuse for doing nothing? What do we say to a school that wants to tackle bullying, but which also wants to do something about child protection, racism and equal opportunities? Where is the time to come from? Developing an anti-bullying policy in a way that involves the whole school community takes a long time. To be effective this process must have a place in the school's development plan and must include provision for evaluation and modification. This will take years rather months. Perhaps the answer lies in developing a more holistic approach to protecting children from bullying and abuse of all kinds. This would be an approach which examines existing policies and brings together their common features in a statement about the relationships and rights of everyone in a school community – child and adult. This may also involve a re-examination of values and discipline and a recognition that this process is central and not peripheral to the education of individuals and the success of our schools.

REFERENCES

Carter, L. and Carter, M. (1976) *Assertive Discipline*. Santa Monica, CA: Lee Carter and Associates.
Johnstone, M., Munn, P. and Edwards, L. (1992) *Action Against Bullying*. Edinburgh: Scottish Council for Research in Education.
Lorenz, K. (1974) *On Aggression*. New York: Harcourt.
Mellor, A. (1990) *Bullying in Scottish Secondary Schools* Spotlight 23. Edinburgh: Scottish Council for Research in Education.
Olweus, D. (1993) *Bullying at School – What We Know and What We Can Do*. Oxford: Blackwell.
Pikas, A. (1989) 'The common concern method for the treatment of mobbing'. In E. Roland and E. Muntle (eds) *Bullying – An International Perspective*. London: David Fulton Publishers.

FURTHER READING

Byrne, B. (1993) *Coping With Bullying in Schools*. Dublin: Columba Press.
Byrne, B. (1994) *Bullying – A Community Approach*. Dublin: Columba Press.
Cullen, Hon. Lord *The Public Inquiry into the Shootings at Dunblane Primary School on 13 March 1996* (Cullen Report) Edinburgh: Scottish Office.
Elliott, M. (1997) *Bullying – A Practical Guide to Coping for Schools*. London: Pitman.
HM Inspectors of Schools (1997) *Special Inspection of the Nicolson Institute – Western Isles Council*. Inverness: Scottish Office Education and Industry Department (SOEID).
Maines, B. and Robinson, G. (1992) *The No Blame Approach* (video). Bristol: Lame Duck Publishing.
Mellor, A. (1997) *Bullying at School – Advice for Families*. Edinburgh: Scottish Council for Research in Education.
Mellor, A. (1994) *Finding out about Bullying*, Spotlight 43. Edinburgh: Scottish Council for Research in Education.
Mellor, A. (1995) *Which Way Now? – A Progress Report on Action Against Bullying in Scottish Schools*. Edinburgh: Scottish Council for Research in Education.
Scottish Council for Research in Education (1993) *Supporting Schools Against Bullying*. Edinburgh: SCRE.
Smith, P., Morita, Y. *et al.* (1999) *The Nature of School Bullying – A Cross National Perspective*. London: Routledge.

CHAPTER 7

Adult Bullying
Working with Victims

Peter Randall and Jonathan Parker

THE INTENTION TO HURT

Mary felt that she was being foolish when she entered the room of the employee assistance counsellor. She had taken three months to pluck up the courage to come and seek help. It had seemed so childish to her that she should be coming to complain that she had been bullied. After all only children got themselves bullied. Part of her worry was that no one would believe that a grown woman could allow herself to be subject to such a childish prank.

She had worked for five years in the small boutique attached to a large departmental store; the work was pleasant and most of the customers were pleasant. Things had been fine until a new regional manager was appointed, a younger woman who was tipped to move up the ladder quickly.

Mary had never wanted to move up the ladder; she had her two young children and a loyal husband. She only did the job because it helped with expenses. She certainly didn't need to be harassed nearly every day because her 'homely nature' didn't fit into the new boss's view of a modern boutique.

The biggest problem that Mary had in coming to terms with the constant criticism was the reason for it. She asked the counsellor if the new manager wanted rid of her: 'If that's it, I'll go quietly, ' Mary said. But that did not fit with all the times that the new woman was charming and friendly, a trait which stopped Mary thinking about resignation and start hoping that all would work out well. But of course nothing did get better. Mary was still being humiliated, scorned and vilified on a daily basis.

The biggest of Mary's difficulties in dealing with what was happening to her was that she simply could not understand that the bully wanted nothing more than to inflict pain upon her. Like many workplace bullies in positions of power, this woman was prepared to abuse her position in order to hurt Mary and enjoy the outcome.

Many instances of human aggression at school, workplace and community may be analysed systematically leading to the inevitable conclusion that, whatever else bullying may be and whatever form it may take, bullies are always aggressive individuals who intend to cause pain or the fear of pain (Randall 1996). The operational definition of bullying employed here makes this explicit: bullying is the aggressive behaviour arising from the intent to cause physical or psychological distress to others.

When Mary considered this definition and talked through examples of other bullies and their victims she began to recall the air of satisfaction the new manager had about her after she had scored another hit; how she was then nice for a while until her triumph wore off. Mary came to realize that the manager was more likely to harass her if some frustration or stress came from further up the hierarchy. At these times the manager needed to release her tension by bullying Mary.

In common with many adult victims of bullying Mary found it hard to come to terms with the fact that other adults could gain pleasure in this way. It was not until she had really accepted this that she felt able to develop the strategies of assertiveness which ultimately stopped the bully's predations on her.

In our experience it is quite common that victims of adult bullying cannot move on from being paralysed by the terrifying strangeness of what is happening to them to adapting a frame of mind that allows them to assert themselves appropriately and effectively. Some never make this transition and remain with the bullying as 'their problem', coming to believe that they must deserve it and losing every shred of self-esteem as a result.

Some adults use bullying as a means of obtaining pleasure or some other positive reinforcement because most of them have discovered in childhood that there are benefits from bullying. They continue this behaviour, albeit in a more refined way, in adulthood. The transition of childhood to adult aggressive behaviour patterns is well researched. For example, Eron et al. (1987) followed up 518 American children from the age of 8 years at a time when all of them were in their forties. One very significant finding was that the children who were designated as most aggressive at age 8 had committed more crimes, and more serious crimes, as adults. They also had more driving offences, more court convictions, a stronger tendency for alcohol and drug abuse and many were classifiable as anti-social personality disorder (psychopathy).

Of particular relevance was a review of their progress at the age of 30 which involved interviews with them, their spouses and partners. There was significantly more abusive behaviour within their relationships and such poor prosocial behaviour that their conduct interfered with routine everyday activities. Not only were they more abusive to their partners, but their aggressive behaviour often ruined their chances at work because they were regarded as disruptive bullies.

This is clear evidence that highly aggressive children often grow up to be aggressive adults with poorly controlled anti-social behaviour, leading often to negative outcomes in most spheres of human activity including relationship building and employment.

Another study (Jacobson 1992) demonstrated that early bullying behaviour is strongly associated with domestic violence. Women who experience domestic violence often described their partners as bullies, with battering constituting the worst form of this behaviour.

Jacobson and Gottman (1998) also reported that the 'batterers' were of two distinct types: the first was an angry, impulsive and excessively reactive type (the pitbulls). The second was calm, calculating and proactive (the cobras), using the battering as part of the subjugation of his partner and striking with particular venom at times. Both types exist among bullies of all ages but there is a very clear similarity between the description of the second type and the cleverer managerial workplace bullies as described by their victims.

It is illuminating to go back in time to discover what sort of children many adult bullies were in order to understand how they become hooked on the reinforcement that bullying brings them.

THE BULLYING CHILD

We have investigated several hundred bullying situations and been able to study both bullies and victims as well as hearing about the bullying events from their parents. Our work and that of many others demonstrates that bullying children are significantly different in social learning and awareness from non-bullying children and victims. As with many other researchers (Dodge and Crick 1990) we found a particular style of thinking, a distinctly hostile bias which invariably attributes hostile intentions to other children no matter how slight the provocation might be. Often there is no real provocation; an invented one is used to justify the bully's aggressive behaviour. Child victims tell of accidentally jostling bullies as they move between classrooms or accidentally wearing the same clothes, having a better toy in the playground or scoring a goal against the bully's side. Whatever the trivial reason the bully assesses it as an insult and a legitimate reason for aggression. Not surprisingly, we found that bullies of all ages do not process social information accurately and seem unable or unwilling to make realistic judgements about the intentions of their victims. These intentions are invariably viewed as hostile and the bully assumes a need for revenge.

The need for revenge causes bullies to have a positive attitude towards aggression to meet this need and solve problems. This short-term effect is a positive reinforcer and foundation for subsequently refined bullying behaviour. The bullies form the belief that aggression is the best remedy to social problems, no matter how complex they may be.

It is not a distant transition from this reinforcement to the learning that the domination of others can prevent problems arising in the first place and operates on the basis of causing pain or threatening to do so. It is not clear whether this trait develops because the bullies cannot develop prosocial behaviour which would help them relate properly to other children or whether this prior learning interferes with the development of acceptable social awareness. Whatever the cause, some childhood bullies do not develop empathy and so fail to understand the suffering they cause.

Many bullies have a high opinion of themselves (Randall 1997). They are relatively unaffected by anxiety, which normally provides a degree of behavioural restraint. Instead they believe they are superior and powerful and have little awareness of what other children actually think of them. Olweus (1993) found that bullies are of average popularity up to the end of primary school perhaps extending into secondary and have a few reasonably close friends who are also generally aggressive. In time, however, their popularity diminishes such that by early teenage years their only acquaintances are other 'toughs'. Although they may get what they want through their bullying behaviour and are respected because of it, this 'respect' is based on fear.

Several researchers (DeRosier *et al.* 1994) have found the self-confidence of bullies is generally strong enough to withstand rejection by their peer group. This is probably due to an inability to perceive themselves correctly in social situations. DeRosier *et al.* (1994) conclude that because other children with normal prosocial skills are afraid of them and therefore do not approach them, they have less opportunity than non-aggressive children to acquire socialization through the imitation of alternative peer models. Not surprisingly, they keep right on behaving as bullies rather than relinquishing the only strategy they have for dealing with others.

This process is maintained in the workplace where other adults, just like other pupils, refer power to the bullies out of fear, trepidation or just for the sake of peace and quiet. The ways in which they behave make a statement about their emotional need for dominance. The incidence of workplace bullying is, in fact, high as shown by a recent study (Rayner 1997). She found that 53 per cent of respondents to her large survey of part-time students reported being bullied, while a further 78 per cent said they had seen the bullying of others. Those most frequently associated with the bullying were line mangers or senior managers (80%). This takes the issue away from its simplistic location with school children and playground incidents. Interestingly, Rayner saw a fairly equal balance between men and women reporting being bullied at work. However, while women appeared to be bullied in equal proportions by men and women, men rarely reported being bullied by women.

Case Study

Max was a 'powerful' bully in the staffroom of the secondary school where he and 62 other teachers worked. The product of a minor independent boarding school where his size and dirty fighting made him king, his moderate ability enabled him to aspire career-wise less gloriously than his merchant banking father, a source of shame to them both.

He had learned that the younger boys would satisfy his desire for supremacy by crying almost as soon as he threatened them and the respect he could not achieve through attainment and industry he gained through fear.

His bullying ways served him well at college and buffered him from his family's disappointment that he had not made university. There was a period of bitterness and resentment during his time as a junior teacher, but soon he was no longer the new boy in the staffroom and he was able to misuse the opportunities he had for assisting newly qualified staff. He challenged them for not being able to keep discipline, for 'being too soft' and 'acting more like the kids than the kids themselves'. His vitriol was corrosive and belittling. Two new staff members left teaching altogether because he demeaned them so much.

Case Study (continued)

Once several of his victims had been through the local authority's employee assistance programme, the nature of his behaviour came to light and action was taken. This involved an interview with the headteacher, assistant director of education and a union representative. Instead of being castigated for his behaviour, he was treated gently but firmly. His 'problem' as an insecure individual was examined in the context of his constant belittling of other teachers and he was asked if he needed therapeutic help to overcome it. Although he protested his innocence, there was little he could do in the face of the observations made by the headteacher. Typically he said that he did not need help but he knew that he could not carry on as he had been for fear of a further interview. It was impossible to believe in his own supremacy when that had been aligned with weakness and insecurity.

Adult bullying and workplace bullying have not been dealt with as extensively as the problem of childhood bullying. Like childhood bullying, however, much of the work that has been done was conducted in Scandanavia (Einarssen and Skogstad 1996), although British research has also begun to contribute much in this area (Field 1996; Randall 1997). In Sweden, in fact, the matter has been taken so seriously that legislation has been passed which deals with bullying at work, the Offensive Discrimination at Work Act 1994. An excellent review of contemporary research into adult bullying is provided by Rayner and Hoel (1997).

Tim Field's superbly helpful book *Bully In Sight* (1996) provides a list of the most common reasons for people to be selected as victims (pp.109–112). This list includes personal characteristics such as having minor disfigurements or, conversely, being too good looking or too popular, having a different sexual orientation or disability. Also included are skills-based characteristics such as being 'too good' at the job or showing too much professionalism, being more highly qualified than the bullies or too successful in the workplace. These victims often need supportive counselling rather than intensive psychotherapy. They are generally able to understand the reasons and come to see the bullies for the sad people they are.

Other victims have more fundamental characteristics that are a source of emotional pain, which the bullying accentuates to the point of the level of hurt becoming unbearable. These victims need more than supportive counselling. They often need psychotherapy to assist them to restructure their feelings about themselves. We have stated that many of the adult victims of bullying wonder how bullying could be happening to them. Yet, for a substantial proportion, they have been bullied at different times of their lives going back into their childhood. Their experiences at work or in their community are often a repetition of what happened to them in school or at home when they were children. This is the case because they lack strategies to assert themselves against would-be dominant people. An important issue for the therapist working with these people is to enable these strategies to be learned while ensuring no self-blame is internalized as a result of not having developed an air of assertion before now.

Many are the unhappy products of dysfunctional parenting systems; some have been over-indulged, over-protected or kept socially inept by parenting styles that reinforces dependency. The following example is drawn from our Employee Assistance Programme (EAP) case files and used previously (Randall 1997). Bullied local government officer Simon was an example of over-dependency.

> I never got on well with people. My mother was obsessed with me, she dominated me with her love and never let me depart from her ideal view of what I should be like ... I could never do anything like the other kids, such as going off to play football or taking a ride on my bike. I had a nice bike but it stayed in the shed all the time because Mum thought it was too dangerous for me to ride it.
>
> She couldn't help herself; she'd had three miscarriages before I came along and she was besotted by me.
>
> When I finally escaped her by going to work it was only to find that I didn't know how to get on with people – they wouldn't take any notice of me except to be rude. I almost use to invite them to bully me in order to gain their attention.

Simon realized that being a victim had become a habit and that he lacked assertiveness.

There is another less common variety of victims who are the products of rejecting parents who have no affection for and interest in their children: they become so anxious to please their parent that they develop this as a habit which is maintained into adulthood.

Nick was one of three children, all sons. His mother told him that she had wanted a girl instead of him because she had had enough of boys. This attitude seemed to have permeated even the warmest of her interactions with him. It did not help that he had been born with a severe squint and feeding reflux problems. Later he developed problems of dentition which left him with bunched and protruding teeth. His mother made a cynical joke out of calling him 'The Buck Tooth Boy Wonder'.

The last three years of his primary education were filled with incidents of daily bullying. He was picked on verbally, mainly by girls because of his appearance, but being good at football spared him the attentions of male bullies for the most part: 'The girls made my life hell and my mother just laughed at me; Dad got it stopped eventually but it was too late. I just kept right on trying to appease my Mum and these girls.'

At work in the dispatch room of a large electrical goods manufacturer, Frankie was subjected to levels of verbal harassment by the women on the packing line. Two of them in particular made disgusting jokes about his sexual appeal and the chargehand made a point of complaining loudly about him being slow, getting too much overtime and making a mess of the dispatch tables. There were comments also about his state of hygiene (which was good) such that he would deliberately wash his hair each day just before going into work. He felt the wet look of it would convince people that he was a clean person. 'I also took in sweets and cakes to make them like me and always offered to help anyone who needed it.' Not surprisingly, his efforts to appease were taken full advantage of without any lessening of the harassment. Frankie undertook many sessions of non-directive therapy and some cognitive behavioural work to help him understand that his submissive and appeasing nature was an adult recreation of the life he had led with his mother.

Sadly, people with this background often learn to be submissive in order to avoid further parental conflict and rejection. Unfortunately, the strategy becomes a trait that pervades all aspects of social life. This, of course, is a trait that bullies can exploit and often have the support of co-workers who would not necessarily become bullies themselves.

Typically the stages through which people pass to become victims throughout their working lives are multi-faceted and partially conditional upon the social environments they encounter. It is rare that any one antecedent is prevalent. Indeed different but related variables emerge according to the nature of the working group they are with. Many reveal that they were bullied for years at school or in their families. Perhaps as children they wept readily or did not fit within the friendship groups. Often they were isolated or ignored by their peers who did not protect them when they were being bullied. Some allege that their parents had not only been power assertive but also sexually abusive. The majority of the long-term victims feel that they did not enjoy normal peer relations.

Several research studies have been published about social withdrawal, which includes shyness, reticence and quietness, that have associated it with psychological maladjustment and difficulties of internalization (Rubin, Chen and Hymel 1993). Such findings have given rise to research about parenting, parent attitudes and parents' beliefs about socialization. Many of the characteristics of both child and adult victims of bullying are incorporated in these studies, including reduced exploration in novel social situations, social deference, timidity, submissiveness, social wariness and anxiety about interactions, negative attitudes about self, including poor self-regard, low self-esteem and acceptance of low status (Hymel, Woody and Bowker 1993; Randall 1996).

HOW TO BEGIN TO WORK WITH VICTIMS OF ADULT BULLYING

The serious nature of workplace bullying is reflected in the response of many proactive industries and occupations to set up, organize or contract employee assistance schemes and occupational health measures. While these are designed to look after the general well-being of employees, it is clear that many of those seeking assistance do so because of their experiences of harassment and bullying. Our own involvement in operating one of these schemes provides a wealth of evidence indicating the need for them.

In the workplace one can look to no better source than Andrea Adams (1992, 1997), herself a tireless campaigner against workplace harassment until her untimely death in 1995, for suggestions concerning a constructive response to protect workers from bullying behaviour. She suggests:

- development of clear policies on bullying which set out the disciplinary actions and sanctions for bullying
- wide dissemination of the policy among staff through leaflets and posters
- clear identification and definition of types of bullying and what staff can do, emphasizing confidentiality
- employer should be vigilant in identifying stress in employees
- complaints should be dealt with quickly and shown to be taken seriously
- development of training in stress and anger management for aggressive employees.

A detailed examination of the development of anti-bullying policies for the workplace is provided by Randall (1997) where a sample policy is made available.

However, it is the individual approach to the victim that counts for most in the recovery process. The opportunity of being listened to and valued as a person with an important report to make for the good of others as well as themselves is a major part of the healing process. Tim Field (1996) makes the point that the process of recall can take months or years in some cases. That is also our experience. Many victims need to test out a listener's response over time before they have the confidence to unburden themselves completely. In addition, post-traumatic blocking of severe experiences is not uncommon and conversely some victims experience flashbacks for years after the incidents have ceased. For these reasons, it is not helpful always to offer only brief therapy approaches. Valuable as these are, there also has to be a potential for longevity in the therapeutic relationship which enables the victims to come back in their own time. Telephone counselling is often useful so that victims can make a call at particularly stressful times.

AWARENESS

Many victims of long-term bullying feel helpless and at the mercy of any would-be aggressor. To start the healing process they should be encouraged to understand that the bullying, whether psychological or physical, does more harm if they give it undue personal significance. Victims need assistance to learn that they have not been diminished in any way as worthwhile people by the unpleasant experiences. Field (1996) states this well by pointing out that many people are bullied because they possess attributes of which the bullies are jealous. He suggests that the aggressors are actually paying their victims a 'backhanded compliment' (p.330). Often these attributes include dedication, a capacity for hard work, fairness, honesty and empathy; all strong positive traits that can be explored with the victims and encouraged to replace the corrosive self-constructs of blame, guilt and shame.

The awareness-raising process should be moulded into another stage. This concerns a primary requirement that victims must ultimately take responsibility for rejecting the aggression that future bullies may seek to inflict upon them. In our experience a golden rule for working with victims of bullying is that they remain as potential victims as long as they accept the passive role. Thus the client who keeps asking 'help me cope with this' needs to become aware that 'coping with' is just a compliance with the passive role. It implies acceptance and a lack of assertiveness in tackling bullying proactively. This vital awareness is 'the foundation on which you [the client] can begin to rebuild your battered self-esteem and eventually learn how to prevent the nightmare from recurring' (Crawford 1985).

It is the case that non-assertive behaviour is strongly correlated with low self-esteem (Back and Back 1991), a lack of respect for oneself and a mal-adaptive desire to appease and gratify others. A fear of confrontation that is explicit within this behaviour is associated with anxiety and is a common antecedent for victim status (Adams 1992). Aggressive behaviour, by contrast, is fundamentally manipulative in that it involves trying to control and subjugate other people. It is crudely manipulative and demonstrates a lack of respect for other people in its refusal to acknowledge their need for a life without fear and degradation. Such regular aggressive behaviours are invariably reinforced by the submissiveness of victims. They accept bullying rather than tackle it.

The key to this non-assertive behaviour lies in mastering appropriate techniques associated with the client beginning to judge his or her own performance independently of the resulting behaviour from the bully or, indeed, from the outcome of the interaction (Guirdham 1990). The beginnings of such adaptive behaviour are to be found in the use of the word 'I'. The therapeutic process should empower the client to say, for example, 'I think that', 'I want to'. This is a first step in taking ownership of one's own feelings, opinions and attitudes without attempting to embed and disguise them in placatory remarks. As this process starts to work the clients are less likely to express themselves in long-winded and roundabout ways, failing to give a clear message. A simple but gradual movement towards clarity and brevity will create an impression in the minds of the bullies that this person is unlikely to submit to their aggressive manipulation. Randall (1996) provides a stepwise procedure for enhancing the assertiveness required.

IMPORTANCE OF GOOD SUPERVISION

Supervision is increasingly recognized as essential for good and ethical practice in all areas of counselling, psychotherapy and social work (British Association of Counselling 1997; Pritchard 1994). Supervision is to some extent defined by its purpose and context. This is no less the case for practitioners receiving supervision when working with victims of adult bullying and harassment or for supervisors working with practitioners in this area of practice. All supervision, however, is designed to provide support in clinical practice, professional development, identifying education and training needs and personal support (McCann 1999). Supervision also ensures accountability by overseeing the work undertaken and providing a management and evaluative function (Kadushin 1992).

Our own experience in working with adult victims of bullying has demonstrated the importance of consultative supervision in which various aspects of casework and clinical practice are discussed, challenged and further developed and in keeping a close yet supportive eye focused on the response of the agency to the problem of adult bullying. The following anonymized case study helps to show the importance of supervision.

Case study

Mollie worked for a regional employee assistance programme. She had voiced a number of concerns about her cases. Most pressing was her view that an increasing number of people on her caseload were contemplating suicide or serious self-harm as a result of their experiences of workplace harassment. Her main objective in supervision was to develop effective ways of reducing the risks of harm if possible and to share ethical and professional concerns resulting from these perceived risks. She sought reassurance about her responsibility towards her clients and their choice of action. The supervisor looked with Mollie at her cases in a systematic way, reviewing the work achieved, plans developed with clients and skills needed to continue the work. While this activity achieved her main objective of identifying existing skills and methods to work with the cases it also helped fulfil an agency objective. The number of high-risk cases were logged and the health and safety of the counsellor assured. Also, once the cases had been reviewed it was clear that the number of high-risk cases involving self-harm and suicidal ideation were far outweighed by other cases presenting much lower risks.

A central issue in supervision concerns the open negotiation of the relationship between practitioner and supervisor (Carroll 1996). Roles, responsibilities and reciprocal tasks are made explicit. The aims and objectives of the supervision are clearly stated. A useful tool that aids clarity and explicitness is the production of a written contract that sets out the detail of the negotiated supervisory relationship. We have found in our practice that supervisory contracts add a sense of safety in knowing that supervision is available and regular. It also helps make the purpose explicit by delineating the areas that will be covered. This alleviates some of the fears and also the bravado that can exist in emotionally draining work with people who have often suffered extreme and prolonged acts of harassment. While a degree of standardization is useful we have also found that a personally negotiated element encourages ownership and allows the individual to maximize the benefits of supervision for personal and professional development. The following example shows how a negotiated supervision contract helped the counsellor we have already met in the preceding case study.

Case Study

Mollie received regular supervision once a fortnight on Thursday mornings for one and half hours. She understood this as her time and ensured this was a priority in her schedule. The supervisor was her line manager who also practised in the field and was aware of the emotional, practical and learning demands the work raised. Informal supervision or consultation was available at other times and debriefing after a particularly difficult, worrying or stressful counselling session was actively encouraged. Formal supervision sessions included a discussion of all cases being worked with, the negotiated counselling plans, methods of working and proposals for evaluation and review. This provided clinical support, attention to learning and development needs and ensured that casework responsibility was shared appropriately throughout the organization. Mollie wished to develop skills in cognitive approaches which severed the connections between the person's feelings of guilt and inadequacy and thoughts about personal responsibility and self-blame for the harassment occurring in the first place. Alongside the standard supervision arrangements, there was space to negotiate training needs and casework practice in these areas.

The stress placed upon supervision allowed all counsellors in the agency to feel valued and to accept constructive developmental advice and support. Any desire to take on large caseloads and unmanageable workloads was reduced as supervision encouraged a collegiate and co-operative approach to the work that valued individuals and their health. This method and approach developed from the experiences of the employee counsellors working with victims of adult bullying and harassment in the workplace.

Working with the victims of adult bullying demands a great deal from individual practitioners, agencies and funding bodies. These demands and expectations traverse the personal, professional and organizational levels in a way that makes regular and purposeful supervision fundamental to good practice.

REFERENCES

Adams, A. (1992) *Bullying at Work*. London: Virago.

Adams, A. (posthumous account, J. Beasley and C. Rayner, eds) (1997) 'Bullying at work.' *Journal of Community and Applied Social Psychology* 7, 3, 177–180.

Back, K. and Back, K. (1991) *Assertiveness at Work*. Maidenhead: McGraw Hill.

British Association of Counselling (1997) *Code of Ethics*. Rugby: British Association of Counselling.

Carroll, M. (1996) *Counselling Supervision: Theories, Skills and Practice*. London: Cassell.

Crawford, N. (1985) *Power and Powerlessness in Organisations*. London: Tavistock Clinic. Paper No. 52, unpublished.

DeRosier, M.E., Cillessen, A.H.N., Coie, J. and Dodge, K.A. (1994) 'Group social content and children's aggressive behaviour.' *Child Development 65*, 1068–1079.

Dodge, K.A. and Crick, N.R. (1990) 'Social information-processing bases of aggressive behaviour in children. Special issue: Illustrating the value of basic research.' *Personality and Social Psychology Bulletin 16*, 8–22.

Einarssen, S. and Skogstad, A. (1996) 'Epidemiological findings of bullying.' *European Journal of Work and Organizational Psychology 5*, 2, 185–201.

Eron, L.D., Huesmann, L.R., Dubow, E., Romanoff, R. and Yarmel, P.W. (1987) 'Aggression and it correlates over 22 years.' In D.H. Gowell, I.M. Evans, and C.R. O'Donnell (eds) *Childhood Aggression and Violence*. New York: Plenum.

Field, T. (1996) *Bully in Sight*. Wantage: Success Unlimited.

Guirdham, M. (1990) *Interprersonal Skills at Work*. Hemel Hempstead: Prentice Hall.

Hymel, S., Woody, A. and Bowker, A. (1993) 'Social withdrawal in childhood: considering the child's perspective.' In K.H. Rubin and J.B. Asendrpf (eds) *Social Withdrawal, Inhibition and Shyness in Childhood*. Hillsdale: Lawrence Erlbaum, 237–262.

Jacobson, N.S. (1992) 'Behavioural couple therapy: a new beginning.' *Behaviour Therapy 23*, 493–506.

Jacobson, N. and Gottman, J. (1998) *When Men Batter Women. New Insights into Ending Abusive Relationships*. New York: Simon and Schuster.

Kadushin, A. (1992) *Supervision in Social Work*, 3rd edn. New York: Columbia University Press.

McCann, D. (1999) 'Supervision.' In R. Bor and M. Watts (eds) *The Trainee Handbook. A Guide for Counselling and Psychotherapy Trainees*. London: Sage.

Olweus, D. (1993) *Bullying at School: What We Know and What We Can Do*. Oxford: Blackwell.

Pritchard, J. (ed) (1994) *Good Practice in Supervision*. London: Jessica Kingsley Publishers.

Randall, P.E. (1996) *A Community Approach to Bullying*. Stoke-on-Trent: Trentham Books.

Randall, P.E. (1997) *Adult Bullying*. London: Routledge.

Rayner, C. (1997) 'The incidence of workplace bullying.' *Journal of Community and Applied Social Psychology 7*, 3, 199–208.

Rayner, C. and Hoel, H. (1997) 'A summary review of literature relating to workplace bullying.' *Journal of Community and Applied Social Psychology 7*, 3, 181–191.

Rubin, K.H., Chen, X. and Hymel, S. (1993) 'The socio-emotional characteristics of extremely aggressive and extremely withdrawn children.' *Merrill-Palmer Quarterly 39*, 518–534.

CHAPTER 8

Working with Victims
of Workplace Bullying

Helge Hoel and Cary L. Cooper

INTRODUCTION

In order to survive and sustain competitiveness a large number of UK organizations have downsized or are in the process of downsizing. As a consequence, fewer people have been left with more work in a climate of uncertainty. This uncertainty is further exacerbated by the increasing number of temporary contracts and voluntary redundancy schemes in operation. Employees in the prime of life are often considered to be too 'expensive' and they face graduates and school leavers competing for and often taking over their jobs. At the same time people are working longer hours, often against their will (Stewart and Swaffield 1997). There are also signs that an increasing number of managers are adopting an authoritarian or macho leadership style, partly as a response to the increasing pressures. Such factors create a climate where insecurity is rife, providing a work environment in which the potential for inter-personal conflict and bullying becomes endemic.

The label 'workplace bullying' did not appear in the UK until Andrea Adams's book *Bullying at Work: How to Confront and Overcome It* (1992) was published. Growing interest in the related problem of school bullying appears to be one explanation for the emergence of the label at this particular time. Application of the term 'bullying' in a work setting was influenced by studies in Scandinavia, which focused on hostile and unethical communication of a persistent nature, predominantly directed towards one person (Hoel 1997; Leymann 1990). UK unions appear to have easily embraced the 'new' concept, as it enabled them to brand a range of unfair treatment as a type of workplace harassment or bullying at a time when the union movement was weakened and collective solutions were often giving way to more individualist approaches (Lee 1998a, 1998b).

Many cases of offensive and bullying behaviour are resolved at an early stage, without turning into bitter personalized conflicts. While it should be the aim of all organizations to reduce levels of organizational conflicts, focusing on those factors which may contribute to increased conflict levels, this chapter concentrates on those cases where the conflict has already escalated to a level where a victim has emerged. At the centre of our attention is the victimization process itself and the effects this may have on individuals and organizations alike. The first part of the chapter focuses on the phenomenon of workplace bullying and its effects, while the second part concentrates on the organizational response to workplace bullying and victimization.

UNDERSTANDING THE PROBLEM
What is 'workplace bullying'?

Lisa, a district nurse, describes what happened to her:

> I was extremely happy and fulfilled in this position until the last two years when there was a change in the style of management.
>
> Bureaucracy and additional paperwork were increasing at a rapid rate. It seemed every day there were threatening and demanding faxes from management. I felt that I was carrying an enormous weight on my shoulders and from having great job satisfaction I felt I had never done enough, even if I'd worked through the night, starting at 7.30, never taking a lunch break to keep 'on top of things'. This was causing increasing stress and health problems.
>
> I had an exemplary record and rarely took any sick leave, until I suffered a crucial spine injury on my way home from work. This, as will be explained later, had serious repercussions for me. Throughout 1997, though I had returned to the job I loved most, managerial pressures became more and more oppressive and I had absolutely no support as the previous supportive manager was made redundant. The service, I felt, was being run on a knife edge and I informed the current manager of this verbally on numerous occasions, and in writing.
>
> The GP could see the stress and exhaustion I was under and wrote to management asking for another part-time secretary to help me. This of course was not forthcoming and the letter ignored – in fact I was told by my line manager 'to keep my mouth shut' to the GP ... At every meeting with my line manager (X) she asked me if I was going to leave and why I didn't change my job so I could spend more time with my patients. I always replied that I was totally committed to district nursing but I did not like or approve of many changes that were taking place, which in my opinion were not for the better. In short, we were constantly in conflict. As she realized I was not going to leave so easily, she decided I needed an urgent assessment at occupational health to see if my previous injury (though I was well and asymptomatic) was in any way preventing me from meeting the needs of the service. I asked where all this was leading and she informed me that I would be sent off indefinitely. By now I was getting very worried as I could feel the weight of power of the organization. I knew she was no longer acting alone. But these were serious moves to redeploy or get rid of me.
>
> Not long after, this particular manager (X) found a reason to start an investigation into my record keeping, and was determined to go back several years to find flaws or technical imperfections which in no way ever compromised patient care. The immediate effect caused me to have an acute anxiety attack, and I had to leave work, see my GP and be prescribed tranquillisers

... The support left me feeling better for a few days until I received a letter in the post, informing me there would be a formal meeting to investigate my record keeping under the Trust's Disciplinary Procedure. This was also extended to case-load management. I asked the manager if she could please put all her concerns in writing as I would willingly respond. She was furious, threatening and annoyed as it would be a lot of work for her photocopying notes, etc. but had to agree eventually. She insisted that on her completion I would have only five days to respond.

Management made everything as difficult as possible for me. Diaries which had been removed were not returned, and I was given no additional resources, which was even more frightening as an even higher level of management decided to take over. I was determined to fight on as I knew that I had done absolutely nothing wrong and had an unblemished record with only high accolades from patients, consultants and GPs. However, the more I fought for justice, the more heavy handed management became, not to mention the financial costs. After completing my response I was summoned to another meeting which I was told was to discuss general matters. My written response was never at any point mentioned, let alone discussed, yet I was given a verbal disciplinary warning to act as a 'marker' and which was to be on my file for six months (I was told I was lucky it was not for longer). I was also told I had to be supervised by a senior district nurse team leader on a weekly basis to ensure I achieved all the management competencies required by the Trust. My team was further reduced to 1.5 staff nurses and the shame and humiliation caused me to become very ill and psychologically unbalanced.

Before we take a closer look at the experience of bullying and the effects exposure to bullying may have on the individual (and the organization), we need to define the problem. In line with definitions used in Scandinavia and other European countries, we will define bullying as follows:

> Bullying emerges when one or several individuals/persons persistently over a period of time perceive themselves to be on the receiving end of negative actions from one or several persons, in a situation where the one at the receiving end has difficulties in defending him/herself against these actions. (Einarsen *et al.* 1994, p.20).

Let us take a close look at the central features of this definition one by one:

1. *Negative actions against one or several people.* We will later describe in more detail what type of negative actions are frequently experienced in connection with bullying, which is often identified with being singled out for negative treatment. However, recent reports suggest that frequently more than one person and in some cases an entire workgroup report being the target of negative and aggressive behaviour (UNISON 1997). Even in such cases, bullying remains a lonely experience.

2. *Persistent.* Bullying will normally refer to behaviour which is repeated and persistent. Therefore, while it can be unpleasant to be the target of someone's occasional aggressive behaviour, such behaviour would normally be considered to fall outside the definition. An exception

here would be intimidation of such a severe nature that the target is left in a situation of permanent uncertainty or fear. Physical violence or the threat of physical violence may serve as an example here.

3. *Long term.* Some cases of workplace bullying may be resolved early on by means of organizational intervention or private conflict resolution. Others are terminated by the exit from the organization of one of the parties involved. However, it is a predominant feature of bullying cases that they may go on for a very long time. From the literature, we know that it is not unusual for a case to go on for three years or more (Einarsen *et al.* 1994). It is important to bear this in mind as the prolonged nature of the situation would affect the state of the victim and the possibility of finding a solution to the problem.

4. *Imbalance of power.* It is essential to the experience of bullying that the targets or recipients perceive themselves to have less power than the perpetrator. For that reason, if there is an equal balance of power between two individuals in a conflict situation, we should not refer to it as bullying. Power, as used in this connection, may be drawn from a formal position within the organizational hierarchy or from more informal sources. Personal contacts, organizational standing and experience, as well as knowledge of the target's potential vulnerability or 'weak points', may all qualify as sources of informal power.

5. *Subjective versus objective.* It is important to note the role assigned to 'perception' as reflected in the above definition. As far as bullying is concerned it is the individual's subjective perceptions of events that are important. In other words, it is our interpretation of the situation that determines the meaning we assign to it (Einarsen 1996).

6. *Sexual and racial harassment and bullying.* Some will argue that sexual harassment is a particular form of bullying (Einarsen *et al.* 1994). Others will suggest that here we are faced with different problems rooted in different causes, in need of a separate response (Leymann 1996). We will argue that there are obvious cases where sexual or racial discrimination may play a part in the bullying scenario, for example, where bullying tactics are politically motivated. Many women who have entered traditionally male-dominated workplaces can report such behaviour. However, since we do not intend to explore the causes of these phenomena, we will let this debate rest and for the purpose of the current discussion we will exclude such cases.

7. *Conflict or bullying.* Most of us would see conflict and disagreement as a natural ingredient of life. Some will even argue that disagreement and conflict are a precondition for any development. However, what decides whether a conflict may be constructive or destructive is how it is being resolved. Unfortunately, what may sometimes start as a conflict between two parties may escalate out of all proportion, ending with a serious case of bullying.

When we look at cases of bullying it may be helpful to make a distinction between predatory and dispute-related bullying (Einarsen 1999). The latter group refers to cases arising from a situation of conflict. Predatory bullying refers to those cases where the victims find themselves the target of aggressive behaviour without any previous personal involvement in the situation. Such examples may be personally motivated, sometimes even pathological in nature, fulfilling certain needs of the perpetrator (Randall 1997). At other times, the situation may contribute to the aggressive behaviour. It is not unusual for a stressful work environment to elicit aggressive behaviour in individuals, with predatory or dispute-related bullying as possible outcomes.

Describing bullying

Even though the experience of bullying varies greatly, several attempts have been made to classify the actions of perpetrators most frequently involved in cases of bullying. According to Leymann (1990), who pioneered research into workplace bullying, bullying may be categorized as follows according to the effects the behaviour may have on the victim. According to Leymann these negative acts intend to damage:

- the victim's reputation (ridicule, gossip, slander)
- the opportunity for communication (accusations, denial of self-defence)
- the victim's social relationships or standing (isolation)
- the potential for victims to perform their work tasks (denial of access to information, misinformation, relocation to an unsatisfactory working environment)
- victims by use of physical coercion or the use of threats.

Not only do the recipients tend to perceive the treatment as deeply humiliating and unjust, but particularly damaging is the effect of the behaviour on the target's self-esteem and ultimately self-respect.

From the examples of behaviour given above, we can make a distinction between actions which are work related and those which are person related. Another way of looking at the behaviour would be to divide the actions into direct and indirect actions.

On their own many of the above actions may be considered normal and quite harmless, even if judged to be unacceptable. However, when the behaviour endures and the abnormal becomes the normal, a case of bullying is likely to evolve.

What is the scale of the problem?

There is currently no agreement as to the size of the problem of workplace bullying in the UK. Scandinavian research has focused on figures of approximately between 5 per cent and 10 per cent (Hoel 1997), depending upon how strictly the concept is operationalized. Figures from the UK vary from 14 per cent to over 50 per cent, where 14 per cent refers to experience over the last six months (UNISON 1997) and 53 per cent when the question referred to experience throughout working life (Rayner 1997).

Victim profile

Is it possible to establish a profile of the typical victim? While the answer to this rhetorical question is a qualified 'no', we can draw some conclusions. Women and men appear to be equally vulnerable to becoming victims of bullying. However, while men predominantly report being bullied by other men, women may be bullied by both genders. Still, the majority of female victims report being bullied by men. This difference in experience between men and women may be explained largely by reference to labour market inequalities (Hoel, Rayner and Cooper 1999). For a large majority of people it is still the case that women work with other women and men with other men. At the same time far more men than women hold positions of authority. It is suggested that women's experience of bullying may vary from that of men. Women may face more negative and aggressive actions of a covert nature than men (Björkqvist, Österman and Lagerspetz 1994). Such actions may be referred to as social manipulation, focusing on behaviour such as spreading rumours or making insulting comments on somebody's private life. Being interrupted or ignored are also actions experienced far more frequently by women than by men.

It has been envisaged that older people may make up the most vulnerable group. Potentially lower pace at work and less flexibility in responding to change as one grows older are possible explanations here. Sensitivity may also increase with age. However, recent UK studies found no differences in the experience of bullying with respect to age (Rayner 1997).

Based on findings from research, there is a belief that bullying is more widespread in white-collar than blue-collar occupations (Rayner and Hoel 1997). However, there is little real evidence in support of this view. This finding is probably more indicative of the self-selecting groups who make use of helplines and self-help groups, which so far have often informed our views.

Bullying should not be seen simply as a product of personal features such as habits or particular personality traits. On the one hand, there is some evidence that individuals with a particular personality profile (introverted, conscientious, neurotic and submissive) may be more likely to be targeted for negative treatment and subsequently victimized (Seigne, Coyne and Randall 1999). On the other hand, it can be argued that such personality features may result from the bullying process (Leymann 1996). There is no doubt that being exposed to bullying has a major impact on a person's personality and identity. We will look into this issue in more detail when we explore the effects of the bullying experience on the victim. However, we would tend to agree with Einarsen *et al.* (1994) who state that bullying is 'neither the product of chance nor of destiny'. Instead, bullying should be understood primarily as an interplay between people, where neither situational nor personal factors entirely suffice to explain why bullying develops.

Effects of bullying

My life is devastated, the effect of the condition denies commitments of any kind, confidence is zero, as is self-esteem. Motivation and will are a much reduced feature of life. I am void of physical, mental, social and emotional stamina. There are frequent periods of utter misery and black moods. The continuing effect of restless sleep, early waking and nightmares creates feelings of guilt and anxiety. Preoccupation with and flashbacks of the experience create a deeply negative perspective. I am daily living in fear of a crisis occurring that I simply won't be able to cope with. Panic, dry mouth, aching limbs, tremors and palpitations are frequent. (John, 51, Sales Manager)

We will examine below the 'victim experience' in more detail. Here we will consider in more general terms the effects of bullying on the individual as well as the organization. The effects of bullying on health are not straightforward. It is likely that people with a history of health problems may be more vulnerable to become victims as well as to develop psychological or physiological problems as a result of their treatment.

The experience of bullying is found to be related to a number of health problems. Psychosomatic stress symptoms such as stomach upset, muscular aches and tensions, as well as sleeping problems or insomnia are among the most common. Psychologically bullying frequently manifests itself in depression, anxiety and nervousness (Hoel et al. 1999). An examination of the relationship between bullying on the one hand, and stress and psychiatric problems on the other, found that the greatest difference between bullied and non-bullied people was to be found in two groups of symptoms referred to as 'cognitive effect' and 'psychosomatic symptoms'. Cognitive effects in this context refer to symptoms such as concentration problems, lack of initiative, insecurity and irritability.

Being exposed to bullying is also likely to manifest itself in behavioural patterns. Increased sickness absenteeism and premature exit from the organization are two likely outcomes. However, again cause and effect are far from clear cut. While some victims of bullying may stay away from work as a result of the bullying experience, either directly as an avoidance strategy or more indirectly as a result of severe health effects, others may carry on despite pains and growing health problems. For the individual a 'presenteeism' strategy may be deemed necessary in order to prevent a further escalation of the conflict as well as disproving any suggestions that they are 'not up to the job'. For some victims this may obviously be seen as a 'catch 22' situation. Tim Field, himself a victim and campaigner against workplace bullying, describes this situation:

> The person becomes withdrawn, reluctant to communicate for further criticism; this results in accusations of 'withdrawal', 'sullenness', 'not co-operating or communicating', 'lack of team spirit', etc. Dependence on alcohol, or other substances lead to impoverished performance, poor concentration and failing memory, which brings accusations of 'poor performance'. (Field 1996, p.128)

Reliable figures of the economic impact on the organization, industry and society as a whole are not available. The CBI calculates the cost of sickness absenteeism alone in the UK in 1998 at £12 billion (CBI 1998). It is not unlikely that bullying accounts for a significant amount of this figure. Increased turnover rates as a result of premature exit from the organization further contribute to the cost. Moreover, it may be suggested that some of the effects of bullying are of an indirect nature, where lack of initiative, motivation and creativity may affect productivity (Bassmann 1992). Such effects may not be limited to the individual targeted for negative treatment, but may severely affect the effort and productivity of fellow workers and colleagues who observe what is going on. As far as cost is concerned, such factors may turn out to be as important as the more direct costs due to increasing rates of absenteeism and turnover.

It should be noted that some victims of bullying pay the ultimate price by committing suicide. The seriousness of the problem is most clearly expressed in the high number of bullying victims (40%) who report that at times they have considered taking their own lives (Einarsen *et al.* 1994).

Post traumatic stress disorder

Post traumatic stress disorder (PTSD), is most commonly identified with the experience of a single traumatic event such as a severe accident. The medical diagnosis of PTSD is identified with the following symptoms: a re-experience of the event or frequent flashbacks, a tendency persistently to avoid stimuli associated with the trauma as well as a persistent feeling of irritability sustained for a relatively long period of time (Scott and Stradling 1994). However, in recent years it has been recognized that similar symptoms to those identified with PTSD may arise from the experience of persistent, work-related extreme stressors such as victimization. On the basis of their work at a Swedish rehabilitation clinic for victims of workplace bullying, Leymann and Gustafsson (1996) state that many victims of bullying may be given the diagnosis PTSD, which also may result in a personality or 'characterological' change. In other words, the individual is no longer the same person as he or she was before the series of traumatic events took place.

It has also been argued that compared with patients who have been diagnosed as suffering from PTSD resulting from involvement in traumatic accidents, victims of bullying showed significantly higher levels of PTSD. This has recently been confirmed in a Norwegian study of long-term sufferers of bullying (Einarsen *et al.* 1999). Not only were 76 per cent of the victims studied found to be suffering from the same symptoms as traditional PTSD patients, compared with individuals who had been involved in very serious traumatic events, the bullying victims were found to have far higher PTSD scores. Furthermore, as many as 45 per cent of the victims whose experience of bullying goes back five years or more reported symptoms at a level above the threshold value for PTSD. How can we explain these findings?

Victimization: The experience of workplace bullying

In order to throw some light on this question we will draw extensively on the report by Einarsen *et al.* (1999) on long-term effects of bullying. To make sense of the fact that victims of severe, long-term bullying suffer extreme effects on their health, the authors make reference to Janoff-Bullmann's (1992) work on trauma and traumatic life experiences. According to Janoff-Bullmann, an event becomes traumatic when it challenges our most fundamental assumptions of the world:

- the world as benevolent
- the world as meaningful
- the self as worthy.

According to this perspective, we gradually build up our view of the world from childhood. To most of us, this picture appears to be generally positive. Furthermore, having our outlook and world picture confirmed provides us with a sense of security. Obviously, the picture is in need of minor adjustment from time to time when our experience is somewhat at odds with our basic beliefs about the world. An event becomes traumatic, however, when this well-established picture is fundamentally challenged to the extent that our basic assumptions about the world collapse.

This model has been successfully applied to the experience of workplace bullying (Einarsen et al. 1999). From a belief that people generally happen to be positive and well meaning ('the world as benevolent'), victims of bullying find themselves in a situation where they feel 'hounded' or they have a strong feeling that somebody is trying to 'get them'. Lack of support from close colleagues or other people they trusted may be very hurtful. In such situations victims would ask themselves: 'why did this happen to me?' ('the world as meaningful'). The assumption of a generally meaningful and just world is now no longer sustainable. This may be particularly hard to understand for the hard-working, apparently successful victim. The victims now find themselves portrayed in the most humiliating way as incapable and useless. It is not surprising that in such a situation many victims feel that a serious injustice is being committed and that the world is conspiring against them. To the victim it seems unexplainable that someone who has always attempted to do their utmost for the best reasons, and frequently appeared to be both successful and popular, is now on the receiving end of a stream of negative and aggressive behaviour (Einarsen et al. 1999).

For some victims the situation may turn from bad to worse when they experience that those around them do not believe them or their version of events. This experience has been referred to as 'secondary bullying' and bears close resemblance to the experience of many rape victims (Leymann 1990). Nothing seems more important to the victims than clearing their name and seeing justice done. In such a situation, we should not be surprised if victims, out of a need for self-preservation, go out of their way to portray themselves as hard-working, honest employees, at times to an extent which may be at odds with reality (Hoel et al. 1999).

The third assumption ('the self as worthy') implies that as a decent human being one deserves to be treated well. This assumption is closely related to the idea that we have some control over outcomes of our actions and that what we do will normally turn out well. In cases of bullying, neither appears any longer to be true. The central role of work in most people's lives also means that a failure at work turns out to be very threatening to our sense of identity. The result of constantly experiencing that their value as a human being is challenged finally results in loss of self-respect undermining victims' own self-worth. For many victims, the questionmark over their own self-worth is accompanied by suicidal thoughts, threatening their very existence.

RESPONDING TO WORKPLACE BULLYING

We discuss now the response of management (employers) and other agencies. Some references are made to prevention and preventive strategies which may contribute to reducing the likelihood of bullying taking place. However, the focus of our attention is above all on the organizational response in those cases where there is already a victim of workplace bullying. While the needs of victims are the focus in this discussion, organizations also need to address the rights of alleged perpetrators. The fact that cases of workplace bullying have the potential to instigate organizational turmoil should also be acknowledged.

The text does not provide the reader with a DIY instruction kit with regard to organizational initiatives in cases of workplace bullying. Instead, it focuses on central issues that the organization and those agencies likely to deal with complaints and victims of workplace bullying would have to confront.

ROLE AND RESPONSIBILITY OF MANAGEMENT

The situation with respect to the law is complex (see Andrea Adams Trust 1998). Here we will simply remind the reader about the general duty of care on the part of employers laid down in the Health and Safety at Work Act 1974.

For the organization the main priority must be to create an environment where bullying has no place. According to Brodsky (1976) bullying cannot exist without being either directly or indirectly condoned by the organization. An environment free of bullying can only become a reality if the organization puts in place the necessary mechanisms to read early warning signs, provides support for individual targets where necessary and demonstrates commitment to eradicate particular behaviours from the organizational repertoire.

It is recognized that the presence of particular stressors may contribute to bullying (Hoel 1997). Conflicting demands and expectations, as well as particular leadership styles, are examples of 'stressors' which are seen to affect bullying. As far as leadership is concerned, the lack of leadership as well as abuse of power are seen as potentially bringing about bullying (Einarsen et al. 1994). This suggests that it should be a priority to include such factors in a risk assessment strategy.

Where a manager discovers that bullying is taking place within a peer group, a fine line needs to be drawn between abdicating responsibility by ignoring the problem altogether, or taking over the entire responsibility for resolving the problem. For example, in cases where bullying arises as a result of norm violation, it is vital to involve the actual work group in solving the problem.

Identifying the victim: looking for vital signs

Unfortunately, we still know too little about victim behaviour to present a reliable checklist of behaviours frequently identified with bullying. However, on the basis of our own experience and what we already know about victim behaviour, we will briefly attempt to point out some of the signs:

1. *Absenteeism.* We have discussed the relationship between bullying and health. Bullying will frequently manifest itself in shorter or longer spells of absenteeism, for which there may sometimes be no physiological explanation. However, it is as likely that some targets of bullying deliberately avoid taking sick leave and increase rather than decrease their effort. Organizational as well as individual factors play a role here, for example, presenteeism may be a common occurrence in organizations whose culture frowns upon sickness absence.

2. *Making unusual mistakes.* Problems of concentration are likely to result in unusual mistakes in victims' work. The individual's fear of making mistakes may even make them more likely. It should be noted that the ability to communicate, not least in writing, is reduced under psychological pressure arising from the bullying experience.

3. *Loss of commitment and morale.* A loss of self-confidence and impaired performance are often identified among victims of bullying. This frequently manifests itself in a reduction in victims' commitment to work and organization.

4. *Irritable and obsessive behaviour.* People who normally have acted calmly may suddenly become short-tempered and volatile with rapid swings in mood from anger to tearfulness. Other signs of extreme psychological strain caused by bullying are obsessive and erratic behaviour.

ROLE OF HUMAN RESOURCE PRACTITIONERS
Policies and procedures

All organizations need to have a policy for handling cases of bullying. This is a sensitive issue and the success of policy implementation hinges not least on the degree of ownership and commitment to the policies which exist within the organization. This implies that the development of an anti-bullying policy needs to involve the entire organization.

So that all members of the organization have a clear picture of what bullying actually refers to, a definition needs to be established. While a general definition may serve as a useful starting point, this needs to be complemented by behavioural examples, taking into account the local culture and local understanding of the issue. Such understanding may be explored by means of discussion groups, or possibly by a more scientific approach whereby local perceptions of the problem are teased out by means of a focus group approach (Liefooghe and Olafsson 1999). Lancashire County Council (1997) provides a local definition of bullying:

> Bullying can be defined as intimidation on a regular and persistent basis which undermines the competence, effectiveness, confidence or integrity of the target. It involves a misuse of power, position or knowledge to criticise, humiliate or destroy a subordinate or colleague. (Lancashire County Council 1997)

Complaints and investigation procedure

There is a strong case for using an informal complaints procedure where possible. Potential misunderstandings, sometimes culturally linked and possibly coming to light when a new member of staff enters the work group, may be addressed and resolved. Bringing in the formal procedures often tends to escalate the conflict. Local variations with regard to use of complaints procedure will play a role here. However, there will be times when the severity of the situation or the nature of the negative behaviour is such that a formal procedure needs to be activated straight away. Furthermore, in cases of repeated or persistent negative behaviour (repeated complaints), it may be wise to invoke the formal procedure immediately. It has also been argued with some weight that informal complaints often leave conflict situations and bullying unresolved and that the conflict may continue, possibly in other forms and other arenas.

The issue of *confidentiality* is a very contentious one and has given rise to considerable discussion; whether it is possible to offer a target unconditional confidentiality. Not only is this at odds with the opportunity to investigate the case but, more importantly, it may be in breach of the employer's legal obligations. According to UK law (Health and Safety at Work Act 1974), the employer is liable for what s/he knows about or ought to know about as well as anything that may be damaging to employee's health. According to Vicki Merchant, one of the leading practitioners in the field, confidentiality should not be offered unconditionally. Instead she suggests that the complaint should be treated in confidence 'insofar as it is consistent with' progressing the complaint (Merchant 1997). At the same time the complainant needs to be given maximum protection with regard to possible victimization or retaliation as a result of the complaint. Any negative experience in this respect would necessarily have a major impact on the willingness of future complainants to come forward.

Any organization needs to be aware of the potential damage a formal investigation may cause with respect to future relationships between individuals, as well as between groups of people. Immediate response, fast progression resulting in a timely conclusion and consistency of approach by people trained in and dedicated to complaints investigation should help to minimize any potential damage of a formal investigation.

Another issue of concern is what standard of proof is needed in cases of bullying. Here, most organizations would take the view that a judgement of whether the complaint should be upheld or not should be based on a 'balance of probability' and 'reasonable belief' for which the burden of proof is less strict than it would be in any criminal case (Merchant 1997).

To ensure fairness it is recommended that the investigation is independent. This means that the investigators should, as far is practically possible, come from another part or section of the organization to avoid the presence of any conflict of interest. In the case of bullying occurring in smaller organizations or in organizations in which independence appears to be difficult to maintain, an independent investigation may be a good alternative option. For the same reason, the investigation should be divorced from the ensuing decision-making process. In other words, the independent investigating team's report forms the basis on which the organization makes its decision. It is important to note that any perceived bias is likely to lead to an appeal.

Should records be kept? In cases where the complaint is not upheld, it appears fair to suggest that no records are kept. However, the fact that recurrence seems to be very common (Rayner 1999) means that it may be wise to keep the record on file for a certain period of time.

Disciplinary action

For a first offence, a warning should normally be given, depending upon the severity of the behaviour. There may also be times when behaviour which many people may consider to be acceptable may be perceived as unwanted and offensive by the target. In such cases, any disciplinary action would be judged inappropriate if the alleged perpetrator had not been made aware of the effect of the behaviour. In such cases, staff development may be seen as an appropriate reaction. However, it is often the defence of the alleged perpetrator that their lack of awareness of the implications of their behaviour should result in diminished responsibility on their part. If the behaviour continues, it should be considered a 'punishable' offence.

Where disciplinary action is taken, relocation and separation of alleged perpetrator and target is in many cases the most likely outcome. Unfortunately, very frequently organizations choose to move the recipient or victim. Not only would victims perceive this as further victimization on the part of the organization, but such a move also gives a negative signal suggesting that the perpetrator 'can get away with it'.

It is strongly recommended that the organisation provides the victim with practical and social support in regaining their work confidence, which will frequently have been undermined as a result of the bullying experience. Where necessary, similar support should also be made available for the perpetrator.

When the boss is the bully

In many cases, the complainant's supervisor or manager is the alleged perpetrator. The procedure needs to reflect this reality. There should therefore be alternative channels for complaints available, in principle, at all levels of the organization. While this may help the target in coming forward, it is not a guarantee against retaliation. In such cases, the alleged offender should be made aware of the fact that no form of retribution will be tolerated. Unfortunately, the literature is full of cases where the organization, not least the personnel function, has adopted the perpetrator's view and has actively colluded in the victimization, often resulting in exclusion of the victim from the organization (Leymann 1990).

Advisors and buddies

A system for appointing formal advisors in cases of bullying may provide targets with a useful first point of contact. More easily accessible and often perceived to be more 'independent' than a personnel practitioner, they may fulfil an important function. When the target decides to go ahead with a complaint, the advisor may provide practical assistance with case preparation. However, when it comes to the issue of confidentiality the appointed advisor may run into the same problem as discussed above, as employer's liability may extend to the advisors. For this reason, a system of 'buddies', where new employees are allocated a senior employee as their informal advisor, may avoid the problem of 'liability', while possibly providing the target with a useful first point of contact to assess their situation.

Mediation

It is recognized that mediation may play a useful role in preventing inter-personal conflicts from escalating into severe cases of bullying (Hoel *et al.* 1999; Whieldon 1997). Mediation is an instrument for conflict resolution in a non-adversarial way, often at an early stage. The process is based on openness, voluntary participation and confidentiality and is facilitated by an independent third party.

The introduction of the method into the workplace is based on the assumption that the parties in conflict are likely to have to continue their relationship in the future. A non-adversarial solution is therefore seen to be most productive. The strength of the method lies in its ability thoroughly to explore the situation based on interaction, whereby both sides of a conflict are brought into the open (Whieldon 1997).

Mediation should not be attempted in serious cases of workplace bullying. When the conflict has escalated beyond a certain point, the target is unlikely to settle for anything less than total victory. A search for compromise would, at this stage, be seen by the victim to militate against achieving justice and redress.

ROLE OF OCCUPATIONAL HEALTH AND THE MEDICAL PROFESSION
Spotting the problem

Many victims would agree that among the worst experiences of their ordeal is not being believed or taken seriously. The obsessive and compulsive behaviour frequently seen in victims of severe examples of bullying, combined with the absence of physical symptoms of illness notwithstanding complaints of psychosomatic symptoms, have unfortunately often misled the medical practitioner, without any prior knowledge of bullying and its consequences, to reach a wrong diagnosis of mental illness or personality disorder (Lennane 1996; Leymann 1996). However, the victims' behaviour must be understood as a response to their experience of bullying and as such represents a normal response to what can be described as an abnormal situation (Leymann and Gustafsson 1996).

The fact that until recently bullying has not been recognized in the psychiatric literature also plays an important part here (Leymann 1992). In line with this view, GPs and occupational health practitioners are advised not to jump to conclusions regarding the presence of pathological problems or psychiatric illness.

For the practitioners it is important to be aware of the fact that they may be dealing with two main groups of victims: those who perceive themselves to be bullied and those who recognize that something is wrong but have yet to label themselves as targets of bullying (Einarsen and Hellesøy 1998). Einarsen and Hellesøy argue that the subtleties of the experience may sometimes make it hard to identify the behaviour for what it is. However, while it is important to identify the core of the problem in order possibly to provide helpful advice, for example, as regards conflict management, there is no value in 'helping' victims to label themselves as victims of bullying. This is more likely to cause further suffering as such a label carries with it a connotation of failure and defeat. Moreover, when the label 'bullying' enters the equation, conflict resolution may become more difficult. Conflict is more likely to escalate as a result of accusations of bullying. The medical practitioner should also be aware of the fact that there will be situations where the victim's perception of bullying may be at odds with the objective situation. However, it is the perception or the subjective experience of being bullied which determines the outcomes as far as negative health effects are concerned, and as such this should be at the centre of attention (Einarsen and Hellesøy 1998). Furthermore, even at times when one may get the impression that the victim is trying to rewrite the past for reasons of self-preservation, it is important to take the story seriously (Hoel et al. 1999).

Working with victims

Is therapeutic treatment the answer? The answer to this question depends on a number of factors such as the state of the victim, the wishes of the victim, how far the victimization process has escalated and whether personality change has taken place. (For a further discussion on rehabilitation of victims of severe bullying see Leymann and Gustafsson 1996). However, it is recommended that under no circumstances should therapeutic treatment be seen as a solution to the problem itself (Einarsen and Hellesøy 1998). This would be further confirmation of not being believed. Any proposal of this kind from the practitioner is therefore likely to get a cool reception from the victim. Instead victims need help in exploring their own situation, trying to improve their understanding of the process in which they have been involved and establishing the current situation. Moreover, they need help in restoring their faith in themselves, which would include actively combatting feelings of worthlessness.

In most incidences, counselling will form part of an intervention strategy. The main aim of any intervention strategy would be to improve the victim's chances to cope with the situation (Einarsen and Hellesøy 1998). From what we know of the negative impact of bullying on partners and close family, it may be wise to consider including them in the counselling process. A typical question would be whether the victim should be encouraged to 'fight on' or whether 'exit' from the organization might be a better long-term solution. To answer such a question it is necessary to consider the victim's coping resources, socially and financially, as well as potential opportunities in the labour market. What is the victim's standing in the organization? Can s/he draw on support from close colleagues and family? What is the chance of finding a similar job? Does the financial situation allow for an extended legal process? Whatever the choice, there is seldom a win-win situation. For those who decide to stay and fight their case, they may retain their self-respect but simultaneously face increasing health problems and the risk of becoming increasingly isolated within the organization. While recovery appears to be more likely for those who leave, they often pay a price in terms of potential guilt and self-hatred for not having fought for justice. However, as Kile (1990) puts it, 'is the struggle worth 20 years of your life?'

A proactive role for the occupational health practitioner

It is possible to envisage a more proactive role for occupational health in prevention and early intervention in cases of bullying. By taking an active role in the risk assessment process the practitioner could provide the organization with vital feedback. Monitoring patterns of sickness absenteeism, stress levels, styles of management and other factors conducive to bullying could form part of such an approach. However, in order to fulfil such a role improved methods for risk assessment in connection with the psychosocial work environment need to be developed to take account of complex phenomena such as workplace bullying. It can also be argued that in order to fulfil their proactive and mediatory potential the profession may have to reconsider its relationship with employers, aiming for a more independent role within the organization.

CONCLUSION

There is an increasing awareness of the problem of workplace bullying and its potential effects on individuals and organizations. However, the complexity of this issue, combined with those related to power and control within the workplace, has often left targets of bullying without any organizational support, exposure to open hostility and attempts at exclusion. Only further organizational insight into the phenomenon, not least with respect to the behavioural effect of bullying, may change this situation. Seemingly inexplicable changes in behaviour have to be taken for what they are – natural responses to extreme situations. Instead, organizations should as a starting point take complaints about bullying seriously and offer victims support of a practical as well an emotional and social nature to present their case and to build up their coping resources. To provide such support, however, does not mean that the organization has to accept the victim's version of events as the only true account of the conflict. Only a thorough investigation would tell whether the alleged perpetrator has a case to answer.

REFERENCES

Adams, A. (1992) *Bullying at Work: How to Confront and Overcome It*. London: Virago.
Andrea Adams Trust (1998) *Workplace Bullying: The Legal Position*, Issue 1. Portsslade: Andrea Adams Trust.
Bassman, E. (1992) *Abuse in the Workplace*. Westport CT: Quorum Books.
Björkqvist, K., Österman, K. and Lagerspetz, K.M.J. (1994) 'Sex differences in covert aggression among adults.' *Aggressive Behaviour 20*, 27–33.
Brodsky, C.M. (1976) *The Harassed Worker*. Lexington MA: Heath.
CBI (1998) *Sickness Absence Report*. London: CBI.
Einarsen, S. (1996) 'Bullying and harassment at work: epidemiological and psychological aspects.' PhD thesis, Department of Psychological Science, University of Bergen.
Einarsen, S. (1999) 'The nature and causes of bullying at work.' *International Journal of Manpower 20*, 1 and 2, 16–27.
Einarsen, S. and Hellesøy, O.H. (1998) 'Når samhandling går på helsen løs: Helsemessige konsekvenser av mobbing i arbeidslivet.' *Medicinsk årbok 1998*. Copenhagen: Munksgaard.

Einarsen, S., Raknes, B.I., Mathiesen, S.B. and Hellesøy, O.H. (1994) *Mobbing og Harde Personkonflikter. Helsefarlig samspill på arbeidsplassen.* Oslo: Sigma Forlag.
Einarsen, S., Matthiesen, S.B. and Mikkelsen, E.G. (1999) *Tiden leger alle sår: Senvirkninger av mobbing I arbeidslivet.* Bergen: Institutt for Samfunnspsykologi, University of Bergen.
Field, T. (1996) *Bully in Sight: How to Predict, Resist, Challenge and Combat Workplace Bullying.* Vantage: Success Unlimited.
Hoel, H. (1997) 'Bullying at work: a Scandinavian perspective.' *Institution of Occupational Safety and Health Journal 1*, 51–59.
Hoel, H., Rayner, C. and Cooper, C.L. (1999) 'Workplace bullying.' In C.L. Cooper and I.T. Robertson (eds) *International Review of Industrial and Organizational Psychology 14*, 195–230. John Wiley and Sons Ltd.
Janoff-Bullmann, R. (1992) *Shattered Assumptions: Towards a New Psychology of Trauma.* New York: Free Press.
Kile, S. (1990) *Helsefarlige ledere og medarbeidare.* Oslo: Hjemments Bokforlag.
Lancashire County Council (1997) *Harassment and Bullying at Work: Investigation Good Practice Guide.* Lancaster: Lancashire County Council.
Lee, D. (1998a) 'The gender dynamics of workplace bullying.' Paper given at the International Harassment Network Annual Conference, Oxford, May 13–14.
Lee, D. (1998b) 'The social construction of workplace bullying.' Unpublished paper.
Lennane, J. (1996) 'Bullying in medico-legal examination.' In P. McCarthy, M. Sheehan and W. Wilkie (eds) *Bullying: From Backyard to Boardroom.* Alexandria, Australia: Millenium Books.
Leymann, H., (1990) 'Mobbing and psychological terror at workplaces.' *Violence and Victim 5*, 119–125.
Leymann, H. (1992) *Psyciatriska Problem Vuxenmobbning.* Delrapport 3. Arbetarskyddstyrelsen, Stockholm.
Leymann, H. (1996) 'The content and development of mobbing at work.' *European Journal of Work and Organizational Psychology 5*, 2, 165–184.
Leymann, H. and Gustafsson, A. (1996) 'Mobbing at work and the development of post-traumatic stress disorders.' *European Journal of Work and Organizational Psychology 5*, 251–275.
Liefooghe, A.P.D. and Olafsson, R. (1999) '"Scientists" and "amateurs": mapping the bullying domain.' *International Journal of Manpower 20*, 1 and 2, 39–49.
Merchant, V. (1997) 'Investigating formal and informal complaints: best practice.' Paper given at the International Harassment Network International Conference on Harassment and Bullying in the Uniformed Services, 29–30 October, Birmingham.
Randall, P. (1997) *Adult Bullying: Perpetrators and Victims.* London: Routeledge,
Rayner, C. (1997) 'The incidence of workplace bullying.' *Journal of Community and Applied Social Psychology 7*, 249–255.
Rayner, C. (1999) 'From research to implementation: finding leverage for prevention.' *International Journal of Manpower 20*, 1 and 2, 28–38.
Rayner, C. and Hoel, H. (1997) 'A summary of literature relating to workplace bullying.' *Journal of Community and Applied Social Psychology 7*, 181–191.
Scott, M.J. and Stradling, S.G. (1994) 'Post-traumatic stress disorder without the trauma.' *British Journal of Clinical Psychology 33*, 71–74.
Seigne, E., Coyne, I. and Randall, P. (1999) 'Personality traits of the victims of workplace bullying: an Irish sample.' Ninth European Congress of Work and Organizational Psychology, 12–15 May, Espoo, Finland.
Stewart, M.B. and Swaffield, J.K. (1997) 'Constraints on the desired hours of work of British men.' *Economic Journal 107*, 520–535.

UNISON (1997) *UNISON Members' Experience of Bullying at Work*. London: UNISON.

Whieldon, J. (1997) 'Mediation in employee relations disputes.' Paper given at the National Harassment Network Second Annual Conference on Workplace Bullying, 26–27 June, University of Central Lancashire.

FURTHER READING

Stone, M. (1998) *Representing Clients in Mediation: A New Professional Skill*. London: Butterworths.

ACKNOWLEDGEMENTS

We would like to thank Vicki Merchant, as well as Lyn Witeridge, Aileen Hay and Val Chapman of the Andrea Adams Trust, for their help in preparing this chapter.

CHAPTER 9

Mediation and the Victims of Violent Crime
A Practitioner's View

Barbara Tudor

THE CONTEXT OF VICTIM MEDIATION

In 1985 the Home Office invited bids from interested parties to pilot reparation to victims within the criminal justice system. Four pilot areas were chosen to explore the possibility: Cumbria where reparation with young people at the pre-court stage was explored; Coventry within the Magistrates court; Wolverhampton at the same stage but set within a voluntary agency; and Leeds at the Crown Court. After the first six months all the pilots reported that, whereas there were some difficulties, the main one being that courts cannot sentence victims to reparation, everyone had found that engagement with the mediative process to explore the possibilities for reparation was invaluable for both victims and offenders. Eventually mediation became an integral part of the West Midlands Probation Service's working across the whole system. Cases could be taken from the stage of pre-caution and conviction, through Youth, Magistrates, Crown Courts and custody to the release of prisoners and their re-integration into the community. In Wolverhampton, the West Midlands Probation Service is currently making use of long standing experience in the Youth Offending Team, which is one of four piloting the whole raft of the new youth legislation, including reparation orders and reparative interactions throughout the range of youth sentencing which will be implemented fully from April 2000. The promotion and debate surrounding 'restorative justice' have breathed new life into work that has been developing in Britain since 1985.

Restorative approaches embrace many different models of intervention between victim and offenders, and indeed any parties in dispute with one another which can cause escalating risk of violence. In the area in which I work, West Midlands Probation Service, we no longer use the term 'mediation' to describe this work. We feel that 'victim–offender' work more adequately reflects the many varied types of intervention which may be appropriate in different cases involving contact with both or all parties. Another reason for the change in terminology was the very substantial lack of understanding about the work undertaken in our units – the major problem being the assumption that mediators are always determined upon arranging for participants to meet one another. This is far from being the case. The people with whom mediators work are the determinants of the best course of action in their particular circumstances. But the advantages of being able to gain a holistic view of potentially violent situations gives professionals a more realistic perception of what has happened and is currently happening so that more effective decisions and actions emerge. However 'mediation' is often still used as an overarching term of convenience.

MEDIATION IN PRACTICE

There are well-known myths surrounding the understanding of mediative approaches to working in the criminal justice system, one of which is that this work is applicable only in minor offences. Indeed many of the early rather short-lived interventions would not accept referrals of assault cases. However, for those practitioners who have worked in the area for a long time there has been a clear awareness that violent offences are very appropriately dealt with through this approach, particularly in the interests of the victims of such offences. There are a number of reasons why work should be undertaken between victim and offender in cases of violence, not least because the aftermath for victims may have a serious, pervasive and ongoing effect on their confidence and feelings of security and safety. It is obvious that anyone who has suffered a violent offence will have an increased wariness and fear of repeat victimization. Clearly in some cases this fear is a realistic one and the information victims may have to give, and indeed may wish to give, about past occurrences or ongoing problems should be taken into account when decisions are made by police officers, court personnel, probation and social work agencies, etc. In many cases, however, information available from offenders may do much to allay the fears of victims and enable them to return to a more relaxed state of mind and to re-establish normal patterns of activity without fear of repercussions. One area of particular relevance here relates to offences committed by young people upon other youngsters and between teenage males. A great many of the victims of violence are middle to late teenage males whose needs are often neglected or ignored. The consequences of offences frequently ripple out and have significant and unpleasant effects upon other family members, friends and peers as some of the examples here will indicate.

In trying to come to terms with their own feelings about a violent offence perpetrated against a child, sibling or close relative, the adults involved may inadvertently ignore the needs and feelings of the young victims. It is notoriously difficult to work with youngsters and empower them to express and explore their feelings and come to terms with the aftermath of events which may cause severe trauma. When we are also aware that services specifically for young people are very limited, the level of often unnecessary suffering which can have serious long-term effects becomes more apparent.

Case study

A boy of 11 years was cycling with his brother, 13 years, in a particular area of undulating land adjoining a local park when they were approached by a gang of youngsters around the same ages on foot. The younger boy's bike was grabbed by one of the group and he was thrown off as the offender pulled the bike away, mounted it and rode off, with the others following. The two brothers had been intimidated by the group, surprised and overtaken by the speed of the actions. The younger boy was shocked by the event, very upset by the loss of his bicycle and fearful that the group were still around somewhere and could reappear and threaten himself and his brother again. The two made away as fast as they could to what seemed a safer vicinity, the nearby road. As luck would have it, as they reached the road a police car was passing and they flagged it down. The officers took the youngsters around the local area where they recognized the group who had approached them and indeed the particular youth responsible – although the bicycle was no longer in his possession but was being ridden by another youth. The officers arrested the youngster identified as the offender and took possession of the bike. As the offender was apprehended the victim heard him say 'I'm sorry' and saw that he was ashamed, embarrassed and upset. However, he made the reasonable assumption that he was 'sorry for himself'.

When the case was brought to the Youth Liaison Panel it was noted by a number of the agency representatives that the offender came from a well-known family, his brothers having been involved in offending for some time along with other known youngsters from the area, but that this was a 'first offence' for him. The age of the victim was noted and the fact that he was likely to have been frightened by the speed and violence of the offence, although he only suffered a few cuts and bruises as he was pushed from the bicycle while trying to ride through the mêlée of the offender's companions. It was decided that a mediator would see if there was any scope for effecting communication between the parties.

On visiting the offender he was found to be genuinely remorseful and ashamed of his behaviour. This was exacerbated by his mother's openly expressed sadness and disappointment that he was getting involved with the 'wrong company and going the same way as his brothers'. However, she was clearly supportive and insisted that he told the full story, which was that he had been 'set up' to take the bike by his 'mates' as a dare. At the time he simply thought he had to grab the bike from the 'posh boys' and then leave it for them to take back. Only when he had taken it did he realize that the others had selected the bike for some of its features and intended to keep it and dismantle it to use the parts themselves. He felt very bad when he saw the young victim shocked and crying and realized that he had been fooled into causing distress and actually initiating an action that had worse consequences than he had anticipated. When his mother was called to the police station he was critically aware of her feelings and shared her fear of the trouble he had got himself into. Although his mother felt anxious about the reactions of the parents of the victim to her son, she was pleased that he wished to apologize, should the victim's family agree to a meeting, and immediately offered to support him in any way she could.

When the mediator visited the victim's home he told the story and said that although the bike had been returned to him he had not been out on it again. Indeed neither he nor his brother had since visited the 'devil's dungeon', although they and their friends had played there a lot in the past. Their parents were pleased to know more of the offender's position and felt relieved to hear of his mother's strongly expressed views about her son's behaviour, immediately feeling some sympathy for her. Similarly they said that the choice of whether their son wished to meet with the offender or not was a matter entirely for him, but they would support him in whatever decision he made. When revisited, the victim decided that he would like to meet and say what he had not previously had the opportunity to say about how he felt at the time of the offence.

The young people expressed the wish to meet with only the mediator present and then invite their parents to join them later. This gave the best chance for them to relate to one another on their own terms with a minimum of embarrassment, although both were nervous. They found a common interest in computers and through that relaxed enough for the victim to receive an appropriate and clearly genuine apology. The very obvious differences in their lifestyles and abilities were bridged and the victim was reassured that he need have no fear of a chance meeting with the offender, which he had been secretly dreading. By the time they invited their parents to join them they had developed a comfortable rapport and both had the satisfaction of having sorted the matter out in a dignified, mature manner.

When the victim was visited later his mother described her amazement at what a difference the meeting had made. She also admitted rather sadly that not until afterwards had the family realized how badly the offence had affected the brothers, particularly the younger victim. They had not noticed how withdrawn and introverted the boys had become until they started racing around the home again in their hurry to get out to play after school. In all the turmoil of the aftermath, the changes that had taken place in everyone's behaviour had become accepted; the boys' state of fear had become a normal though restrictive part of life.

Here is an example of being able to offer an opportunity of communication between victim and offender at a very early point. The meeting between the two boys took place immediately after the offender had been cautioned for his behaviour, only a few weeks after commission of the offence. At that time they lived in virtually the only part of the country where the opportunity to arrange such a meeting could have been offered. Although this offence may seem trivial, the effects were not and could have had far-reaching consequences. In the early days of the scheme's operation another example will highlight the possible results of not addressing issues early on.

Case study

A young man of 22 was referred to the Reparation Scheme by the probation officer writing the social enquiry report for the next court hearing. In discussion regarding the offence the offender said that he had entered an IT training department in a community college. The room was full of people sitting at computers. He saw the victim sitting near the furthest corner. The offender was wearing a black balaclava and wielding a hammer. He cornered the victim, forcing him to jump onto the bench, backed him up against the wall and beat him, causing serious bruising, before the course tutor could fetch help in order to contain the situation. This description was alarming enough, but the offender went on to say that this offence was a response to the last offence against himself when he had been followed by a member of the victim's 'gang' and beaten with a bicycle chain. 'I'm really frightened now, ' he blurted out, 'one day someone is going to get killed.' Although initially apprehensive at the prospect of trying to communicate with the victim, he decided to allow the mediator to attempt to make contact with him and felt that he would trust her judgement about the next move.

The victim wished to meet the mediator at college where she also spoke with the tutor and some of her colleagues who had been somewhat traumatized themselves. The victim explained that there had been an ongoing argument between a group of young men since an incident on the school bus when they were about 13 years old. He was just as nervous about what would happen next and to whom as the offender. He was also afraid that his parents would find out about the situation as his father was terminally ill and his mother was struggling to cope.

After careful consideration about safety and having a positive future focus a meeting was arranged. During the discussion which took place the two men discovered that neither had been responsible for the incident on the bus and clearly it had been wound up out of all proportion by others who had long since lost touch. The whole situation came into perspective. It now seemed trivial and silly. They were rather shamefaced and almost incredulous about how matters had reached such serious proportions. They shook hands and agreed that they would each take responsibility for informing their respective peers about the meeting and its outcome and left together. When the case came to court the offender was put on a one-year suspended sentence supervision order. Two years later the offender called back at the mediator's office. He came to say thank you, laughed about the stupidity of it all and said that they had now all 'grown up', making a wry reference to the fact that if nothing had been done it was possible that some of them may have lost the opportunity of 'growing up at all'.

Indeed, the growing awareness of those of us who have worked in this area for some time led us to make active efforts to encourage colleagues in all criminal justice agencies to look out for the sorts of cases which gave us reason for concern that the situation could easily lead to an occurrence of violence, or further violence involving the same people or others, as the effects rippled out. The cases where we felt it was necessary to make contact with both or all parties were those where there was evidence of relationships, neighbour disputes and offences committed in areas where the victim and offender would be more than likely to come into contact with one another because they lived or worked in the same locality or community. Most people in such circumstances are keen to find a dignified means of extracting themselves. If they are not, it may be that we as responsible professionals need to be quite clear that revictimization will not be tolerated and that arrangements will be put in place to offer the victim protection and to alert appropriate agencies immediately in the event of further offences or potential offences.

Case study

An offender arrived in court with a suitcase. His solicitor told the court that although the offence had involved his wife suffering bruising and a broken arm during a violent argument, everything was now alright between them and indeed as soon as the case was over he would return to the marital home – hence the suitcase. The magistrates thought maybe they should just 'check out' the situation from the victim's point of view. They referred the matter to the scheme.

When the mediator visited the victim she said that it was not the first time she had been in the situation that occurred on the night of the offence, but she did intend that it would be the last. She was not surprised to hear that her partner was planning to return. This formed part of a pattern that had taken place several times before, but on this occasion he was currently on a bail condition not to return while the court hearing was pending. The victim had set her mind on a different future. She felt that the offender might listen more attentively to a third party. She had no desire to meet him but wanted the message conveyed that sadly it would be no good him trying to return. However, she was prepared, through the mediator, to make arrangements for him to see their children as she had a good supportive relationship with his mother, in whose care she felt confident to leave them.

A further meeting with the mediator put the matter into perspective for the offender. Although it was painful for him to accept the reality of the situation, indirect mediation offered a safe and dignified way for the adjustment which had to be made to take place between offender and victim. He was sentenced to a two-year probation order which gave him the support to find permanent accommodation and to prove himself trustworthy and reliable in making responsible arrangements regarding the divorce that his wife wanted and in keeping up contact with the children. He was also aware that if he were to cause his partner anxiety for her safety she would be able to raise the alarm immediately and concerted action by a number of agencies would most certainly follow. A case like this clearly requires contact with other parties; sometimes relatives or supporters but also possibly the police, housing colleagues and social workers, schools, health professionals, etc. A piece of short-term intensive work may save a number of long-term episodes of potentially more serious violence.

THE ROLE OF VICTIM MEDIATION

The Home Office circular (PC 61/95) sets out how victims of serious sexual and violent offences which attract custodial sentences of four years and over are to be offered information about what sentence has been passed, what the stages of its progression are likely to be and plans for release. They are invited to express their views regarding the latter and their wishes regarding conditions on licences can be forwarded on their behalf to decision makers and supervising officers who will take them into consideration and make appropriate arrangements. The first contact made by the probation service with the victim should be within two months of the sentence being passed. This is a important opportunity to make more informed risk assessment and management plans from the commencement of custody.

The introduction of this responsibility in the Home Office (1995) *National Standards for the Supervision of Offenders in the Community* was welcomed by the West Midlands Probation Service, where there has been a tradition of victim work since 1985. With knowledge of the likely trauma that these types of offences cause to victims, the policy was extended to embrace cases where offenders had been sentenced to one year in custody or more. Although the probation service faces ever-tightening resources and ever-increasing demands on its services, it is not alone in becoming increasingly aware of the need for this work to be done, and of the enhanced contribution it can make to reliable risk assessments. Other colleagues in prisons, courts, police forces, social services departments, housing authorities, education and health authorities are also realizing the value of working with both or all parties and sharing information to combine efforts more cogently and economically.

It would appear that a paradigm shift is taking place. The Crime and Disorder Act (Home Office 1998) demands that agencies have to make arrangements to work together. The mediative approach cannot work without interagency co-operation. It is an ideal vehicle to cement joint working which makes the notion of joint responsibility for community safety and protection of the public a reality. It also makes contact with victims an ordinary and expected part of the work, as well as making us much more readily accessible to victims and our work more understandable to them. Consultation re-empowers them and makes us more credible.

BENEFITS TO VICTIMS

There is a myth that victims want nothing to do with Probation Services. The reality is that victims are well aware that the Probation Service has access to offenders. If they wish their views to be acknowledged and information which they have to be known and acted upon, they need to be able to access the probation staff.

Close and active relationships with Witness Support Services are also invaluable. It is possible for these services to play a pivotal role in informing victims of the Probation Service's responsibilities. Further hurt and unnecessary upset being caused to victims and their families can be prevented if we are alerted to problems which may have been caused by or exacerbated during court hearings and the aftermath of sentencing.

The notion of repairing the damage, particularly the emotional damage which victims have suffered, and making offenders aware of the repercussions of their actions and the need for those who have suffered offences to know what really happened, why it happened and whether or not it will happen again, reflects a different, fairer, more common-sense and realistic emphasis on what needs to be done to restore their equilibrium. It places the victim in a more appropriate position and indicates a more humane intention within the law. Within the new youth legislation, the Reparation Order and the intention to arrange for reparation and restorative work to be part of the Action Plan Order and Supervision Orders, if implemented properly, offer a genuine opportunity for victims to have a more central place in the system. Whether they wish to be the recipients of restorative services is unequivocally a matter for themselves. If we add to this the work that Probation Services are currently developing in response to the National Standards, it cannot be long before more agencies become involved in the further development of restorative approaches across the board; i.e. from caution to the release and rehabilitation of offenders from custody. There would be scope for all victims to give information to decision makers, either directly (face to face) or indirectly through mediators, on a completely voluntary basis, and to accept direct or indirect reparative work should that be possible, acceptable and beneficial.

For victims there is the opportunity to give and receive information about the offence, the aftermath and the situation as it relates to them at the time of decisions being made regarding action to be taken, sentencing in the courts and release from custody, etc. There may also be the opportunity to communicate directly or indirectly with offenders, those who supervise offenders and decision makers if they should so wish. This is a much more empowering situation than they generally find themselves in and offers genuine opportunities for restoration, reparation and the ability to move on, to reintegrate into the community and to feel more in control of their lives. Therein lies the dignity of proper acknowledgement of their position, which in many ways the system has long disregarded, 'using' victims to 'hold' cases, provide evidence and sometimes to receive the rather desultory compensation payments.

CONCLUSION

The restorative approach is not a universal panacea. It will not always be the most appropriate or even possible course of action, but it provides us with tools to use either alone or in conjunction with other forms of intervention. In some cases there may be no scope to engage because of the victim's or the offender's attitude, vulnerability or refusal. The utmost attention must always be given to power issues and balance. Insensitivity to such issues could prove at the least demoralizing, at worst positively dangerous. Victim–offender workers can find themselves in a powerful position, being in possession of a great deal of information. This must be acknowledged in their practice and exercised responsibly. We have yet to fully value and explore the scope of indirect work between parties, which has never attained the status within restorative interventions that it deserves. The ability to provide the right service at the right time for all participants may prove impossible for technical reasons, legal difficulties, or because individuals may be resistant to engagement. They may feel they have too much to lose if they begin to empathize with the other/s involved. Timing and pace are crucial factors in terms of good practice. If we attempt to force individuals to engage we set ourselves up to fail by pushing them through a meaningless process which could prove damaging and thereby cause revictimization.

Workers involved in these processes must fully understand their role and feel comfortable working within management structures which enable the mode of operation required to work with both victims and offenders in a genuine, ethical way. We must make sure that victims realize the benefits of the process and are not 'used' for the benefit of others (e.g. the offender, an agency or the system). They must be treated respectfully and listened to carefully. The key to this work must be the provision of what is really meant by the concept of restoration, not a cosmetic corruption.

The very substantial contribution that these approaches can provide for risk assessment, management and rehabilitation of victims and offenders is yet to be realized. The examples here are drawn from the first fifteen years of experience within a probation service. So far these interventions have been on a small scale, but the indicators are clear. The focus of the Crime and Disorder Act 1998 is on a reparative dimension throughout the whole system from dealing effectively with youngsters through to anti-social behaviour and some of the most difficult offences to define and manage: domestic violence and racially motivated crime. Space and time do not allow for more than an outline of the contribution of the restorative and mediative approach to victim–offender issues, but there is undoubtedly a strong trend towards its wider application. This trend brings new challenges to a small group of long-term practitioners: to uphold the key principles necessary for good practice as outlined in the Mediation UK practice standards and the current development of Community Justice Standards which will cover all aspects of this work. The ability to do this work also raises major implications regarding resources, training and maintenance of service implications which must now be faced.

REFERENCES

Home Office (1998) *Crime and Disorder Act*. London: HMSO.
Home Office (1995) *National Standards for the Supervision of Offenders in the Community*. London: HMSO.
Probation Circular (PC) 61/95 (1995) *Probation Service Contact with Victims*. London: HMSO.

CHAPTER 10

Good Practice Around Domestic Violence in Solihull

Judy Woodfield

The Crime and Disorder Act 1998 requires that statutory agencies work together and develop a strategy that will reduce crime and disorder at a local level. Domestic violence is a crime and as such should be addressed by each local authority as part of their aims as required by the Act. Solihull Metropolitan Borough Council has identified domestic violence in its *Crime and Disorder Strategy* document (1999). Its aims are:

1. To reduce the number of victims of domestic violence by improving awareness and understanding to improve reporting and action in response to domestic violence.

2. Focusing on repeat victims of domestic violence.

3. Supporting victims of domestic violence.

4. Taking positive action against offenders.

5. Improving the sharing of information between agencies and departments.

6. Developing a domestic violence perpetrator intervention programme.

7. Developing person safety initiatives.

In 1995 an Inter-agency Circular was produced that outlined the roles and responsibilities of the key statutory and voluntary agencies. As a result some areas such as Solihull formed their domestic violence forums with a view to sharing information, developing a consistent approach towards domestic violence and improving services. It has been through the Solihull forum that the aims of the crime and disorder strategy were drawn up in relation to domestic violence.

To achieve consistency a clear definition was required in order to prevent any misunderstanding between agencies and as such to ensure that each victim is treated in the same manner and without minimization of that person's experiences. Some examples:

A domestic dispute is any quarrel including violence not only between family or household members but including non-household partners or ex-partners. Domestic violence occurs when a person or persons causes or attempts to cause, or threatens to cause emotional, physical or sexual harm to another family or household member. (West Midlands Police Policy and Procedure)

Any form of physical, sexual or emotional abuse which takes place within the context of a close relationship. In most cases, the relationship will be between partners (married, cohabiting or otherwise) or ex-partners. (Home Office Affairs Committee 1993)

Domestic violence includes any form of physical assault, sexual abuse, rape, threats and intimidation. It may also be accompanied by other kinds of intimidation such as degradation, mental and verbal abuse, humiliation and systematic criticism. (Home Office and Welsh Office Circular 1995)

It is this definition that was adopted by the Solihull Domestic Violence Forum.

Any incident of violence or aggression whether that be physical, sexual, emotional or psychological abuse of an individual by a family member, partner or ex-partner in an existing or previous domestic relationship regardless of gender, culture or sexual orientation. (Leicestershire Inter Agency Strategy 1997)

Violence from a person with whom he is associated, or threats of violence from such a person which are likely to be carried out. (Housing Act 1996)

Of the police forces that produced a policy document in relation to domestic violence, a majority were based on the Home Affairs Committee (1993) definition. Whatever the definition used, it is important not to be too narrow. The emotional and controlling ingredients that make up domestic violence can be identified in many various forms of relationships, from husband–wife, boyfriend–girlfriend, homosexual and lesbian relationships and those of adult children and their parents. Child-related incidents should be dealt with by the way of child protection investigations.

In 1990 a Home Office circular was issued (60/1990) and as a result domestic violence units developed within police forces across the country. The Police Research Group (1998) produced a paper that looked at the organizational structures of police forces in relation to domestic violence. Only 24 per cent of the forces specified that their definition applied irrespective of the gender of offender or victim. Some forces had chosen to identify only physical violence as domestic violence when across the country the range of offences forces claimed to be domestic violence could even include damage to property. Repeat victimization has been identified as a factor in domestic violence and yet only nine forces in England and Wales recognized it in their force policies.

Out of 42 police forces surveyed, 24 have a dedicated unit to deal with domestic violence; some within the units had other tasks as well such as child protection, victim support and missing persons. Huge differences were highlighted in the number of households a single domestic violence officer has to cover ranging from 2, 000 to 286, 000. In respect of job description there are also variations, although liaison with other agencies and supporting victims were identified as part of the role by over 90 per cent of the officers. Other duties included taking witness statements from victims and collecting other evidence.

Only 27 per cent of the officers interviewed the offenders. The report recommends an evaluation of this practice, as it is thought that there would be more prosecutions and fewer cases being withdrawn by victims after the initial complaint. It would also provide a more positive status to the role of domestic violence officer.

The West Midlands Police area is divided into operation command units (OCUs). The borough of Solihull is one OCU within the West Midlands Police. It is unique within the force as due to its geographical location it is not further divided, unlike the rest of this metropolitan force. It has the benefit of sharing the same boundaries as the local authority, housing, health authority and social services department. This assists with the communication between agencies and enables the domestic violence officer to be aware of the facilities available and the limitations of each agency, preventing the victim an unnecessary trail from agency to agency seeking the help and support required. Unfortunately, even within this small borough it very much depends on the individual whom a victim sees as to the response given and the level of help provided. There is clearly a need for interagency good practice guidelines to be drawn up in areas with a view to ensuring consistency.

When drawing up the strategy for tackling crime and disorder in Solihull, the role of the domestic violence officer was considered and, as a result, the strategy mirrors the facilities the West Midlands Police at Solihull provide. It assists me in the imparting of knowledge and in stating my expectations as it provides a legal base to support the often difficult tasks that I have in trying to implement new as well as tried and tested ideas with a view to tackling some of the problems. For example, with regard to repeat victimization, together with senior officers I am constantly trying to find ways of reducing the number of victims, without increasing their vulnerability and without making them feel that the contact with the police is not the route to take. The current method is positive action, i.e. arrest where possible and routine uniform checks at the address of victims, with a view to ensuring that both the offender and victim are clear domestic violence is crime and will be treated as such.

The provision of statistics is part of my role as domestic violence officer. The accuracy of these figures is imperative; 'fudging figures' can affect the resources which are allocated to the area and in some cases this could put more people in a position of greater vulnerability. Solihull Police and the Housing Department are the only agencies within the borough that keep accurate records of victims of domestic violence, so increasing the need for accuracy. Currently, the figures are collated monthly. They are categorized by means of referral, the total number of incidents and victims along with ethnicity and the percentage of repeat victims. Incident types are broken down along with arrests and percentage of arrests to compare with the number of incidents. The disposal of offenders is also recorded. The number of children present or who witness an incident are also recorded, although certainly in the Solihull borough this figure is not used to compare with other referrals, such as those to the child care teams within social services.

Support has to be a key word within the job description of a domestic violence officer. Providing accurate recording and information can be of great assistance to patrol officers who find themselves confronted by the tangle of problems peculiar only to domestic violence situations, i.e. non-molestation and occupation orders issued under the Family Law Act 1996, and restraining orders granted by the courts under the Harassment Act 1997. The domestic violence officer should be a readily accessible link between the victim and the patrol officer who in many cases works unsociable hours and cannot easily access information in order to update the victim, such as court dates, etc.

In respect of the victim support is vital. On receipt of a domestic violence referral the officer should attempt to make some contact with the victim, either by letter, telephone call or visit. The approach should be very much guided by the information they receive as to how contact with the victim is made. An ill-timed telephone call could have horrendous consequences should the offender answer it or be present when the call is taken. On more than one occasion I have found myself cross-examined by an abuser when s/he has answered the telephone. Only saying 'Sorry, I've got the wrong number' results in twenty questions. An important point to remember is where possible use a telephone where the caller's number is withheld from the receiver's telephone.

The role of the domestic violence officer requires the provision of accurate information. In many cases they are the victim's first contact with the support networks. It is imperative that the victim's options are placed clearly before her in order that she can make her own decisions. In doing so it can provide her with the feeling that she is in control of at least a part of her life. Even if we feel those decisions are wrong, apart from reiterating the pitfalls we should still support that victim. It is difficult to trust the stranger who is advocating action and providing information that is in complete contrast to what you already believe. The information held should not just be in relation to the outcome of criminal proceedings, but also regarding options such as civil court, housing and other agencies that may be able to provide the assistance which each individual victim requires, not only in relation to social matters such as housing and benefit agencies, but also those of a voluntarily or caring nature. All agencies should offer a consistent approach to domestic violence.

There are other agencies that can assist victims of domestic violence. Victim Support is an organization of volunteers who can offer practical help and advice to victims of crime. They will also provide a listening ear. Witness Support Service provides a service at the Crown Courts. They will arrange to show potential witnesses the make-up of the court and explain court procedures. I have found this particular service invaluable. Warwick Crown Court, where many of the boroughs' more serious domestic violence cases find themselves, are blessed with a service that prides itself in caring for the witness. The procedures are explained with patience and understanding. During the weeks preceding the trial, the witnesses can be regularly kept updated with the ever-changing court hearing dates. The court process is traumatic for the victim; lack of knowledge and understanding of the procedures, together with the long months of waiting are nerve-racking. As police officers we should always remember that this may be the only time a witness has been in a court of law. They are not professional witnesses and the only ideas they have come from the world of television and films.

Being a witness can be a very lonely experience and the support of the domestic violence officer is invaluable, particularly in the Magistrates Court and Civil Court where there is no witness support to date (although there are plans to increase the service to the Magistrates Courts in all areas). It is imperative that officers have a good liaison with the court and a sound knowledge of procedures in order to increase the confidence and reliability of the witness.

Accurate records of all incidents of domestic violence should be recorded, including County Court injunctions and non-molestation orders. Information relating to these should be accessible at all times in order that uniform officers are able to act on the injunctions immediately. If there is a power of arrest attached to the order then there is a requirement for the officer to arrest the offender. It does not have to be found committing and it is at the officer's discretion.

LEGISLATION

Domestic violence is not a legally defined offence in respect of criminal law, but there is legislation that covers much of what the victims experience, from physical and sexual abuse to the emotional aspect. This can be tackled by looking at offences in relation to property and including the recent Harassment Act 1997. This was devised with a view to protecting people from stalking, but is coming into its own in relation to domestic violence.

Offences Against the Person Act 1961

The act is divided into sections depending on the severity of a physical assault:

- Section 47: Actual Bodily Harm
- Section 20: Wounding or grievous bodily harm without intent
- Section 18: Wounding or grievous bodily harm with intent
- Section 16: Threats to Kill (it is essential that the person threatened believes that the threat would be carried out).

All these are arrestable offences with a term of imprisonment prescribed as possible punishment. They can be dealt with by either the Magistrates Court or the offender can choose to go to the Crown Court, or in serious cases the magistrates can elect that a case is best heard at the Crown Court.

Section 39: Common Assault, is found under the Criminal Justice Act 1968 and deals with minor assaults, i.e. reddening to the face following a slap. It is not defined as an arrestable offence. It can only be tried at a Magistrates Court. In this case a prosecution must be brought within six months of the occurrence. There is no time limit for the more serious offences.

Sexual Offences Act 1956

Section 1: Rape. This definition has been amended and now reads:

> A man commits rape if he has sexual intercourse with a person (vaginal or anal), who at the time of the intercourse does not consent to it and he knows that the person does not consent or is reckless as to whether that person consents.
>
> Contrary to the myth, *R v R (A Husband) 1991* a man can rape his wife.

Rape is an arrestable offence and carries a term of imprisonment that could include life. It is indictable which means that the case can only be heard at the Crown Court.

Criminal Damage Act 1971

This Act deals with damage to property, including arson. It covers threats to cause criminal damage, all of which are arrestable offences.

Criminal Law Act 1977

Section 6(1) and (5) of this Act refer to Using Violence to Secure Entry or Threats of Violence to Secure Entry. These offences can carry up to six months imprisonment.

Public Order Act 1986

Disorder: Section 4 of the Public Order Act 1986 deals with threatening words or behaviour. This includes abusive and insulting words or behaviour with the intention of causing the other person to be in fear that violence would be used against him/her.

Breach of the Peace

This dates back to ancient times. It is not a criminal offence, but it is very important to police officers and can be used effectively to deal with domestic situations, although in *McConnell v CC 1990* one judge stated, 'A purely domestic dispute will rarely amount to a Breach of the Peace.' By this he meant that an angry shouting match that was likely to remain as that would not constitute a breach of the peace, but a real fear that harm would be done to a person or to his property would be required.

Harassment Act 1997

The Harassment Act 1997 was introduced in an effort to tackle stalking and persistent anti-social behaviour. It is the nature of this persistence that makes it a perfect tool for dealing with some of the difficult domestic violence cases, many of which would fall into the category of emotional abuse. It can be used in both the Criminal and the Civil Court. In order to prove an offence of this nature two or more instances of harassment are required. The term harassment is not specifically defined, but if the conduct of the offender causes alarm, distress, violence or fear of violence it is possible that this may fit the bill. Speech is included in the term conduct.

The court has the power to sentence up to six months imprisonment and or a fine. It can also impose a *restraining order*. A breach of this order is viewed very seriously. The matter can be dealt with at either the Magistrates or the Crown Court. At Magistrates Court a term of six months imprisonment and/or a fine can be the sentence. If heard at the Crown Court a sentence of five years imprisonment can be imposed. In the case study of Frances this was the ideal solution, a restraining order with no expiry date, the order to remain in force until revoked or another order made.

Case study

Frances is 38 years old, a divorcee with two children, a girl aged 13 and a boy aged 14. Her first husband, although a hard worker, was a heavy drinker. Frances has worked hard all her life. She is currently employed as a school cleaner and has struggled to keep a three-bedroom council property in beautiful condition and well furnished for her and her two children.

Frances met Eddie who is also in his late thirties. He lived mostly with his mother who was a neighbour of Frances. Eddie was charming, considerate and wanted to be with her. Without actually agreeing or even being asked Eddie had moved into her home, although he never gave up his own tenancy. Suddenly, overnight almost, he became violent. He caused so much trouble that her parents no longer wished to visit her. Because Eddie felt that Frances's ex-husband received more attention than he did from the children he assaulted their father.

Frances cared for her home, so Eddie knew that destroying her property caused her distress. He smashed everything he could lay his hands on. She no longer took care of her home, became ashamed of it and in turn ashamed of herself, which increased her isolation. On one occasion she spent the whole night standing in the gully at the back of her home, nursing serious bruising to her face. It was a neighbour who called the police on seeing her standing there, almost in a trance. Frances made a statement of complaint against Eddie. He was arrested and charged with assault and bail conditions were imposed. She had got him out of her home and now she could keep him out.

Without family or friends to support her, Frances had little hope of feeling safe from Eddie. If she told the police he would kill her; he always said he would. Within two days of being arrested Eddie was back into the house with a threat, along with a promise that it wouldn't happen again; it was her own fault, she was a slovenly slattern; she deserved it and provided she had learnt her lesson all would be well. Frances approached the police wishing to withdraw her statement of complaint. She was seen by the domestic violence officer who took her retraction. It was in the form of a written statement detailing the incident, but claiming that the relationship was over and she was there of her own free will. She claimed that Eddie had not intimidated her in any way. The bruising on her face was still apparent and obviously very painful. For Frances this was the beginning. Details of her history of violence were being collated by the domestic violence officer and Frances became aware that someone had knowledge of her past, would not judge her, and would be prepared to assist her in the decisions she was making.

Case study (continued)

Three months later Frances returned to see the domestic violence officer. This time she brought her daughter who was verbally aggressive towards her mother. She was insisting her mother get Eddie out of their family home. The officer explained the options open to Frances, which included advice regarding criminal proceedings, civil court proceedings and the availability of safe accommodation should she require it. Frances left the station preparing to make her home more secure and to put Eddie's few belongings on the step outside. Information reports were prepared for the local police with a brief history of the violence and confirmation of necessary information in respect of tenancy agreements in relation to the property should Frances have need to call the police.

Weeks later Frances was back into the police station requesting hostel accommodation. This was found for her with the help of the domestic violence officer in conjunction with the local housing authority. Due to the lack of a purpose-built refuge, a homeless unit was used, but unfortunately Eddie knew its whereabouts and after one night he fetched her out. By this time her children were living between their grandparents and their father.

Frances was learning never to argue with Eddie, nor to answer him back. On one occasion the German shepherd dog urinated on the carpet, something it often did when Eddie was angry, but this time he saw it. He hit the dog over and over. Frances stated that she asked him to stop, but instead he kicked the dog and beat it more. After that she never interfered when he hit the dog.

Again Frances visited the police station to 'see what she could do'. Patiently the options were laid out for Frances, reminding her that locks could be changed again, emergency accommodation found, court orders could be applied for to support her in removing Eddie from her home. Then one morning, on her birthday, Frances telephoned the domestic violence officer requesting an urgent appointment. She came straight from her morning shift to the police station. She never went home. Another hostel was found, a reasonable distance away, and with regular visits from a support worker from a local domestic violence support group Frances began to change. She was going to obtain a non-molestation order. Under the Family Law Act 1996, because Frances was in a hostel she was no longer entitled to emergency legal aid. So an application to the legal aid board was made. Fed up with an empty house, Eddie moved out to his mother's. Six weeks later Frances was still waiting for her legal aid. Meanwhile, at her request the domestic violence officer was keeping her family informed that she was safe and well and of the current situation.

Case study (continued)

Under the housing legislation (Housing Act 1996) as a victim of domestic violence Frances was not only entitled to emergency accommodation, but also to a house move. Everything she was offered was greatly inferior to what she was already allocated and her children were refusing to move. This was a hard time for Frances. Eventually it became too much for her and she insisted on going home. She compromised with the professionals working with her and went to live with her parents and agreed to attend the local support group for domestic violence. I feel sure this was to please the people she felt had helped her rather than because she really wanted to.

Eddie began to threaten Frances's mother and followed Frances to her place of work. She was terrified, but she remained with her parents. Her legal aid arrived, requiring £90 per month towards legal costs. This was a week's wages for Frances. By this time Frances could see that Eddie did not have the same hold over her. When incidents of harassment followed, on the advice of the domestic violence officer, she and her mother recorded every incident and telephoned the police. Uniform police attended. However, for various reasons no positive action was taken, even following an incident where Eddie drove Frances and her mother off the road. All the information was recorded in statement form by the domestic violence officer and presented to a uniform inspector who arranged for officers to arrest Eddie and charge him with harassment. Eddie pleaded guilty on the advice of a solicitor and was issued with a restraining order not to threaten, intimidate or pester Frances or her mother. A breach of this order is an arrestable offence and can warrant a term of five years imprisonment. The order has no expiry date and will only be revoked if another order is issued.

For Frances it was a positive step. She returned to her own home with the assistance of a police attack alarm. She still has to put up with smirks and even the odd comment when she sees Eddie, but at the moment appears to be strong enough to cope. Her children are back with her. The house is completely redecorated and when her ex-husband sends cakes for the children he puts an extra cake in for her. The family are taking their first holiday for five years, a family wedding in Ireland. Two years prior to this Frances had no family.

LESSONS LEARNT

The important factor in this case was the patience shown to Frances when she ignored advice offered. It is very easy for workers to be confident in the service they provide. We should remember that at the time our suggestions seem drastic and impossible for the victim. She has learnt how to survive

Case study (continued)

from day to day and often the options provided by professionals just add to the uncertainty. The lack of co-ordination within the police service could well have met with tragic results for Frances and highlight the fact that the response to a plea for help can be met in very different ways. We are very dependent on the individual who responds to the request. The fact that each agency provided the same information to Frances was a key to building her confidence in a system that worked for her, but very nearly failed her.

Family Law Act 1996

The second piece of new legislation to benefit the victims of domestic violence is Part IV of the Family Law Act 1996 entitled 'Family Homes and Domestic Violence'. Matters brought to court under this Act are dealt with before the Civil Court. It enables the court to issue non-molestation orders and occupation orders.

Occupation order

An occupation order can be applied for with a view to enforcing the right of the victim to remain in the property by requiring the offender to leave. It can also require the offender to allow the applicant to enter the house and remain within it, or part of it, and it can regulate the occupation of the house by either or both parties. It can further impose who is responsible for the repairs and maintenance of the house and the payment of the rent or mortgage, and even bills. The contents of the house too can be subject of this order, granting possession of items of furniture to either party and ordering that reasonable care is taken of it. Before granting an order the court has to take into consideration the financial position of each and financial obligation to each other and any child. The court must also be sure that the applicant and any child are likely to suffer significant harm at the hands of the respondent, and that in turn must be greater than the significant harm that may befall the offender and any relevant child.

Non-molestation order

A non-molestation order shall be issued if the court feels that it is needed in order to protect the victim or child with a view to ensuring their health, safety and well-being. It will prohibit the victim from molesting the victim and any child that is involved in the relationship. The order can identify specific acts of molestation, such as harassment or threats of violence, or it can refer to simply 'molestation'. It can be made for a specified period or until another order is made.

It is possible that if an offender is prepared to make a promise to the court then instead of issuing either of the orders it can choose to accept an undertaking from the offender. Any breach of this promise will be dealt with by the court. No power of arrest can be attached to an undertaking.

There are times when the court will hear an application for a non-molestation and/or an occupation order without the respondent being present in the court or even being aware of the hearing. This is known as being heard 'ex-parte'. The reasons for this would be that the court decides it would be detrimental to the applicant or any relevant child if the case was not heard immediately, leaving them at risk of the hands of the offender. If this is the case the order(s) can still be made, but the matter must come back before the court as soon as possible in order that the respondent may make representations on their behalf.

Power of arrest

If the court believes that violence has been used or threatened then a power of arrest can be attached to either of the orders. Sec 47(6) Part IV Family Law Act 1996 provides the terms of the power of arrest.

A constable may arrest without warrant a person whom he has reasonable cause to believe is in breach of an order. This means that the offender does not have to be found committing the breach of the order, the evidence of a witness would be sufficient to bring the offender back to court. Having been arrested then the offender must be brought before the relevant court within 24 hours from the time of arrest, excluding Sunday, Christmas Day and Good Friday.

When applying for a non-molestation order and/or an occupation order it is usual to do it through a legal representative, but unless the applicant is entitled to legal aid it can be an expensive process, well out of the reach of many people. If this is the case it does not prohibit them from obtaining an order. They can make their own application without legal representation. At Solihull Family Court, situated in the Magistrates Court building, forms are available for completion along with a blank statement. There is also a guide to assist with the completion of the forms. On being received the magistrates clerk ensures that the forms are filled in correctly and then a decision is made as to whether the situation warrants an emergency hearing. The court clerk cannot help or advise on the content of the application. Should an emergency hearing be deemed necessary, then magistrates will hear the case ex-parte. When the orders are issued a new date will be set, normally within the week. It is the responsibility of the applicant to effect the service of the orders, along with any power of arrest issued, a copy of the applicant's statement, and other necessary forms. These forms have to be served personally, and if not carried out correctly then the orders cannot be enforced. This is often the most terrifying part of the ordeal – to confront the abuser. In some cases a request can be made at local police stations for uniform police officers to accompany the applicant when the forms are served with a view to preventing a breach of the peace.

In the event of it not being considered an emergency, then a date will be fixed and the court will contact the respondent serving the necessary papers. However the orders are obtained, it is important that the local police are made aware and provided with copies of the orders, relevant power of arrest and a statement of service of the order.

Case study

Parveen is a 39-year-old Asian female, married to a professional medical person with two children of that marriage. She had dedicated herself to her family, giving up her own university career to support her husband throughout the years of study and training. None of the family were British citizens; they were resident in the UK as dependants of husband/father. Having been in the country for nearly six years both children aged 8 and 13 years have been educated in the country and have English as their first language even within the family home.

The marriage was not an arranged one and his parents were against it. Parveen believed it was secure and she was happy with her role within the family home. Her husband took a new job in another part of the country. It was then that she became aware that he had been building up a lot of debt on credit cards. He used money inherited by her to pay off the debts. When she challenged him the violence began. The debts increased. He was keeping another woman, yet returned to the family home at weekends and attempted to force her to have sexual intercourse with him as he believed it was his right. He attempted this in the presence of his daughters. She called the police on several occasions, but each time was subjected to the attitude that her husband was a professional person and was therefore to be believed. This occurred even with a short history being available to the officers provided by the domestic violence officer.

The constant threat of deportation if she pursued the matter was yet another concern. Through the domestic violence officer she became aware of a resource centre which could to some degree assist her with advice regarding her immigration status. If she were to take her husband to criminal court for either harassment or physical assault, conviction could result in his deportation and in turn she and the children would be forced to return with him. If they were to divorce she would have to return to the country of her birth, no longer being his wife. The introduction of the Family Law Act 1996 meant that she was able to apply for a non-molestation order to protect her physically and an occupation order to keep him away from the property. Because of the violence a power of arrest was attached. This order was obtained on her own application to the Family Court. As her husband lived away it was not felt to be an urgent matter and papers were sent to him. By using this course of action only if he breached these orders would there be recourse to consider him for deportation.

Case study (continued)

Solicitors became involved and due to other hearings of a family matter the case was transferred to the Civil Court. She was treated in a very mixed way at one point. Her solicitor had misinterpreted her instructions and because they were not in court the orders were allowed to lapse. Immediately Parveen was taken straight to the County Court where she was seen by a judge in his chambers who provided another temporary order to return to the court after the weekend. During that hearing she was humiliated by yet another judge and believed that she was subjected to blatant racism. At that hearing her husband made an undertaking to the Civil Court not to pester or harass his wife and was restricted as to when and how he made contact with his daughters. With that undertaking there was no power of arrest. For the next two years he pushed against the order to its limit, knowing that her immigration status would prevent Parveen from returning to court. In 1999 she obtained leave to stay in the UK indefinitely. She is now able to obtain her divorce.

LESSONS LEARNT

From a police perspective it was extremely difficult to support Parveen as clearly the decisions she had to make were not in line with a police positive action idea, but clearly they were the only decisions she could take. When working with victims of domestic violence professionals should look at each case individually and accept that sometimes what is best for the victim is not always in line with policy. Poor communication between victims and those from whom they seek help can actually increase the sense of confusion and uncertainty of the victims as well as possibly worsening the situation.

CONCLUSION

The Crime and Disorder Act 1998 has placed a clear obligation upon statutory agencies to reduce crime and disorder, including what is increasingly recognized as a serious crime: domestic violence. As the case studies have illustrated 'the system' can work for the victim, but this can take time, a highly individualized response and agency commitment to best practice in a complex and challenging area of work.

REFERENCES

Breach of the Peace Common Law. London: HMSO.

Crime and Disorder Act 1998. London: HMSO.

Criminal Damage Act 1971. London: HMSO.

Criminal Justice Act 1968. London: HMSO.

Criminal Law Act 1977. London: HMSO.

Family Law Act 1996. London HMSO

Harassment Act 1997. London: HMSO.

Home Office (1990) *Circular 60.* London: HMSO.

Home Office Affairs Committee (1993)

Home Office and Welsh Office Circular (1995) Home Office Public Relations
    Bureau.

Housing Act 1996. London: HMSO.

Leicestershire Interagency Strategy (1997)

Offences Against the Person Act 1961. London: HMSO.

Police Research Group (1998) Home Office Research, Development and Statistics
    Directorate

Public Order Act 1986. London: HMSO.

Sexual Offences Act 1956. London: HMSO.

Solihull Borough (1999) *Crime and Disorder Strategy Document.* Solihull: Solihull
    Borough.

West Midlands Police Policy and Procedure

CHAPTER 11

Working with Domestic Violence in Knowsley

Brenda Fearns

HISTORICAL BACKGROUND

In the early 1970s activists discovered that battered women were treated poorly within the criminal justice system. Particularly the police service did not take positive action against men who assaulted their wives or co-habitees and rarely offered assistance to women. Police officers, like society itself, were unable or unwilling to see situations of domestic abuse for what they were – misuse of power and crimes. Instead, they were an interruption of policing more important areas of work that resulted in cases being played down and officers failing to take any action. One of the reasons for this was that there was an understanding among police officers that the victim of abuse and the offender would get back together again soon after the incident. For this reason little positive action was taken.

Senior police officers gave evidence to the Parliamentary Select Committee on Violence in the Family (1975). They denied complaints and deflected responsibility for dealing with domestic abuse. Their resistance was resolute: there was either no problem, the problem belonged to someone else or the problem was trivial.

By the mid-1980s change began to evolve through police policy and training programmes. Didactic training programmes that provided scripts for non-intervention were outlawed. In its place police officers were told to make their own informed decisions about how they should manage cases based upon their own experiences of police work. The Home Office *Circular 60* (1990) gave advice and guidance to forces on the management of domestic violence cases stating the following:

- Domestic violence is as serious as any other form of assault.
- Secure the protection of the victim and any children from further abuse.
- Consider taking action against the offender.

- Adopt positive interventionist behaviours, i.e. arrest, removal of women and children to refuges, assistance with medical treatment.
- Reinforce the need to work with other agencies.
- Police to be aware of their powers under criminal law and civil law.
- Importance of continuing support and advice for the victim.
- Support during pre-trial periods for the victim.
- Accurate record keeping.
- Police forces to have clear policies on domestic violence.

KNOWSLEY FAMILY SUPPORT UNIT

On 15 July 1991 the first domestic violence unit became operational on Merseyside and led in 1995 to the establishment of police family support units that provided a police response to incidents of domestic violence and child abuse. These units dealt with nearly 18,000 cases of domestic abuse last year.

In Knowsley, an area in Merseyside, police officers respond to 2,000 domestic abuse calls per year. The majority of those calls involve violence against women and children and the minority involve abusive situations that on the face of it seem less innocuous. Knowsley has two domestic violence liaison officers whose office is situated within the Family Support Unit at Prescot Police Station. The principles as laid out the in the Home Office *Circular 60* (1990) have been adopted. Unlike some domestic violence units on Merseyside, Knowsley Domestic Violence Units also arrest offenders if the victim of abuse makes it known to them that they wish to support a prosecution. We have adopted this method of working to provide continuity of service to those women with whom we build up a close working relationship. We do not have the resources to take over cases on behalf of all police officers in Knowsley.

WHAT IS MEANT BY THE TERM DOMESTIC VIOLENCE

Domestic violence includes the physical, sexual, emotional or economic abuse of one person, usually a woman, by another person, usually a man. The abuse takes place in the context of a close personal relationship that may or may not be still ongoing. Police strategies on Merseyside regard domestic violence as being something that happens in families regardless of the relationships between family members, unlike other policies across the country which focus on partner or ex-partner relationships. Most recently practitioners have begun to recognize the consequences for children involved in a domestic abuse situation

Physical Abuse

Physical abuse includes hitting, slapping, punching, pushing, kicking, strangling, headbutting, burning. It can also include violence towards pets and property. Offenders can inflict the assault themselves or they can do so by throwing items such as hot food and drink.

Examples of physical abuse

- Man who broke his wife's jaw told police officers that he only slapped her. He received nine months imprisonment for this offence and the local newspaper reported that 'Man given 9 months for slapping wife'.
- Man who battered his pregnant partner with a mop, hitting her over her stomach.
- Man threw a plate at his partner which hit a child on the leg causing an injury.
- Man threw a telephone at his partner. It hit an infant child causing an injury that required hospital treatment.
- Child was shaken by a father following a row. The shaking caused the child to have a disability.
- Child sustained 66 injuries in a five-week association between a mother and new partner
- Child drowned in a bath while her mother was being beaten by her partner.

Sexual Abuse

Sexual abuse means any sexual act carried out without informed consent and includes touching, fondling, forcing, sexual intercourse and offensive or suggestive sexual language. This is the most under-reported area of abuse. The cases that do come to the fore are generally concerned with sexual abuse which happened many years previously. The humiliation of victims reporting sexual abuse must be difficult to cope with and many choose to remain silent about their experiences.

Examples of sexual abuse

- Woman was raped with a bottle.
- Woman said that she had been forced to perform sexual acts with animals while her partner recorded the events on video. The video was later used by her partner to threaten her to remain silent.
- Woman who had separated from her boyfriend was invited back to his home on the pretext of removing property and then subjected to a harrowing torturous rape that left the victim fighting for her life and suffering from mental illness.

Emotional Abuse

Emotional abuse includes behaviour that results in psychological harm. It could include humiliation, blaming, criticizing, controlling, pressurizing, coercion, fear, threats (of violence, death).

Examples of emotional abuse

- Two women were stalked by their partners prior to forming a relationship with them. The women found it quite appealing to begin a relationship with a man who was so besotted with them and they did not see their futures as prisoners or possessions of that man.
- Women recall their partners constantly mistrusting them: dialling 1471 on the telephone; being made to account for their calls from the itemized telephone bills; having their vehicle milometers checked; having specific journey times monitored and checked.
- Women being called stupid, bad mothers, incompetent, ugly and being made to feel that they are not worthy.
- The goalposts constantly move: the children are too noisy; they are too quiet; the children are in bed, so the woman is lazy.
- One woman disclosed that she was manipulated into giving up her newborn child. The child was exchanged by her new partner in payment for a debt that he owed.
- Child removed the gun from his father and placed it under his own bed because the father had threatened to commit suicide if the woman left him

INDIVIDUAL RESPONSES TO VIOLENCE AND ABUSE

Every woman and child's experience of domestic and child abuse is unique. Police domestic violence liaison officers know that each person will be affected differently by their experience and it is helpful to gain an understanding of the stressful dimension of their experiences. The types of influences that will affect victims are:

- The degree to which it was or is unpleasant.
- The lack of control they have about their situation.
- The unpredictability of their situation.
- The amount of coping strategies available.
- The likelihood of success/failure in their attempts to cope.

These dimensions of victim stress are also affected by:

- Their distorted self-image (unworthy, unclean, blaming themselves, incompetent, hysterical and frigid) that has been wittingly or unwittingly implanted in their minds by the abuser.
- Their own personality and whether they see themselves as being resourceful and able to cope.
- Locus of control, including whether they believe that they can alter their situation or whether they believe that there is nothing they can do to improve things.

- 'Learned helplessness': they have learnt that they might as well not bother to fight against their situation.

The culmination of the abusive experience and the dimensions of their particular stress lead victims to feel isolated, confused, apprehensive, depressed, anxious and completely stressed (Shepherd 1990).

POLICE RESPONSES TO DOMESTIC VIOLENCE

It follows therefore that by the time police officers make contact with women and children in domestic abuse situations they are likely to have little resilience to fight back and help themselves. Some police officers may see women in crisis situations as behaving very badly while the offender appears poised and this may adversely affect police officers' distorted view of the survivors' world. All police officers, but particularly operational and street officers, need to remember that safety of the woman post-incident is crucial to the future wellbeing of herself and her children.

Research conducted on Merseyside (Horn 1998) found:

- There are pockets of police officers who have the right attitude to the subject of domestic abuse.
- Of all contact calls to the police 55 per cent were received via the emergency '999' system.
- The emergency system had to be used twice by 19 per cent of victims to get a police response.

In Knowsley between April 1998 and March 1999 the repeat domestic incident rate is 48 per cent. It follows that nearly half the victims with whom police officers have contact have had to telephone for assistance on a least one previous occasion since 1995.

POLICE RESPONSE AT THE SCENE OF AN INCIDENT

Spontaneous incidents of domestic violence are reported to Merseyside Police and a computer log of the incident is created, the call is prioritized and an officer is sent to the incident. The officer is informed prior to arrival about the type and nature of previous calls for assistance to the venue and is given details of how those calls were concluded by previous officers in attendance. Intelligence information such as this helps to aid the officers' decision making on how to handle the new situation. At the scene, officers will usually establish who the parties are, separate them and establish what has happened. Armed with this information, officers will conduct an assessment of the situation and decide upon the most positive course of action to protect the victim and any children in the family. Officers are told that they must never attempt to reconcile the parties involved in the domestic incident. Actions by police officers at the scene of such incidents include: discussion about hospital attendance; taking the victim to hospital; helping victim to move to another place; giving advice; waiting with the victim for the perpetrator to collect property and leave; returning children; arresting for assaults, breach of the peace; giving out information regarding the existence of the domestic violence unit; giving advice to call again or to call at the police station; taking statements; giving advice on civil and criminal proceedings. In all Horn (1998) discovered 32 main actions taken by police officers at the scene of an incident and myriad other actions that have not been measured. The main problems we have identified about lack of positive response are:

- hospital attendance not followed up by officers
- victims told to seek medical attention and then visit the police station
- lack of arrests to give victim the time and space to think
- too many arrests for breach of the peace resulting in refused charge
- not enough offenders placed before the court for 'binding over' (to be of good behaviour)
- lack of ongoing assessment and proactive management by custody officer
- bail conditions given by the custody officer to allow access to children
- victims not being kept informed about the conduct of cases.

When crises occur victims and offenders come into contact with the police and uniformed police officers see more victims than domestic violence liaison officers. It is therefore important that uniform police officers become the eyes and ears of the police service and do their best proactively to manage the risks that each situation poses to the victim and children. The noting, recording and referral of accurate and complete information to the police family support unit is essential so that contact can be made with victims and the process of problem solving with the victim can commence.

RESPONSE OF THE DOMESTIC VIOLENCE LIAISON OFFICER

In addition to all the computerized logs of incidents that are accessed by liaison officers each day, they also receive referrals from other police officers, other agencies and victims themselves. Each referral is assessed to attempt to identify those incidents that are purely domestic violence and those that involve a child. Incidents which do not involve children are dealt with by the liaison officer who tries to make contact with each of the victims. Where victims are not available on the telephone, letters are sent to their homes. Response from letters sent out is not good and we make assumptions that not all victims receive the letters which are sent. Sometimes a victim will make contact many weeks or months after the event. At the present time the unit is constrained by lack of resources and we would very much like to have the ability to send our liaison officers out into the community to make direct contact with victims rather than sending letters to them. Attempts at gaining more resources have failed so we are having to assess victims according to the nature of the presenting problem and prioritize which families we make contact with. We use the nature of the incident to help us decide which cases to filter in or out. Serious assault cases would always receive our attention along with less serious repeat victimization cases.

During contact the liaison officers explain who they are, what they do and most importantly that they will not attempt to take control of the case by imposing their ideas and solutions on the victim. The victim is informed that they will work with them to prevent them from being hurt in the future. Minor achievements are celebrated, for example, the victim may learn to leave her handbag in a strategic position to allow her to escape during an abusive episode or she may be able to put busfare in her pocket to facilitate her escape to safety. The bulk of our work involves referrals to other agencies and offering a listening ear. Last year in Knowsley 31 per cent of all domestic abuse victims received a service by a referral being made to another agency. Examples of referrals include, women's refuge, housing departments, Victim Support, solicitors, adult social services, community mental health teams, Women's Aid, domestic violence outreach worker, male offender counselling services and Merseyside Probation Service Offender Programme. The objective with this type of service is to establish appropriate and timely positive contacts to increase the options for survivors of abuse.

Practical advice regarding civil and criminal proceedings is discussed along with the triggers of violence and the idea that the victim has to get out of the situation. Criminal proceedings are explored by the provision of information about what would and could happen if the victim decides that she is able and willing to support a police prosecution. Practical assistance in the form of alarms is provided whether or not a prosecution is being pursued. Contact is also made by the police officer to establish what the situation is post event and to answer any questions that may have occurred to the victim since the last discussion. Notes are made by the police officer of what the victim says and these are kept for any future criminal or civil case.

When it is identified that there has been a child involved in a domestic abuse incident the liaison officer will make a child protection referral to the child protection team within the family support unit. The woman is always told that this referral will happen and an explanation is given regarding our role and responsibilities to the children. The victim is asked if she still wishes to work with the police officer who made the referral. If she does not want to work with that officer then another is found. We hope that by doing this we can engender a trusting relationship within the confines of our role. Child protection in-formation is always passed on to social services department and, depending upon the nature of the incident, it will be classified as information only for discussion or as a referral under Section 47 of the Children Act 1989. In some cases information is also shared with the child's health visitor who may then take on a monitoring role. The objective here is to provide the mother with a support mechanism.

Case study

Alan was a respected businessman living in a small community, where he had many influential contacts. He was married to Barbara for 23 years during which time they had three children. Barbara experienced domestic violence in the form of constant monitoring. The marriage ended and Alan began a relationship with Rachel who had children. One child, Catherine, complained about being sexually abused by Alan one evening while she was in bed. The matter was investigated by authorities and closed on the basis that there was no evidence. This relationship ended 18 months later. Alan started following Debbie, showering her with gifts and making her feel important. The couple began living together and after a while Elizabeth, Debbie's daughter, complained to her mother that he had touched her breasts. Debbie was concerned and alarmed by this and the fact that she had suspected that the relationship between him and his daughter, Fiona, was abnormal as he had seemed over-affectionate towards her. She ended the relationship and moved out of his home.

Alan refused to return her property for several months. Then he changed his mind. When she entered the house she was tortured and raped in a manner that caused her to suffer a high level of degradation. She attempted suicide, was admitted to a psychiatric ward and had no voice for several weeks. Medics and family did not know what was wrong with her. Eventually after many months she disclosed to a psychiatrist, without going into detail, that she had been raped. She spent a number of years receiving treatment for her physical and psychological injuries and during this time she made a number of other attempts at taking her own life

Simultaneous to this happening, details of another abusive event were emerging in his ex-wife's home. Fiona disclosed her abuse and decided to report the facts to the police so that her father could be brought to justice. An investigation commenced.

Police officers first made contact with Debbie at her home. She told the officers that Alan had done unspeakable things to her. After a couple of meetings Debbie was willing to give an account of what had happened to her but she was unable to say what she had experienced. Eventually Debbie agreed to speak into a tape machine in a room on her own. Arrangements were made for this to happen at her home and her community mental health nurse was available to assist Debbie once she had recorded her account. This attempt failed as she said that she was not feeling well. Forty-eight hours later Debbie contacted the police. Arrangements were made with her and the tape machine was delivered to her home.

Case study (continued)

Debbie was asked to say who she was, where she was speaking and the time and date of the recording. Debbie recorded her account on the tape; she included great detail of what had happened including aromas that she had smelled. Her verbal account was transcribed into a written format. She gave a written statement formally introducing the recording she had made (this is necessary for court purposes) and clarified some details of her recording.

Alan was arrested and interviewed about the many criminal offences he had committed against Debbie and the other children with whom he had come into contact. Implements were recovered which had been used in the rape. Debbie was provided with an alarm and a telephone machine that had the capability of recording any calls made to her. Alan denied any indecency with Debbie. He said that the implements had been used on Debbie at her instigation. Forensic and medical evidence showed that this was very unlikely due to the scale of the injuries and the location of the forensic evidence. Alan was charged with a number of criminal offences and remanded on bail with conditions to live in another police area hundreds of miles away from Debbie and his other victims. He pleaded not guilty at court.

In the months leading up to his trial arrangements were made for Debbie to receive professional help and counselling. The Victim Support service visited and spent time with her. Arrangements were made for respite care in a local victim support establishment. This enabled her to spend time in a confidential and secure setting with access to 24–hour counselling should she need it. At this time it was found that the drugs she was taking were being duplicated. Arrangements were made for her to be admitted to another unit that specialized in the treatment of people dependent upon prescription drugs.

Nearer to the trial arrangements were made for Debbie to visit the court where she was going to give evidence. A victim support worker and a police officer who was not associated with the case but whom Debbie had met on previous occasions supported her in the court. Debbie gave her evidence clearly.

Alan received nine years imprisonment for the rape of Debbie.

CONCLUSION

This chapter has reviewed both the changing attitudes and the changes in the roles and responsibilities of police officers in working with victims of domestic violence. Horn's research (1998) and practical work in Knowsley have demonstrated that 'good practice' can be delivered and, more importantly, the areas in which practice can continue to improve. With commitment, learning from practice, and the will to implement practical responses in this area, victim protection can be achieved.

REFERENCES

Home Office (1990) *Domestic Violence Circular 60*. London: HMSO.

Horn, R. (1998) *An Evaluation of Domestic Violence Units in Merseyside* (Unpublished).

Merseyside Police Force (1999) *Policy on Domestic Violence*. Liverpool: Merseyside Police.

Parliament Select Committee on Violence in the Family (1975) *Report from the Select Committee on Violence in Marriage, Vol II, Report, Minutes of Evidence and Appendices*. London: HMSO.

Shepherd, E. (1990) *Investigative Interviewing: A Trainer's Workbook*. London: Investigative Science Associates.

CHAPTER 12

Violence in prisons

John O'Connor

Much has been written about violence in prisons. Remarkably little about it has been written by prisoners themselves. There are myriad reasons for this apparent reticence. For many the experience of imprisonment is sufficiently unpleasant not to want to dwell on it any longer than necessary. Get your head down, do your 'bird' (time) and upon release forget about it. There are more important and far more pleasurable things to think about in the meantime. For a sizeable majority of prisoners their lack of literacy skills[1] ensure that personal tales of violence remain untold.

Another reason for this pervasive silence is the threat of physical retribution. A prisoner deemed to have 'grassed' (informed) on fellow inmates often risks serious personal injury. In most prisons this threat alone ensures an extremely effective silence. But while enforcement of a no 'grassing' culture can at times be as brutal as the Mafia's vow of *omerta* it does not necessarily guarantee total success. In fact, prison staff depend greatly on 'grasses' for otherwise unobtainable information. They want to know about escape attempts and, as importantly, the wheelers and dealers of illicit activities, principally drugs – now regarded as the scourge of present-day prison life and the main cause of violence among inmates.

Undoubtedly prisons are places of violence. Inmates are never far from the possibility of attack, disfigurement and even death, which is not surprising when the nature of prisoners' offences is analysed. In 1997 the number of adult males sentenced to imprisonment for crimes of violence accounted for 23 per cent of the total prison population. In fact such crimes accounted for the largest single segment of the seven categories of recorded offences for which adult males were imprisoned. In descending order the separate categories of burglary and drugs came in at an equal 16 per cent, followed by robbery 12 per cent, theft and fraud and (jointly) 'other' offences 11 per cent, and sexual offences 10 per cent.

---

1   Sixty-five per cent of prisoners are so bad at reading, writing and counting that they were considered ineligible for 96 per cent of jobs, according to Martin Narey, Director General of the Prison Service (quoted in *Daily Telegraph*, 1 June 1999).

Interestingly, once sentenced there is a marked drop in prisoners' propensity to resort to violence. This can be deduced from the types of offences against prison discipline recorded in 1997. Of the six main categories, disrespect accounted for 38 per cent, followed by the inexact 'other offences' 33 per cent, with violence coming in at 13 per cent of the 108,000 proven offences (Home Office 1998).

Incidences of violence and wilful damage were the most common in remand centres and closed and juvenile institutions. Included in the commentary accompanying these Home Office 1997 figures is the statement:

> Male black prisoners had an adjudication rate about 25 per cent higher than male white prisoners. The difference is particularly marked in violent offences, where there were more than twice as many proven offences per head for blacks, whereas black males had fewer adjudications for wilful damage or escape. South Asian, Chinese and other male prisoners had fewer adjudications than either group, especially for disobedience or disrespect. (Home Office 1998, p.139)

The willingness of Home Office statisticians to identify ethnic minorities in the context of their criminality may well be a thing of the past. This is because the publication of the Macpherson report (1999) into the death of Stephen Lawrence has resulted in a long overdue sensitivity when using race as a peg on which to hang a plethora of statistical information to disguise latent racism.

In facing up to the threat of actual and threatened physical violence prison management adopts a number of strategies. The most obvious is initial control and restraint training for uniformed staff who then undergo regular refresher courses. Another strategy is aimed at prisoners personally. Courses are targeted at inmates with offence-related convictions and/or histories of personal violence inside and outside of prison. It was the aftermath of one such course that acted as the catalyst for my willingness to write about violence in prisons.

An inmate had been awarded a certificate for successfully completing an anger management course. A few hours later he attacked a fellow inmate, breaking his jaw in several places and causing some fairly startling colouration to his nose and both eyes. Needless to say, the perpetrator was someone with a history of violence stretching way back to his teens. Breaking his cycle of aggression will be no easy task.

There is no escaping the miasma of violence that swirls through the long galleries of multi-tiered prison cells, penetrating the numerous nooks and crannies of mainly Victorian edifices. As a prisoner, wherever you turn you are confronted by it. Just the wrong facial expression is sufficient to cause the beholder to launch a bodily attack on the perceived transgressor. To survive requires a crash course in interpreting body language. The most innocuous gesture or verbal remark can result in a split lip, blackened eye or cracked rib. Shower rooms are a popular place for such assaults. A naked inmate is extremely vulnerable to a physical going-over.

Fortunately for all concerned, spontaneous physical clashes are often over as quickly as they occur. It is the planned, contrived acts of violence which can cause greater and possibly permanent injury. Forethought and malice are the lethal mix of ingredients used when wreaking vengeance. Traditional weapons include the stocking containing several PP9 batteries – sizeable, heavy objects used in prisoners radios. To be whacked over the back of the head with such an easily made weapon risks receiving a hefty dent in the scull.

Prisoners foolish enough to earn the enmity of others can also expect to find crushed glass in their food. Their unoccupied cell might be 'dirtied' – prisoners will slip in and smear everything with excrement. Property could be smashed or stolen, or the inmate's possessions placed in a pile and set ablaze. The occupant might respond to a polite knock on the door, only to have a blanket thrown over his head and then be kicked and beaten senseless by a group of unidentifiable thugs. Often the officers in the vicinity know about these things and condone them because the inmate concerned has made himself as obnoxious to the staff as he has to his fellow prisoners.

But a more painful retribution because it lasts far longer is when a hapless inmate is doused in boiling water. Not ordinary boiling water straight from the kettle, but water which has first been mixed with sugar. Not too much, not too little – just enough to ensure a liquid sufficiently viscous to stick to the victim's skin as he (invariably a male) desperately attempts to rid himself of the searing pain. You soon know when someone has been doused. It is not the sight but the scream which tells you what has happened. A slight variation on this theme of dousing occurs when the target approaches a communal cooking area and, instead of sugared water, the victim is splattered with boiling fat.

A more traditional prison weapon is the knife or, more precisely, a razor blade. This can be the thin blade extracted from prison-issued shaving razors which has been melted into a toothbrush handle for grip, or the Stanley-knife type blade prisoners are allowed to use for model-making, etc. Many a scar-faced inmate acquired his markings since coming into prison. But knives do kill. In June 1988 Alan Averill was stabbed to death during a cookery lesson at Stoke Heath Young Offenders' Institution. He died on his eighteenth birthday.

At this point a distinction has to be made between those types of assaults which in the main are not intended to kill and those which most certainly are designed to be fatal. One particular incident of the latter which left a lasting impression on me was when an undoubted psychopath wired up a bath with the intention of electrocuting his targeted victim. It required patience and attention to detail to succeed and months to set up. The distance between bath and power point was far, so it was essential that the long strands of wire used remained undetected. This was achieved by the perpetrator painting the wire the same colour as the floor tiles.

Although stretching credulity to think that such a madcap scheme could have succeeded in a prison environment, it almost did. The intended victim got into the water-filled bath and fortunately was able to leap out instantly he felt the electric shock. Youth and peak physical condition were on his side. His reaction was so fast that he escaped death. To be sure he was left shocked and shaken. Because of this incident his subsequent aversion to taking a bath is akin to that of some filmgoers who saw the shower scene in Alfred Hitchcock's *Psycho*. It was little consolation to know that his assailant received a 15-year sentence for attempted murder.

The intended victim is presently claiming compensation from the Home Office alleging breach of its duty of care. That such a duty exists in law was confirmed in 1998 in *Hartshorn v Home Secretary*. Robert Hartshorn, a convicted murderer, was badly scarred after a razor attack on him by fellow inmates at Gartree Prison, Leicestershire. A court ruled that he was entitled to compensation on the ground that the Home Office failed to ensure the prison was run in a safe and secure manner. The significance of this legal victory is that prior to it only prisoners who were known to be at risk of attack such as child abusers could mount such a claim. The *Hartshorn* ruling means that the Prison Service must be far more vigilant when ensuring the safety of prisoners. It can no longer afford to turn a blind eye to inmates meting out punishment on each other.

This readiness to resort to violence is not only explained by the testosterone-charged environment in which male prisoners are placed. It also has much to do with the mental illnesses from which many suffer. In 1994 Christopher Edwards, a mentally ill young man being held on three days' remand, was put into a cell at Chelmsford Prison with another young man suffering from paranoid schizophrenia. He was known to be extremely dangerous. Christopher was beaten to death by his cellmate so violently that he could only be identified by his dental records. His ear was eaten. Four years later an independent inquiry criticized all agencies involved, particularly the prison service for 'disastrous deficiencies on a multitude of issues'.

For far too long prisons have been used to accommodate people who should be in special hospitals. Peter Sutcliffe, the Yorkshire Ripper, was obviously raving mad when he embarked on his series of killings and evidence given at his trial by psychiatrists confirmed this. Yet because the jury (highly unlikely to be versed in the nature of mental illness) did not accept this expert opinion, Sutcliffe had first to spend a few years in prison. He was eventually certified and transferred to a special hospital.

That prisons house so many inmates who are undoubtedly certifiable is a situation which has only recently received belated recognition. It can now be successfully argued by inmates when seeking legal redress following attacks on them by mentally ill prisoners that the Prison Service was in breach of its duty of care in allowing deranged people to remain in prison. In May 1999 it was announced that steps are to be implemented to expedite the removal of seriously mentally ill prisoners to more suitable accommodation. Such decisions have to be based on Section 37 of the Mental Health Act 1983 which requires a minimum of two psychiatrists to independently assess and confirm certification under this Act.

In the not too distant future it could also be a biologist's signature which is accepted. Recent developments in medical science have revealed more about the genetic nature of mental illness, including recognition that violence may have a biological basis. This is a major milestone in the understanding of antisocial behaviour which traditionally has been regarded as an acquired behavioural trait. It could also provide an explanation of the behaviour of one inmate I got to know personally despite his horrendous reputation for unpredictable mood swings. Genetic aberrations have been discovered in his brothers and sisters which match a similar pattern found in a convicted Dutch criminal and his siblings. The search is being widened to identify more prisoners with similar behavioural patterns and to establish a statistical correlation in their

DNA. One has already been established with the so-called 'gay' gene. With this and the presently hypothetical 'violence' gene, much more research is required to give either of them credence. But the implications of research into both types of genes are profound: they have ramifications in the area of eugenics as well as law and order.

Who is most likely to be a victim of violence in prison? Surprisingly, in my experience it not necessarily the obvious Darwinian candidate – the weakest at the mercy of the strongest. Whether this is a result of peer group pressure among aggressive types or simply the realization that there is no mileage in pursuing inadequates, those inmates deemed obviously inadequate are generally left alone, confined to their limited social group. Inadequates are defined as those having a combination of limited educational, vocational, social or sporting abilities. Having little or no access to money makes some prisoners distinctly inadequate in the eyes of their peers. Violence is more likely to be found within social groups as distinct from the lone psychopath roaming his solitary path through the prison.

The prison soccer pitch is often used as a venue (and excuse) for throwing punches. But off-pitch violence more often takes place in cells unless the aggressor feels a public message has to be delivered. Then it takes place in front of an audience – usually queuing for meals or the prison canteen. The upside of this tactic is that officers can quickly intervene before too much bodily damage has been inflicted, but not too soon to negate the whole point of the public assault: that physical retribution has been inflicted. The public message is abundantly clear: 'Don't anyone else mess with me.'

Once upon a time tobacco was the root cause of most violent disputes. Today the scene has changed drastically. Health awareness means fewer prisoners are smoking. Undoubtedly drugs are now the predominant cause of much violence. Purely subjectively, I have the impression that when drugs are involved more extreme violence is meted out than was the case when tobacco was traded. Are drugs and violence synonymous? Enormous sums of money are at stake, such is the addictive nature of some of the 'gear' which finds its way to prisoners via their visitors and/or co-operative prison staff.

Given a choice most prison officers would turn a blind eye to cannabis because of its calming effect on users. Unfortunately for them, it is the drug most likely to be detected in a mandatory drug test because it stays in the blood stream the longest, far longer than heroin or psychosis inducers such as metamphetamines – the scourge of the prison drug scene. These types of drugs can clear the bloodstream within 48 hours – sufficiently long enough for a Friday night fix to be undetected following a Monday morning drug test. Ironically, the justification given by many prisoners for their drug use is to survive imprisonment. That drugs can help is confirmed by the ready availability of psychopharmacological medication doled out by the prison doctor.

Many observers of penal environments would argue that in practical, pragmatic terms cannabis is the least harmful and most beneficial of mood conditioners, and a fraction of the price currently spent on 'legitimate' medication. These could be reasons enough for legalizing it. Perhaps the final arbiter will be the avaricious Treasury when persuaded of the revenue raising potential of legalized cannabis. A cost-benefit analysis is urgently needed to assess and confirm the claims of the many proponents of legalization. Apart from many prison officers, also among those urging for decriminalization is *The Economist*, whose track record for accurately predicting and forming public opinion cannot be overlooked.

The public image of prisons as violent, conflict riven environments is compounded (if not actually created) by the way penal environments are dramatized on film and television. Literature too plays its part. Two great Russian writers – Dostoevsky and Solzhenitsyn – and more recently the young English writer David Willocks of *Green River Rising* fame (1994) have portrayed horrific scenes of unimaginable violence when men (invariably men) are forced to live together in alien, hostile conditions. For a factual description of violence in Scottish prisons particularly, Jimmy Boyle's (1985) *The Pain of Confinement* remains a classic of the genre.

More realistic but no less violent pictures have also been painted by official inquiries into major incidences such as the spate of riots which broke out a little under a decade ago in a number of prisons, including several high security establishments. The initial spark was ignited at Manchester's aptly named Strangeways Prison. The death of at least three people can be directly attributed to these disturbances. Strangeways was an appalling example of mob violence. In the report of the official inquiry chaired by Lord Woolf, the present Master of the Rolls, he said: 'The first 25 days of April 1990 saw the worst series of prison riots in the history of the British penal system' (Home Office 1991). The report then describes in forensic detail the extent to which violence was used as the principal weapon in a wave of protest and destruction which also spread to five other prisons. 'Strangeways acted as a beacon which provided the signal for unrest and disturbances across many parts of the prison system,' said Lord Woolf.

Strangeways brought about a profound rethink regarding the way the Prison Service deals with violence. It also taught senior managers that the ways in which prison discipline and regimes were being enforced could not continue unchanged. Violence as a tool of control is ineffective. It might appear successful in the immediate term, but long term it contains all the dynamics of an emerging volcano. Strangeways was the name of the Prison Service's own Krakatoa.

I entered prison a few months after Strangeways erupted and fortunately have never personally experienced or witnessed mob violence during the ensuing nine years. I have had ample opportunity to observe and absorb the nature of violence in the three prisons to which I have been sent. I have also had a considerable number of conversations with long-term prisoners, many of whom, when reminiscing, express a discernible nostalgia for the pre-Strangeways regime. 'At least you knew where you stood' is a typical refrain, and not only from inmates. What has become most apparent post-Strangeways is the way training has affected the attitude of uniformed staff to threats and real acts of violence. Originally their initial response to either scenario was that of an uncontrolled mob. Officers would materialize from all directions and just pile in. It would look more like a rugby scrum than a serious attempt to take control of a volatile situation.

Nowadays the benefits and obvious advantages of a more reasoned, re-strained approach are notably evident. Staff have much greater insight into the psychological forces at play. They are encouraged to talk through a con-frontation rather than exacerbate it by mirroring the inmate's behaviour. However, this enlightened approach is not yet the norm in all prisons. There are still too many where uniformed staff have a vested interest in maintaining or exacerbating tensions. These prisons are mainly those where inmates are being held on remand or serving short-term sentences. Notably, Wormwood Scrubs, Brixton, Wandsworth, Armley, Liverpool, Bristol and Winson Green have unenviable reputations for brutality.

At the time of writing, a major police inquiry into allegations of beatings and racism is in progress at Wormwood Scrubs. And 12 months after commencing their initial probe the same team is investigating similar claims against prison officers at Brixton and Wandsworth gaols. At Wormwood Scrubs accusations have been made against 43 officers and so far 27 have been charged with criminal offences. In the course of this police investigation into allegations of brutality made by prisoners and their legal representatives some uniformed staff have already left the Prison Service.

The broadening of this police investigation coincides with a warning by the newly appointed Director General of the Prison Service that he will not tolerate abuse of prisoners. Martin Narey (*The Guardian* 1999), while stressing that he was not referring to officers currently accused and suspended, told delegates attending the Prisoner Officers' Association annual conference that a 'tiny handful' of officers were causing irreparable damage to the profession. He said: 'They do not treat prisoners and visitors with dignity. Sometime they abuse prisoners. However small their number they do irreparable damage to your profession. There is no place for them in our service.'

The type of behaviour to which Martin Narey referred was aptly described in the Woolf Report – a description as valid today as it was nine years ago:

> The single and most important contributory factor in my opinion (in the causes of riots) – is the attitudes of prison officers ... What makes prison more difficult more than anything else is the often disgusting, ignorant and apathetic attitudes of prison officers. Any prisoner will know exactly what I am talking about. Being shouted at like a dog, being constantly verbally de-graded and being belittled as part of the game. Nobody (unless of course they went in blue jeans and striped shirt) can understand just exactly what sinister goings on actually take place within a prison environment ... a new world opens up to you. Officers bullying, telling lies at adjudications, disre-garding rules. Prison officers seem to thrive on enforcing to the limit the of-ten petty rules which constitute the prison rule book ... Generally the incidents I talk about occur more in local prisons than in dispersal or Cate-gory C prisons. I watched young recruited officers coming to the job with many good points, e.g. talking to prisoners, smiling, saying hello ... trying to help a prisoner if possible, even if that only meant opening a door to allow him to go to the toilet. However, within a space of a week or two these excel-lent attitudes were quickly and efficiently knocked out of all but the stron-gest willed by the old school of prison officer who growls and grunts like an animal. (*Prison Disturbances* 1990, p.493)

Justification for these brutal regimes is the belief by prison officers of the need to make new inmates understand who is in control. Yet strangely, those prisons managed by private contractors such as Group Four do not deem it necessary to impose oppressive, intimidatory regimes when establishing the status quo. This says more about effective, accountable operational procedures based on clearly defined and understood duties and responsibilities than it does about a prison management held in thrall of a recalcitrant, unco-operative trade union more concerned with job security than with norms and standards of humanity and respect.

It is important when writing about violence in prisons that a clear distinction be made between different types of prisons. These range from those holding remand and short-term prisoners and other prisons, particularly those accommodating long-termers and those with a lower security category. By the time prisoners transfer to these latter groups the likelihood of violent behaviour has diminished significantly.

Undoubtedly, prisons are hostile, violent places. The psychodynamic sequence of the initial confusion of inmates upon first entering prison turning into fear and then anger which finds an outlet in physical violence is well recognized. But in reality this violence takes on a form more dangerous and insidious than the general bloody image of split lips, blackened eyes or cracked ribs. Occasionally these assaults are fatal. However, such displays of physical dominance are few and far between. In fact they are profoundly counterproductive. Far more effective is the threat of physical violence. This is the basis of bullying, be it in a school playground or a prison exercise yard.

Unsurprisingly, the notion of violence in prisons as an everyday occurrence is not readily accepted by the Prison Service. However, substitute 'bullying' for violence and suddenly everyone knows what you are talking about. In fact the Prison Service has an official anti-bullying policy. This is confirmed by announcements to be found on notice boards throughout prisons, usually placed alongside a statement about its suicide prevention policy. In too many establishments this is the full extent of what is done about alleviating these twin evils of prison life

The purpose of bullying is to dominate and gain materially from victims in the face of specific or generalized threats. Usually the reputation of the bully is sufficient to produce the desired result. In prison desirable items include phone cards, postage stamps, tobacco, tea, coffee and particularly sugar. Coveted objects can also include trendy trainers and fashionable clothing. The essential commodities of prison life are obtained almost as a form of taxation. The trained eye soon recognizes the inmates in the canteen queue and relates them to other prisoners hanging about in the immediate vicinity. They are there to waylay their victims before they can travel too far into the depths of the prison. For the victims it is pay-up time.

HM Inspector of Prisons claims as many as 40 per cent of prisoners suffer from psychological or psychiatric problems. In these circumstances it is often bullying which can finally drive a vulnerable prisoner over the edge. Then inquiries are held, inmates suspected of involvement are transferred and the knuckles of staff who knew or should have known about this risk are occasionally rapped. Rarely is anyone sacked for dereliction of duty, for how can individual blame be apportioned to what is a collective responsibility? But prison managers are not unmindful of this failure in their duty of care towards weak and vulnerable inmates. The appointment in April 1999 of the present Director General of the Prison Service brought with it his personal pledge (*The Guardian* 1999) to reduce the suicide rate which in 1998 totalled 82 deaths.

Tokenism pervades even when yet another inadequate soul succumbs to the misery of imprisonment and takes their life. Many enter prison already over-burdened: the nature of their offence coupled with a sense of guilt and remorse, its impact on themselves, their partners and possibly children, present and future employment prospects, loss of accommodation, etc. And many prisoners are mentally ill prior to custodial remand. Imprisonment undoubtedly exacerbates an existing delicate, confused or unbalanced mind.

Irrespective of where it occurs, obvious acts of violence between inmates or against prison staff are usually dealt with quickly and conclusively. In some prisons it is still the unquestioned norm for violent, recalcitrant prisoners to be seized by staff and escorted (more usually dragged) to the 'block' while held in vicelike armlocks. Invariably located in a basement, the block is a self-contained prison-within-a-prison noted for its Spartan conditions: unheated cells lacking internal sanitation, sometimes containing only papier-mâché furniture, plus a mattress on the floor (often removed during the daytime to discourage sleeping).

Officially known as a special cell or as the segregation unit, 'refractory or violent' prisoners who are placed in it under Prison Rule 48 (the old Rule 45) must now have any period of confinement over 24 hours approved by a member of the Board of Visitors (Rule 48 (2)) or 'an officer of the Secretary of State (not being an officer of a prison)'.[2] Prison blocks have a notorious reputation of being the place where violent (or just recalcitrant) prisoners get their come-uppance. That such violence is inflicted by uniformed staff is without doubt. The injuries rained by officers on the Birmingham Six when remanded in custody at Winson Green Prison brought lasting shame to the Prison Service.

The death in Winson Green in the late 1980s of an inmate named Prosser actually resulted in manslaughter charges against a number of prison officers, all of whom were acquitted. Barry Prosser was a physically large man, with voice and attitude to match. Assertive, boisterous, questioning and unfazed by his imprisonment, he was deemed a 'control' problem by certain officers. Rather than place him in the segregation unit, he was confined to a padded cell in the prison hospital. While there he suffered severe physical injuries including a burst spleen and eventually died. For many years his widow would spend most Saturdays silently picketing the main entrance to the prison while displaying a placard protesting over the death of her husband.

The death of an inmate in privately operated Blakenhurst Prison at Redditch in 1998 while being 'restrained' by five uniformed staff en route to the block sparked an enormous outcry. Not so much for this loss of life, but more for the disappearance of a video which recorded what happened at the time death struck. Compounding this tragedy was the claim by the then Director General of the Prison Service that, unlike white people, those of African-Carribbean

---

2   The Prison Rules 1999 (S1 1999 No 728) came into effect April 1 1999. The new Rules (Stationery Office) revoke and replace the 1964 Rules, as amended.

origin were physiologically predisposed to sustaining neck injuries when pressure from a head lock was applied; in other words, making black people more susceptible to die from asphyxiation when held down by prison officers. Needless to say, the moment the enormity of this egregious gaff was realized a stream of profuse apologies flowed like a torrent from Prison Service HQ. This devastating remark sounded more like a line from Dario Fo's farce *The Accidental Death of an Anarchist* (1987) than a considered statement by a senior civil servant.

As the loss of the Blakenhurst video demonstrates, proving violence is virtually impossible although recently there have been rare exceptions. The police inquiry launched in early 1999 into allegations of violence perpetrated in the block at Wormwood Scrubs is indicative of the seriousness with which the Prison Service now views claims by prisoners. This change of heart could have much to do with the courts upholding prisoners' claims for compensation. Courts appear increasingly willing to accept that it is not just in police cells or the back of police vans where injuries are inflicted on people held in custody.

As with the police, Britain's prison officers are poorly managed, weakly disciplined and insufficiently accountable for unlawful assaults on prisoners. Officers whose conduct is being investigated are more often than not allowed to escape into early retirement with pensions intact before disciplinary proceedings against them have been completed. Bringing the Prison Service within the ambit of the Race Relations Act, from which it should never have been excluded in 1976, particularly in view of the disproportionate percentage of black people jailed, will do much to reduce race-based assaults on prisoners. It will also put an end to the unconscionable provocation by some uniformed officers at Brixton Prison of openly wearing National Front tiepins. These changes will be a lasting legacy of the Macpherson report (1999) into the death of Stephen Lawrence.

It is against this background of violence in prisons that offence-related courses are provided. But the incident I describe earlier involving the inmate awarded a certificate for successfully completing the anger management course confirmed my growing impression that the motivation for such courses is principally tokenism. Yet these courses form a key element of the Prison Service's strategy to bring about change in inmates offending behaviour. There is no compulsion to participate, but those who do know they will find requests for early release on parole considered far more favourably than prisoners who decided such courses were not for them.

Unfortunately, prison-based probation and psychology staff responsible for running these courses appear inclined to regard them in a quantitative rather than a qualitative context. From personal experience I have discerned that the integrity and therefore effectiveness of these courses is being undermined by a fraying at the edges of the necessary degree of quality control. These courses will only be provided if a minimum number of inmates participate. Specialist staff therefore have a strong incentive to get bums on seats rather than be ultra-fussy about targeting solely those prisoners able to benefit from such courses. To adopt the latter approach could result in too few attendees to warrant running them and the continued employment of specialist staff delivering them. So staff know their jobs depend on a high headcount. Inevitably, quality is being undermined at the expense of quality.

For those prisoners attending courses, unless there is a genuine commitment to change they will be among the 56 per cent of prisoners who were reconvicted within two years of being released (Home Office 1998). To be effective, these courses also require a greater commitment and expertise from the Prison Service. I have personally participated in courses where everyone made all the right noises and appeared fully committed to learn from the 'insights' revealed. But the moment participants left the meeting room the true response of many was articulated. Typically, 'load of bollocks, rubbish, bullshit' are among the views expressed about these courses. Such responses confirmed that inmates' prime motivation for attending them was simply as a means of getting out of prison sooner. The instinct to resort to violence remains unchanged. So has imprisonment for the purpose of reforming violent behaviour failed? On the evidence of current rates of recidivism the answer must be a depressing 'yes'.

REFERENCES

Boyle, J. (1985) *The Pain of Confinement*. London: Pan.
Fo, D. (1987) *The Accidental Death of an Anarchist*. London: Methuen.
Interview in *The Guardian* 14 April 1999.
Home Office (1991) *Prison Disturbances April 1990*, Cm 1456. London: HMSO.
Home Office (1998) *Prison Statistics 1997*, Cm 4017. London: The Stationery Office.
Macpherson, W. (1999) 'The Stephen Lawrence Inquiry.' London: HMSO.
Report in *The Independent* 1 June 1999.
Willocks, D. (1994) *Green River Rising*. London: Arrow.

CHAPTER 13

Violent Men in Prison
Confronting Offending Behaviour
Without Denying Prior Victimization

David Webb and Brian Williams

INTRODUCTION

Men who commit crimes of violence have often experienced extreme violence themselves. This does not excuse their offending, but in some cases it may form part of the explanation for it. Demonstrating an understanding of this context can be crucial to effective engagement with individuals, and gaining the trust of a service user is usually an essential first step when attempting to 'confront' offending behaviour as part of pre- or post-release work. Taking a full and informative history of previous experiences of violence may increase the effectiveness of such work.

There are obvious difficulties in paying special attention to the previous victimization of violent offenders. Some offenders will attempt to hide behind their 'victim' status as a way of avoiding discussion of the harm they have done to others. The worker's sympathy can also get in the way of appropriate vigilance: we all want to believe that people can change for the better, but we must not allow this to cloud our judgement or to prevent us from asking difficult questions when working with serious violent offenders (see Prins 1995). These obstacles can, however, be overcome in practice.

In this chapter we consider the connections between violent offending, socialization into violent behaviour and earlier experiences of violence at the hands of others. We review the experience of male prisoners and the difficulties facing those who try to work with them on issues of violence and aggression. Using case studies, we explore some of the implications for professional practice with violent males.

THE ROOTS OF VIOLENCE

Different academic disciplines favour their own widely varying explanations of aggression and violence, but there is considerable agreement that early experience is important. Although most writers in the psychoanalytic tradition have tended to assume that violence is innate, Freud (1908) argued that there were links between resentment, hostility and aggression (Siann 1985). Social learning begins at an early age and continues throughout life. Parental aggression, conflict and cruelty are significant factors in the development of violent offenders (Farrington 1994; Storr 1970). Not only do violent parents model violent behaviour in front of children, they may also create feelings of impotence and worthlessness which manifest themselves in violence later in the children's lives (Toch 1972). Being brought up in a subculture in which people look up to 'hard men' and violence is seen as an answer to problems is also influential (Boyle 1977; Levi 1994; Wolfgang and Ferracuti 1967). People who are bullied, judged less intelligent and perform badly at school are likely to fail to develop feelings of self-worth and to grow up as aggressive adults (Devlin 1997; Patrick 1973; Siann 1985).

Men who learn to deal successfully with fear and feelings of impotence by using violence are likely to repeat the pattern (Toch 1972). Relatively trivial incidents may spark off violence where the self-esteem of men is at stake. Daly and Wilson (1988, p.128) went so far as to assert that: 'In most social milieus, a man's reputation depends in part upon the maintenance of a credible threat of violence.'

This may be an exaggeration, but it takes seriously the working-class machismo and violence arising from challenges to personal honour which many commentators are inclined to dismiss (Polk 1994). In the prison context the need to maintain one's reputation is highlighted both by the continuous threat of violence and by the humiliations of imprisonment. Toch (1979) showed that the indignities and domination routinely involved in prison life create a dangerous situation where men with a propensity for violence are concerned. Everyday instructions from those in authority are likely to be taken as threats to autonomy and personal affronts, and resentment can be manifested in unpredictable ways. When authority is abused, such resentment can become general and threaten the orderly running of a prison and its legitimacy in the eyes of its inmates (Sim 1994b).

VIOLENCE AND VICTIMIZATION IN INSTITUTIONS

Prisons and at times other institutions such as children's homes make enormous demands upon the personal resources of their inmates. Not everybody copes well under such circumstances: 'Survival in prison demands recourse to a set of personal resources which may exceed the abilities of those it confines. Assessing risk in prison, and addressing it, requires a sensitivity to the subjective world of the prisoner, and a hard look at the nature of the regimes involved' (Liebling 1997, p.202).

Suicides and self-mutilation, intimidation and bullying, physical and sexual assault, and various kinds of mental distress are common in prisons. As well as containing substantial proportions of people prone to such stresses, prison creates the conditions for victimization. Some groups are particularly vulnerable, and not only those who have committed sexual offences. All those who are segregated for their own protection are likely to be targeted for violent attack by other inmates, as are the very young and elderly prisoners. Younger offenders and women prisoners are over-represented among those involved in suicidal and self-harming behaviour. Prisons are violent and dangerous places and their regimes tend to encourage the development of brutal survival mechanisms. It is not only an abnormal minority of prisoners who resort to violence: 'Violence and domination in prison can ... be understood not as a pathological manifestation of abnormal otherness but as a part of the normal routine which is sustained and legitimated by the wider culture of masculinity' (Sim 1994a, p.105).

This raises a host of questions about the possibility of rehabilitating violent men in such an environment. People's behaviour in prison may not be a very good predictor of their likely behaviour after release (Hirschmann 1996), although this has been the subject of considerable academic debate, with some authors arguing that prison misbehaviour does indicate a need for caution about early release (Clark 1994).

In any event, the prison environment is hardly conducive to serious questioning of common stereotypes of appropriate male behaviour: 'Prisoners and staff alike share stereotypical views of gender roles. A woman ... is conscious of entering a male domain. Despite legitimate reasons for being there, she is an intruder' (Knox 1996, p.13).

While female workers, and men who challenge macho norms, have developed strategies for raising these issues in prisons, it may not feel (or be) safe for male prisoners to do so. In prisons, the use of force is legitimized. A particular version of masculinity is institutionalized. The gender inequalities rampant in society as a whole are intensified. As Sim puts it:

> The institution sustains, reproduces and indeed intensifies this most negative aspect of masculinity, moulding and re-moulding identities and behavioural patterns whose destructive manifestations are not left behind the walls when the prisoner is released but often become part of his 'taken-for-granted' world on the outside. (Sim 1994a, p.103)

In such an environment, there are dangers in encouraging men to challenge the negative aspects of their socialization, although in a prison system which gives priority to engaging effectively with serious offenders, this is an important and unavoidable task (Knox 1996). For the prisoners, it can be extremely risky to become involved in work which breaks down their denial and defensiveness about the nature of their offending. Not only does the personal change involved in such work make it harder to survive emotionally in the prison environment, but some offenders may literally be putting themselves in danger by undertaking group work which identifies them as sexual offenders. They are much more vulnerable to random attack by other prisoners once this becomes known. At a more mundane level, the prison system is profoundly ambivalent about the need to challenge male violence:

> Frequently, for example, the Parole Board recommends that a prisoner examines his attitudes and relationships with women. This represents a formal recognition of the problem and yet issues such as the display of sexual images of women within the prison are not tackled in a more general way. (Knox 1996, p.18)

For the staff, there may also be a price to pay for raising gender issues, particularly as they relate to offending. 'Welfare' workers in general and women staff in particular, represent a challenge to some prison officers by their mere presence. This can result in petty obstruction and constant challenges to the legitimacy of the probation task. When women challenge sexist behaviour or simply act assertively, this can be taken as a threat to the authority of male prison officers. It will, however, have a cumulative effect (Knox 1996).

Some prisoners invite outsiders to feel sorry for them. Some may deserve our sympathy, but it should not be allowed to get in the way of effective work. The probation and youth justice mandate for involvement with incarcerated offenders is specifically to do with crime prevention (see Part III of the Crime and Disorder Act 1998 and the Criminal Justice Act 1991). We may work with prisoners for humanitarian reasons, but primarily with a view to successful rehabilitation. When prisoners present themselves as victims of circumstances, our personal concern needs to be tempered by balancing this against the need to protect past and potential victims of their offending. Serious sexual offenders, for example, may play up the difficulties they are facing as a way of distracting attention from the damage done to their victims. Careful questioning about the details of offences is always necessary with serious offenders and can help to break down the defences of those who play 'poor me' in the counselling context (Prins 1995). Personal experience of victimization can also open up unexpected opportunities for encouraging men to examine the consequences of their own offending upon victims (Knox 1996).

This is not to suggest that claims of victimization in prison are necessarily a smokescreen. It is a necessary part of the 'civilian' professional role in total institutions to make sure that such claims are properly investigated, and indeed inmates will judge the trustworthiness of representatives of outside agencies such as probation partly by the way in which they conduct themselves in such situations. We cannot ignore the risks to which service users are exposed as a consequence of their incarceration (Williams 1997). Probation officers have a role in trying to make prison regimes less destructive, for example, through their involvement in suicide prevention projects, race relations committees and group work programmes. They also need to support the prisoners whose offending they are challenging, both as part of the work on offending behaviour and as part of the professional role in the prison setting.

The need both to support offenders and to challenge their behaviour may seem contradictory, but this paradox is central to constructive work with prisoners who are likely to be living with either the experience or the fear of victimization. The connection between someone's experience as a victim and their own use of violence is complex and resists easy categorization. In practical terms it can be important to acknowledge that there is a connection and that offenders may well perceive themselves, rightly or wrongly, as being victims as much as perpetrators.

Violence can be seen as a product of external factors (such as social conditions, childhood abuse, alcohol or drug use) and of internal processes, which may well be shaped by memories and fears of victimization. Not all those who experience the external factors associated with violence (what Slaby (1997) calls 'violence toxins') become violent themselves. The difference between them and those who do act violently may lie in their psychological resources for resolving problems and conflicts. The way people interpret and respond to events has a critical effect on their behaviour. Looking at the difference between peaceful and violent children, Slaby concluded that the explanation 'probably lies not so much in the objective experiences themselves as in the way the child organises, interprets and emotionally responds to these factors' (Slaby 1997, p.182). This means that good practice with violent offenders requires us not just to assess and monitor the situations they encounter (for example, in deciding the suitability of a proposed address on release) but also to discover and work with the way they perceive and interpret situations and relationships.

BEHAVIOUR CODES ENDORSING VIOLENCE

Writing about 'confrontational homicide', Polk (1994) noted how often men-on-men murders arise from an apparently trivial cause. He refers to the work of Daly and Wilson (1988) in concluding that the conflict quickly escalates to a 'contest over honour or reputation'. The role of bystanders is important in motivating the men to aggressive action in order to save face. Slaby (1997, p.174) suggests that 'the mere presence of a bystander often increases both the volatility and the stakes of an encounter'. Edgar and O'Donnell's research (1998) into the victim's contribution to assaults in prison found that the roles of aggressor, victim and bystander were often fluid. Sometimes the person who was most seriously injured had instigated the fight, being both aggressor and victim: 'Some of the assaults we examined arose out of a shared willingness to resort to violence. In such incidents, the categories of victim and attacker break down' (Edgar and O'Donnell 1998, p.636).

This 'shared willingness' can represent a common social code based on the use or threat of violence to assert honour, self-respect and 'manhood' (Anderson 1997). Edgar and O'Donnell found that such a code was pervasive in prison. There was: 'a persistent faith among many prisoners in the protective value of the use of force against others ... force is perceived to be a solution in a wide range of situations' (1998, p.649). An inevitable consequence of aggressive masculine stereotypes is male victims, which can lead to further violence in the form of reprisals and revenge attacks.

We have considered the connections between victimization and violence; the influence of confrontational male social codes; the fact that the roles of aggressor, bystander and victim are often interchangeable; and the ways that these problems often tend to be exaggerated in prisons. The following fictional case studies typify some of these dynamics, both in the commission of the index offence and in the implications for work with the offender. They are representative of cases one of us is currently working with as a prison probation officer on a long-termers' wing.

Case Study A

Chris is 23, a black man serving life for murder. He has been in custody since he was 19. He has a 12-year tariff. He was brought up first by his grandmother and then, after her death when he was 7, by a succession of foster parents. He is closer now to his mother but is still hurt by her early neglect of him. He does not know his father, but has become attached to his stepfather. He has not had regular employment, but had started college when he was arrested.

He has a previous conviction for robbery – 'if they won't defend their property they don't deserve it' – for which he served 7 months of a 12 month sentence in a Young Offender Institution (YOI). He admits to similar undetected offences and states that he had a reputation for 'being able to handle myself'. He committed the murder a month after his release from his first sentence. He and his victim Darren had once been friends but they argued over a jacket. Darren accused Chris of stealing it from him and beat him up with a baseball bat. They met by chance a week later. Both men were known to carry knives and when Darren threatened him, in front of a group of their associates, Chris stabbed Darren five times. 'It was him or me. Yes, I feel sorry for him, he was my friend, but if he was alive now, I'd be dead.'

Chris was repeatedly 'nicked' for fighting in the YOI, and was moved to the adult prison system when he was still 20. Since then his behaviour has gradually improved; he is proud of avoiding disciplinary adjudications for two years. He has explanations for a lot of his violence in the YOI, which he did not always instigate himself: 'Those places aren't like adult prisons, you've got to look after yourself. If you don't, they walk all over you. It's all front, everyone's got a front on there.' He has regular meetings with his prison probation officer, attends available offending behaviour programmes and gets on well with his home probation officer who has supervised him since his arrest.

Case Study B

A small white man in his thirties, Maurice is two years into a discretionary life sentence, with a six year tariff. Maurice has two previous convictions for arson, in which he set fires in empty buildings. His offences fall into a pattern of relationship problems, alcohol misuse and self-harm. In this case he and his partner Keith had had a volatile relationship. Maurice states that Keith hit him on several occasions and at other times forced

Case Study B (continued)

him out of their flat, which was Keith's tenancy. On the day of the offence they had both been drinking. Keith took home a friend of whom Maurice was jealous. When Maurice returned, Keith and the friend shouted abuse at him and told him to sleep downstairs. Later that night, Maurice crept into the bedroom and hit Keith over the head with a hammer while he slept. Keith was seriously injured and Maurice was later convicted of attempted murder.

As a child Maurice was physically abused by his father, who was also violent to Maurice's mother. His parents are both dead, his mother having died a few months before this offence. Maurice has mild learning difficulties and a history of psychiatric treatment, including lengthy spells in secure hospitals. The pre-trial psychiatric reports for this offence concluded, however, that he has an untreatable personality disorder, thus ruling out a hospital order.

In prison Maurice is occasionally bullied and he attempted suicide soon after sentence. He seeks frequent but superficial contact with the wing probation officer, yet resists intrusive questioning about his offence and its origins. He depicts himself as a victim, both currently in prison and during his relationship with Keith. He insists that his apologies for the offence are evidence of remorse, but clearly perceives Keith as being at least as culpable as he. He is willing to discuss his sexuality in individual work but not in front of other prisoners, so that his participation in group work programmes is necessarily restricted.

BUILDING TRUST

These are complex cases involving men who have both perpetrated and endured violence. Productive work with them will require ongoing effort to build a trusting relationship. A sufficiently trusting relationship can only be built by adherence to the basic Rogerian concepts of client-centred counselling:

- unconditional positive regard (acknowledging their intrinsic value as persons)
- accurate empathic understanding (whereby the worker shows a sense of the client's world)
- congruence (the client experiences the worker's responses as genuine)
- presence (the worker demonstrates sustained commitment to the process).

These qualities will underpin the different methods suggested below and are consistent with the theory that violence is strongly connected to the ways a person interprets and perceives the world. They are also consistent with effective practice principles about how workers should relate to offenders (see Gendreau 1996, p.124). With probation officers increasingly constrained by high caseloads and bureaucratic requirements, their contact with clients in prison is usually related to specific pieces of work like risk assessments or parole reports. There is little time to devote solely to developing trust and overcoming client resistance. Instead, these basic social work skills need to underlie the explicit tasks being performed.

We have referred to the need for a trusting relationship with the offender. In both these cases, as with many lifers, the men harbour resentments about their treatment by the police and the prosecution before and during their trial, and about the life sentence system, which has renewed their perceptions of being victimized. Chris and Maurice had previously been attacked by the men they assaulted and both have subsequently endured violence in prison. As well as perpetrating violence, they have been victims of it. Their perception of themselves as partly victims is entangled with their previous negative experiences of professional intervention, in care, in hospitals or in prison. They are therefore sceptical of 'authority', including probation officers. Chris is particularly wary of what he calls 'sly' workers who, in his view, feign friendship in order to obtain material which they then use against him in reports and assessments. He also believes that he suffers from the consequences of assumptions made by professionals about young black men being aggressive. Meanwhile, Maurice's lengthy experience of secure hospitals and now this life sentence have taught him that he is powerless over his own destiny. The differing attitudes of these two men may each lead to irritation or frustration for the worker, who must be careful not to respond in a way which entrenches the men's feelings of being mistreated.

PRO-SOCIAL MODELLING

The way that workers deal with conflicts between them and the offender will be important in conveying implicit messages about how problems can be resolved. Work has recently been done in Cambridgeshire aimed at incorporating principles of pro-social modelling and legitimacy into probation practice (Rex and Matravers 1998). This includes the probation officer acting as a positive role model to reinforce pro-social behaviour. In the context of a prison, the worker's responses to institutionalized inequalities also give an opportunity to demonstrate a constructive use of authority. Indeed, as Williams (1996, p.128) points out: 'If counsellors fail to take proper account of inequality and injustice, they will become unable to form helpful relationships with angry and embittered clients, who will doubt their good faith.'

On the other hand, Chapman and Hough in their Home Office guide to effective practice comment that:

> Reasonableness, fairness and encouragement appear to engender in some probationers a sense of loyalty towards their supervising officers. This positive relationship can motivate an individual to enter into an alliance with the officer and participate in a process even if not convinced of its effectiveness. (Chapman and Hough 1998, p.58)

THE OFFENDER AS AGENT OF CHANGE

In order to enable the offender to get beyond the sense of being victimized, the feeling of being the recipient of experiences rather than the creator of them, the worker can be helped by client-centred methods aimed at promoting individual change. Both Motivational Interviewing and Brief Solution Focused Therapy fit this formula, being characterized by a belief in the possibility of positive change, determined by the client. These methods also have the advantage of being compatible with the reality of much contemporary professional work with offenders, namely that workers are unlikely to see their clients in prison more than once every few months. Brief therapy in particular was devised to fit with the fact that many clients only meet a therapist once. The emphasis in the following discussion of good practice is on the individual as the agent of change. This is not to ignore the need for change in the client's social circumstances, both inside and outside prison, and there may be times when the worker can address such problems. In working with offenders who are also victims, though, there is much to be said for focusing on how they can manage change for themselves.

MOTIVATIONAL INTERVIEWING

Motivational Interviewing has its origins in the field of addictive behaviours which, like offending behaviour, are often characterized by short-term gratification and long-term harm. Prochaska and DiClemente (1984) developed their theory of the cycle of change to explain how a person goes through different stages in the process of behavioural change. They subsequently refined their theory, moving from a 'cycle' to a 'spiral' to reflect the way people often relapse into the original behaviour before eventually maintaining the change (Chapman and Hough 1998). The stages they identify are:

- precontemplation (the offender does not consider the behaviour to be a problem)
- contemplation (the offender sees problems in the behaviour but is ambivalent about change)
- decision (the offender decides to change)
- action (the person takes action to change)
- maintenance (the person maintains the change against the risk of relapse)
- relapse (the person returns to the original behaviour).

The worker's role is to help the offender move through the stages, obviously aiming to arrest the process at 'maintenance'. The client's perceptions are crucial because the impulse to change must come from them. This fits with our earlier suggestion that violence arises largely from the way the offender perceives the situation. In their review of research into 'evidence based practice', Chapman and Hough (1998, p.58) note that: 'It is the offender's awareness which is critical not the worker's.' They also write that:

> Motivational interviewing avoids the authoritarian, confrontational style. It
> involves listening and acknowledging (though not colluding with) the valid-

ity of the individual's experiences and perspectives. The method stresses the importance of the worker's style in obtaining positive outcomes. (Chapman and Hough 1998, p.60)

One of the worker's first and primary tasks is careful listening. As well as using the notion of stages of change, the method identifies five factors necessary for constructive change:

- concern
- belief in the possibility of change
- knowledge of strategies for change
- self-esteem
- desire to change.

Initially the worker is listening for the client's 'self-motivational statements', which will reveal the extent to which these five factors are present. As a generalization, it can be said that clients who have also been victims are likely to lack self-esteem and belief in the possibility of change. This is true of Maurice:

> *W*: What else could you have done when Keith made you sleep downstairs?

> *M*: Well, what could I have done? I mean, there's nothing I can do, and his friend was laughing at me, and if I try to argue with him my words get all jumbled up.

The worker's next task is to target and build up the depleted areas, in Maurice's case self-esteem and belief in the possibility of change. The technique of positive reframing is particularly useful here. This involves drawing out the positive aspects of the offender's past behaviour, emphasizing their capacity for choice and control over what they do. Thus, the worker's response to Maurice's gloomy comment might be as follows:

> *W*: So you know enough about yourself to know you're better off avoiding arguments you're going to lose. And you didn't react when Keith's friend tried to provoke you by laughing at you. That shows you've got self-control and self-awareness.

The process of reframing should not mean ignoring a client's concerns or problems, but it can help to alter the way they perceive themselves and, by extension, their ability to influence adverse situations.

Careful listening will also reveal much about how the offender constructs and interprets situations. Although Chris has demonstrated a calmer, less aggressive attitude in the adult prison, he still perceives other men as a potential threat. After relating how he successfully defused a possible argument, he then adds, 'But if he'd raised a hand to me, I'd have been ready for him.' Other comments he makes, such as 'I mean, if you pulled a knife on me now I wouldn't be messing about with that anger management stuff', show that for Chris the danger of becoming a victim is still very real, and with that perception goes an increased risk of violence from him. His comments may show a reluctance to shed the macho self-respect which is an important part of his self-image. They may reflect an accurate grasp of the risks of life in prison. They may arise from the traumas of having been a victim. But they also reveal his continuing ambivalence about the possibility and desirability of change, despite his concern about the problem of violence, as shown by his changed behaviour. The worker needs to maintain in Chris a degree of concern, while still showing change to be possible.

Listening to the client's self-motivational statements is also useful for assessments of future risk. As with all risk assessments, the worker needs as much accurate information as possible. Without knowledge of the client's perceptions and attitudes though, the risk assessment will be static and mechanistic. Commentators such as Hudson (1996, p.155) have noted that in the 'new risk penality ... "non-legal factors" such as race, employment record, homelessness and single parentage ... are reintroduced as "risk factors".' In this way, actuarial risk assessment performs a 'labelling' function which may reinforce and entrench oppression, making it harder for people in the 'wrong' categories to change. As Tallant and Strachan (1995) have noted, it is important also to know how an offender 'frames' a situation, including their perception of likely gains and losses. Thus an offender like Chris, convinced of impending victimization, may well become riskily aggressive. Knowledge of the situations that the client is likely to confront, integral to the planning of supervision on post-release licence, must be matched by an awareness of the client's likely reactions.

BRIEF THERAPY

Brief Solution Focused Therapy also offers the worker a way to learn about how clients visualize their future behaviour. Again this is particularly useful for working with victims because it locates the offender as the person choosing and shaping their own destiny. The basis of this approach, summarized by George, Iveson and Ratner (1990), is that clients already possess the solution to their problems. In the case of violent offenders there will have been occasions when they settled conflicts without violence. The worker aims to focus on such occasions, looking at the solution not the problem. In Chris's case this is particularly relevant because, although he describes violence as a first resort for resolving conflict, he has in fact often settled conflicts peacefully. There is a difference between his rhetoric and his behaviour, as revealed in the following exchange:

C: I almost hit someone in the dinner queue yesterday.

W: So you sorted it out without hitting him?

C: Yeah, but he got me really riled.

W: What did you do?

C: I stopped and looked at the bloke, then I asked him what he was doing.

W: What else did you do?

C: I don't know really, well I thought, it's not worth it, he hasn't been here long, and I could see this mate of his he was trying to impress, so I just shrugged and let him get on with it.

W: Was that the end of it?

C: It was then, but the funny thing was that he came up to me later and said sorry and that he'd been out of order.

Chris's initial report of the incident emphasizes its potential for violence. The worker again uses a reframing technique to concentrate instead on the successful outcome, and takes care not to ask Chris for details of the original problem. It is the solution that is of interest, along with eliciting what Chris did. At other times, for example in assessing future risk, the brief therapist will ask the client what will be happening in future when they are successfully avoiding violence. Persistent questioning ('what else?' is a brief therapy catchphrase) will reveal the extent of the client's ability to visualize a non-violent future and will thus be informative for risk assessments. All the time the emphasis is on solutions and on developing the client's existing skills. This is especially useful for people who find it hard to envisage change or to see themselves as agents of change.

WORKING WITH SELF-HARMERS

Brief therapy's relevance for clients who cannot envisage change makes it useful for work with prisoners who may self-harm. Workers may be asked to contribute to prison self-harm procedures, but this should not replace ongoing contact with the client. In fact, anecdotal evidence from affected prisoners suggests that the protective procedures can sometimes aggravate the problem. The experience of being on a 24–hour watch is itself stressful and distressing. Liebling (1997) has suggested practical steps to reduce the risk of self-harm, such as ensuring that vulnerable people have their time occupied; that if possible they are not left socially isolated and that, because they may lack the ability to ask explicitly for help, careful attention is paid to what may appear to be medical or disciplinary problems. She based her observations on in-depth interviews with relevant prisoners who, she found, took time to disclose information and only did so 'when they finally felt that they were being believed' (Liebling 1997, p.198). This exemplifies the patience and skill needed to help such inmates. Liebling also refers to 'Beck's cognitive triad' (no reference given) of the self, the future and the environment, and how all three appear bleak to the prisoner who attempts suicide. Brief therapy's emphasis on the client's already having the skills to effect change, and on a detailed visualization of a more hopeful future, may help to shift the client's perceptions so that the self and the future, if not the environment, may not appear quite so bleak.

ACTION TO AVOID VICTIMIZATION

George *et al.* (1990, p.3–4) note that 'from a systemic point of view, if one significant person in a system begins to change, the rest of the system will have to change in relation to that person'. The problem with identifying the victim as the person who should change is the implication that the victim is somehow responsible for his problems. Yet in reality, inmates already take steps to avoid being victimized. For example, we mentioned earlier the role of bystanders when public conflicts escalate into violence. When Chris described the argument in the dinner queue he noted that the other man was trying to impress his friend, a factor which influenced Chris not to get drawn in further. For Chris this is particularly relevant because his offence occurred in front of a group of onlookers. It is important, therefore, to identify and praise this new restraint and to bear it in mind for future risk assessments. Edgar and O'Donnell's (1998) research into assaults in prison shows how certain behaviours by victims contributed to the assault upon them. Name-calling was an element in 21 of the 96 assaults they investigated; in 15 of the assaults the victim started the violence; involvement in the illicit prison economy increased the risk of being assaulted, as did disputes over access to shared resources. The researchers found that: 'in 3/4 of the assaults we studied the victim had made the attack more likely or had directly brought it about by his own actions' (Edgar and O'Donnell 1998, p.649).

Without falling into the trap of blaming the victim, it can be valuable for workers to help clients recognize any of their behaviours which may precipitate violence and to be aware of the emotional responses their clients provoke in them. For example, the worker may feel irritated by Maurice's self-pity, while with Chris there is a risk of getting drawn into confrontational arguments about his belief that violence is often justified. The way Maurice and Chris make the worker feel may be representative of the reactions they arouse in others. Giving them sensitive feedback may be a way to help them to reduce their chances of being victimized again.

Both Motivational Interviewing and Brief Solution Focused Therapy can be used to reveal the offender's perceptions and to assess their readiness and desire for change. If, in terms of the cycle of change, the person is at the 'decision', 'action' or 'maintenance' stage, then they may need help with strategies for change. Such strategies are often taught on offending behaviour programmes in prisons. These programmes usually share a cognitive behavioural basis: if you change the way the offender thinks in high-risk situations you can reduce the risk of violence. Anger management and thinking skills programmes recommend tactics such as stopping to think, assertiveness rather than aggression or passivity, and weighing up the long-term consequences before acting. Motivational Interviewing and Brief Therapy can be used to complement these programmes by preparing the client for them, through work on their motivation and by reinforcing the learning that is delivered.

Increasingly, the knowledge reviewed above is also being employed to make environmental changes in prisons. For example, induction groups in some prisons have been redesigned to give priority to showing young offenders constructive ways of coping with imprisonment and warn them about the ways in which attempts will be made to involve them in the illicit prison economy. Some prisons have developed anti-bullying strategies that are emphasized during new prisoners' induction programmes, which also highlight sources of help within the institution (Tattum 1997; Tattum and Herdman 1995).

CONCLUSION

There has not been space to go into much detail. Both Motivational Interviewing and Brief Therapy feature a number of techniques which can be found in the literature cited above. These methods focus on the client's own resources. It should be remembered that prison can be a brutal and brutalizing place and that many inmates face daunting social problems both inside and outside custodial institutions. Where the worker is able to improve the client's situation, this should be done. We hope to have set out some basic principles for good practice in individual work with prisoners who have also been victims. In summary:

- Be aware of macho behaviour codes in prison which endorse violence and abhor 'weakness'.
- Acknowledge that the roles of victim and aggressor are often interchangeable.
- Use influence appropriately in contact with prison authorities to improve conditions.
- Use basic counselling skills to improve trust and overcome resistance.
- Be authoritative, not authoritarian.
- Show pro-social behaviour in interactions with the client and with the institution.
- Discover offenders' perceptions and attitudes for more informed, complete risk assessment.
- Listen carefully to self-motivational statements to locate offenders on the cycle of change.
- Target intervention accordingly, for example, relapse prevention strategies for those at the 'maintenance' stage.
- Use positive reframing techniques to boost self-esteem and belief in the possibility of change.
- Concentrate on the solution, not the problem.
- Investigate clients' ability to envisage an offence-free future.
- Help the offender/victim to identify behaviours which precipitate violence against them.
- If the offender makes you angry, feed this back, sensitively and constructively, to heighten their awareness of reactions they provoke.
- As well as contributing to prison self-harm prevention procedures, use Brief Therapy techniques to help suicidal inmates to shift their perceptions.
- Use Motivational Interviewing and Brief Therapy to augment offending behaviour programmes by developing the client's motivation and by rehearsing the problem-solving skills taught on the courses.

REFERENCES

Anderson, E. (1997) 'Violence and the inner-city street code.' In J. McCord (ed) *Violence and Childhood in the Inner City*. Cambridge: Cambridge University Press.

Boyle, J. (1977) *A Sense of Freedom*. London: Pan.

Chapman, T. and Hough, M. (1998) *Evidence Based Practice*. London: HMSO.

Clark, D.A. (1994) 'Behavioural risk assessment: a methodology in practice I.' In N.K. Clark and G.M. Stephenson (eds) *Rights and Risks: the Application of Forensic Psychiatry*. Leicester: British Psychological Society.

Daly, M. and Wilson, M. (1988) *Homicide*. New York: De Gruyter.

Devlin, A. (1997) 'Offenders at school: links between school failure and aggressive behaviour.' In D. Tattum and G. Herbert (eds) *Bullying: Home, School and Community*. Chichester: Wiley.

Edgar, K. and O'Donnell. I. (1998) 'Assault in prison: the victim's contribution.' *British Journal of Criminology 38*, 4, 635–649.

Farrington, D.P. (1994) 'Human development and criminal careers.' In M. Maguire, R. Morgan and R. Reiner (eds) *The Oxford Handbook of Criminology*. Oxford: Clarendon Press.

Freud, S. (1908) *The Standard Edition of the Complete Psychological Works of Sigmund Freud, Volume 9*, edited by J. Strachey. London: Hogarth Press.

Gendreau, P. (1996) 'The principles of effective intervention with offenders.' In A. Harland (ed) *Choosing Correctional Options that Work*. Thousand Oaks CA: Sage.

George, E., Iveson, C. and Ratner, H. (1990) *Problem to Solution: Brief Therapy with Individuals and Families*. London: BT Press.

Hirschmann, D. (1996) 'Parole and the dangerous offender.' In N. Walker (ed) *Dangerous People*. London: Blackstone.

Hudson, B. (1996) *Understanding Justice*. Buckingham: Open University Press.

Knox, J. (1996) 'A prison perspective.' In K. Cavanagh and V.E. Cree (eds) *Working with Men: Feminism and Social Work*. London: Routledge.

Levi, M. (1994) 'Violent crime.' In M. Maguire, R. Morgan and R. Reiner (eds) *The Oxford Handbook of Criminology*. Oxford: Clarendon Press.

Liebling, A. (1997) 'Risk and prison suicide.' In H. Kemshall and J. Pritchard (eds) *Good Practice in Risk Assessment and Risk Management 2*. London: Jessica Kingsley Publishers.

Patrick, J.A. (1973) *A Glasgow Gang Observed*. London: Eyre Methuen.

Polk, M. (1994) 'Masculinity, honour and confrontational homicide.' In T. Newburn and E.A. Stanko (eds) *Just Boys Doing Business? Men, Masculinities and Crime*. London: Routledge.

Prins, H. (1995) *Offenders, Deviants or Patients?*, 2nd edn. London: Routledge.

Prochaska, J. and DiClemente, C. (1984) *The Transtheoretical Approach: Crossing Traditional Boundaries of Therapy*. Homewood: Dow Jones Irwin.

Rex, S. and Matravers, A. (1998) *Pro-social Modelling and Legitimacy*. Clarke Hall Day Conference. Cambridge: Institute of Criminology.

Siann, G. (1985) *Accounting for Aggression: Perspectives on Aggression and Violence*. London: George Allen and Unwin.

Sim, J. (1994a) 'Tougher than the rest? Men in prison.' In T. Newburn and E.A. Stanko (eds) *Just Boys Doing Business? Men, Masculinities and Crime*. London: Routledge.

Sim, J. (1994b) 'Reforming the penal wasteland? A critical review of the Woolf Report.' In E. Player and M. Jenkins (eds) *Prisons After Woolf: Reform through Riot*. London: Routledge.

Slaby, R. (1997) 'Psychological mediators of violence and urban youth.' In J. McCord (ed) *Violence and Childhood in the Inner City*. Cambridge: Cambridge University Press.

Storr, A. (1970) *Human Aggression*. Harmondsworth: Penguin.

Tallant, C. and Strachan, R. (1995) 'The importance of framing: a pragmatic approach to risk assessment.' *Probation Journal*, December, 202–207.

Tattum, D. (1997) 'Developing a programme to reduce bullying in young offenders' institutions.' In D. Tattum and G. Herbert (eds) *Bullying: Home, School and Community*. Chichester: Wiley.

Tattum, D. and Herdman, G. (1995) *Bullying: A Whole-Prison Response*. Cardiff: Cardiff Institute of Higher Education.

Toch, H. (1972) *Violent Men*. Harmondsworth: Penguin.

Toch, H. (1979) 'Perspectives on the offender.' In H. Toch (ed) *Psychology of Crime and Criminal Justice*. New York: Holt, Rinehart and Winston.

Williams, B. (1991) *Work with Prisoners*. Birmingham: Venture Press.

Williams, B. (1996) *Counselling in Criminal Justice*. Buckingham: Open University Press.

Williams, B. (1997) 'Rights versus risk: issues in work with prisoners.' In H. Kemshall and J. Pritchard (eds) *Good Practice in Risk Assessment and Risk Management 2*. London: Jessica Kingsley Publishers.

Wolfgang, M.E. and Ferracuti, F. (1967) *The Subculture of Violence*. London: Tavistock.

CHAPTER 14

Working with Victims of War

Ian Robbins

This chapter looks at working with victims of war and aims to give practitioners a way into working with this group of clients. This includes exploring the impact on civilians as well as combatants and looking at differing approaches to treatment, as well as presenting a model of working which evolved through the practice of working with elderly veterans of very distant wars. The same approach has also demonstrated its usefulness with civilian victims of war as well as combatants of more recent wars.

Mental health practitioners are likely to come into contact with survivors of warfare. This has been a century of warfare. There have been two world wars with massive loss of life and political turbulence. Zvi and Ugalde (1989) point out that in addition to this there have been numerous wars around the globe in Third World countries with over 160 wars since 1945 resulting in an estimated 22 million deaths and over three times that number injured. Many of these wars have involved conflict between a centralized power and a distinct ethnic or religious group. Dejarlais *et al.* (1995) estimated that in 1987 only 3 per cent of the conflicts were between nation states, whereas the bulk of the conflicts involved politically marginalized groups fighting against state governments. Increasingly civilians have become the casualties of war. During World War I it was estimated that civilians made up 5 per cent of the direct casualties but by World War II this had risen to 50 per cent. By the Vietnam War civilians made up 80 per cent of casualties and more recent estimates suggest that civilians account for over 90 per cent of casualties (UNICEF 1986). Alongside the physical injuries there may be considerable psychological damage both to those in the military and civilians caught up in warfare, many of whom may end up as refugees. There is a myth promulgated that psychological suffering which occurs as a result of war is a recent phenomenon and is the creation of a 'trauma industry'. It is helpful to take a historical perspective in order to dispel this myth.

HISTORICAL BACKGROUND

Shay (1987, 1994) points to evidence of the impact of battle as long ago as the Greek wars in Homer's work, but the earliest medical description was by Hammond, a Surgeon General in the American Civil War, who termed it 'nostalgia' (Hausman and Rioch 1967). The aetiology of the condition was unclear, with the emphasis being placed on absence from home, but it was distinguished from other conditions such as paralysis and insanity. The incidence rates of nostalgia were 2.3 to 3.3 cases per 1000 throughout the war. Hammond developed an approach to management of the condition by providing 'occupation for both the mind and the body ... soldiers placed in hospitals near their homes are always more liable to nostalgia than those who are inmates of hospitals situated in the midst of or in the vicinity of the Army to which they belong'.

Subsequently this was largely ignored, only to be rediscovered in later wars. Anderson (1966) has reported similar nostalgia casualty rates for the Franco-Prussian, Spanish-American and Boer wars although there is no evidence that there was any specific treatment of the condition. The high levels of killed and injured during the Russo-Japanese War of 1904–05 brought about awareness of psychiatric combat casualties and the beginning of rudimentary treatment (Anderson 1966).

With the large manpower loss during the course of World War I, a serious attempt at understanding the aetiology and development of treatment was made with a view to returning the casualties to duty. While initially regarding the problem as one of cowardice, the British and the French eventually classified the majority of psychiatric casualties as 'shell-shocked'. At the time it was speculated that brain damage had occurred as a consequence of a nearby explosion and therefore the diagnosis had an organic basis. This theory was fostered when some patients were found to have blood in their spinal fluid. However, casualties with similar symptoms to those in shell-shock but who had not been exposed to exploding shells were not always treated as sympathetically and were judged as cowardly or lacking 'moral fibre' (Moran 1945).

The British and the French armies differed in their treatment of psychiatric casualties. The British, particularly in the early years of the war, evacuated their casualties to psychiatric hospitals for conventional treatment in England. Whereas the treatment was relatively humane, the recovery rate was poor with few returning to duty. In contrast the French treated casualties at either forward or rearward units depending on their initial diagnosis. Those allocated to the forward units were generally classified as neurotic and received rather severe treatment in the form of painful muscular electric shocks, whereas those casualties diagnosed as psychotic were treated more humanely with an emphasis on retraining. The recovery rate for forward treatment was high, with 60–75 per cent of the patients being returned to active duty. It was established that the important factor was the location of the treatment facility rather than the treatment regime. Essentially the best results were obtained with brief therapy and respite near the combat zone, an outcome previously observed by Hammond in the American Civil War.

With the entry of the USA into World War I, Salmon (1919) developed a division-based psychiatric service after assessing the value of the French and British services. The overall theoretical rational was directed at treatment in forward settings within a military context together with an expectancy of returning to duty. The programme proved to be highly successful with a 65 per cent recovery rate which supported the British and French findings while still using a humane therapy. Furthermore the speculation of an organic basis for psychiatric casualties was gradually replaced by a more psychological one. These principles of forward treatment, rapidly applied with an expectation of return to duty, were reiterated in the 1922 Shell Shock Committee as being the most appropriate way to manage acute combat trauma.

With the start of World War II the programme previously established by Salmon failed to be implemented by the Americans until 1943 following the landings in North Africa. The American psychiatric casualty rate for the whole of World War II was 23 per cent of all medical evacuees. The poor provision of psychiatric services was clearly seen in the North African Campaign where 30 per cent of all the casualties were psychiatric, and only 3 per cent of the psychiatric casualties returned to duty. However, with the implementation of an effective psychiatric service a 70 per cent return to duty rate was established (Hausman and Rioch 1967). Similar improvements were made in the management of psychiatric casualties in the Italian Campaign. Following the Normandy landings both the British and American forces had established forward divisionally based treatment facilities for combat stress reactions with favourable treatment outcomes.

With the outbreak of war in Korea (1950) the effective psychiatric programme developed in World War II was rapidly instituted using the premises of proximity, immediacy and expectancy. Prior to implementation of forward treatment principles the extent of the problem was reflected in psychiatric casualty rates and return to duty rates similar to those in World War II. With the implementation of forward treatment sites for mild cases the casualty rates dropped to 6 per cent with a 65 per cent to 75 per cent return to duty rate.

The Vietnam War was thought to have caused a lower number of psychiatric casualties compared to World Wars I and II (Figley 1978). Estimates of psychiatric casualties range between 1 per cent and 5 per cent. DeFazio (1978) compared the psychiatric casualty rates of various wars. In World War II the rate was 101/1000, in Korea it was 37/1000, and in Vietnam only 12/1000. Originally these figures were thought to show that by the time of the Vietnam War the lessons had been learned; that the incidence of psychological disturbance was relatively low because of rotation of duty, lack of prolonged exposure to shelling, the impact of modern psychiatry, including the forward placement of psychiatric personnel. While the rate of acute combat stress reactions was thought to be very low during the Vietnam War there was an increasing awareness of the post war development of problems in combat veterans.

The Falklands War (1982) produced an apparently low rate of acute psychiatric casualties. Price (1984) estimated that 2 per cent of all casualties were psychiatric. However, Abraham (1984) has proposed that this is an underestimate and that 8 per cent of all casualties suffered from psychiatric problems. Subsequently O'Brien and Hughes (1991) found that 22 per cent of Falklands veterans whom they surveyed would have met the DSMIII criteria for post traumatic stress disorder (PTSD) although they were apparently functioning well in their military role (APA 1987).

CIVILIAN STUDIES

Case study

Mrs A was a successful professional from an affluent family when civil war engulfed the town in which she lived in Somalia. Life quickly became reduced to an exercise in survival. A few weeks after the civil war started her house was attacked and in the course of this she saw her husband shot in front of her. She was subsequently repeatedly raped and beaten and was eventually released with her wounded husband. She managed to make her way to the UK via Kenya. She now lives on benefits in a one-bedroom flat and was experiencing repeated intrusive thoughts and images, nightmares in which she re-enacted some of the experiences and prolonged periods of low mood with high levels of anxiety. Her self-esteem was particularly low and while she has asylum status her greatest fear is that she may die in the UK rather than her homeland.

Although there is a literature relating to the impact of war on men there is comparatively little work on the impact of war on women either acutely or in the long term. The experience of women is likely to have been very different to that of men. Until very recently women in the UK were not allowed to serve in branches of the armed services which involved direct combat and as civilians the pressures of dealing with maintaining family life in the context of bombing, rationing and enormous uncertainty were immense. In a descriptive study of general practice attendances Aubrey (1941) suggested that following direct exposure to air raids one-third of female patients as opposed to one-fifth of male patients showed signs of 'neurotic disorders'. Psychological symptoms were more likely in those experiencing damage to their homes as a consequence of the bombing or who did not possess a domestic air-raid shelter. Given the prohibitions of the time with regard to expression of weakness or emotion among men, these differences in observed levels of distress may not be surprising. The impact of bombing on civilian populations was reviewed by Janis (1951) who suggests that the psychological impact of bombing is directly proportional to the level of death and destruction and particularly related to the experience of seeing others dead or mutilated. The experience of a 'near miss' contributed greatly to the development of severe fear reactions as well as to higher levels of anxiety and depression, as did the loss of one's home.

More recently Murphy (1977) looked at Vietnamese civilians evacuated from battlefront areas, finding higher rates of psychological problems among women than men with increased rates of depression being notable. Similarly in a different context Lyons (1979) found higher levels of anxiety and greater vulnerability to stress in women in Belfast in comparison with men. A number of studies in Lebanon (see Farhood et al. 1993) have found that the loss of home and property was positively related to levels of psychological distress. Similarly a number of environmental problems arising as a consequence of warfare such as lack of sanitation, water and electricity, along with overcrowding and the number of children at home under 15 years of age were positively correlated with increased levels of depression among women. The absence of family members has been reported as a factor. McCubbin *et al.* (1974) looked at the families of servicemen who were either prisoners of war or missing in action, finding that their absence engendered high levels of anxiety, frustration and insecurity. The main problems described were loneliness, making important decisions alone and health concerns with 72 per cent of women reporting the lack of their husband's companionship as being particularly difficult to cope with.

LONGER TERM IMPACT OF WAR TRAUMA

Most of the research examining the impact of traumatic experiences has a relatively short time scale although there have been some exceptions. Op den Velde *et al.* (1990) found that World War II resistance veterans were more likely to retire early and to be in receipt of a disability pension. They also found that some veterans having had PTSD symptoms initially then had a symptom-free period before a re-emergence of symptoms in later life. Hovens *et al.* (1994) looked at a sample of 660 male and 144 female Dutch resistance fighters and found that 27 per cent of men and 20 per cent of women met the criteria for a diagnosis of PTSD. Those veterans with PTSD were more likely to score higher on measures of trait anxiety and depression than non-PTSD veterans.

A number of studies have looked at the impact of severely traumatic experiences among survivors of concentration camps during the Holocaust (Chodoff 1962; Eitinger 1961) where high levels of chronic psychiatric symptoms were reported. More recently Kuch and Cox (1992) reported that 52 per cent of concentration camp survivors and 65 per cent of a sub group who had been in Auschwitz met the criteria for a current diagnosis of PTSD. They point to the clear role of severity of the traumatic experience in continued psychopathology. Mazor *et al.* (1990) in a study involving Holocaust survivors suggest that while the majority of those interviewed have got on with their lives and had a similar range of achievements to those who did not experience the Holocaust, they have had to deal with their past in terms of intrusive memories and emotions on a continual basis. For many it was only as they entered their fifties that they started to open up to their experiences and try to give some meaning to their lives.

One of the first studies to look at the continuing impact of war on military populations was carried out by Futterman and Pumpian-Mindlin (1951). In a five year follow up of 200 combat veterans they found a 10 per cent rate of PTSD type symptoms. They pointed to the fact that they were still seeing people who were presenting for the first time with problems five years after the end of the war. In 1955 Brill and Beebe reported a five- to six-year follow-up of soldiers who had experienced breakdowns. They found that 8 per cent remained severely disabled while a further 20 per cent had moderate levels of disability. They noted more severe reactions occurred in those whose breakdowns occurred during combat and felt that issues such as compensation had little impact on presentation. This was in sharp contrast to Kalinowsky (1950) who had previously emphasized the role of pensions, compensation and other forms of 'secondary gain' in symptom maintenance.

Archibald and Tuddenham (1965) in a 20-year follow-up of World War II and Korean War veterans found significant effects of combat stress reactions. They also found an increasing number of new patients who were seeking treatment for war-related neuroses. They suggested that these presentations were the result of traumatic stress, the effects of which had remained latent until reactivated by the process of ageing. They concluded: 'The impact of the war has not been fully realised two decades after its termination. The combat fatigue syndrome which was expected to vanish with time has proved to be chronic if not irreversible.'

Subsequently Hamilton and Canteen (1987) looked at 32 World War II veterans who had seen heavy combat. They found that 16 per cent of these subjects met the criteria for a diagnosis of PTSD. Symptoms of PTSD are more frequent in Vietnam veterans than Korean or World War II veterans, with 46.2 per cent of the Vietnam group scored within the PTSD range as compared to 30 per cent of the Korean group and 18.5 per cent of the World War II veterans. When the rates of problems were examined for veterans who had been prisoners of war (POWs) they found no significant differences in PTSD rates between the three groups which were around the 50 per cent level (Blake *et al.* 1990).

There have been numerous studies examining the long term impact of being a prisoner of war (Zeiss and Dickman 1989; Sutker, Allain and Winstead 1990; Speed *et al.* 1989) all of which have found high lifetime rates of PTSD as well as higher rates of current psychopathology compared to non-prisoner veterans. The strongest predictors of PTSD were proportion of body weight lost and the experience of torture during captivity. They suggested that the persistence of symptoms for so many years is a reflection of the severity of the trauma. Few studies have looked at how veterans cope with traumatic memories and subsequent life events. An exception to this is the work of Fairbank *et al.* (1981) who compared former POWs of World War II with chronic PTSD with those without PTSD and a non-POW veterans group on measures of general psychological functioning, appraisal and coping. Appraisal and coping were assessed under two stressor conditions: memories of war and captivity experiences and recent negative life events. They found that ex-POWs with PTSD had poorer general psychological functioning, significantly less control over intrusive memories and more frequent use of self-isolation, wishful thinking, self-blame and social support in order to cope with the memories than did the other two groups. Differences were not so marked for coping with recent negative life events.

TREATMENT APPROACHES
Immediate Treatments

The assumption is often made that immediate interventions have more likelihood of success but few controlled studies exist. Rose and Bisson (1998) in a systematic review of early intervention studies for a variety of traumas found only six randomized controlled trials and concluded that there was no evidence to support the assumption that early intervention including debriefing approaches was effective or at least benign in their effects.

Immediate treatments for combatants are governed by the principles of proximity, immediacy and expectancy with treatment being offered as close to the fighting as possible, as soon after the onset of problems as is practical and with an expectation of being able to return to duty. Soldiers whose problems cannot be managed with rest, food, etc. at their unit level are treated by field psychiatric teams. They are given rest, allowed to ventilate their feelings and are encouraged to retain their military role. As recovery occurs they take up more military duties. During the Gulf War, Gillham and Robbins (1993) looked at integrating treatment models into the framework of proximity, immediacy and expectancy. Using both Cognitive Behavioural and Cognitive Analytic Therapy they showed how therapeutic principles could be successfully integrated into the framework. Work by Solomon and Benbenishty (1986) has demonstrated the effectiveness of these principles with Israeli soldiers.

There have been attempts to evaluate the impact of group debriefing in ameliorating the impact of trauma but as yet there are no controlled trials. Deahl et al. (1994) looked at the impact of debriefing in body handlers during the Gulf War. For operational reasons two groups of body handlers were going to different locations. One group received debriefing while the other did not. Psychological problems were high in both groups with no significant effect of debriefing being discernible.

Chronic or long-term problems

Ochberg (1995) has described a number of components of post-traumatic therapy. This starts with an educational component and includes sharing books and articles, reviewing current knowledge, teaching about psychophysiology in order to understand the stress response, discussing responsibilities under civil and criminal law and introducing the fundamentals of holistic health. At the heart of most approaches to the treatment of trauma is the disclosure of the traumatic experiences. Ochberg (1995) suggests that treatment is never complete if the clients have not disclosed the details of their trauma. He suggests that people who suffer 'victimization' or PTSD are still captured by their trauma histories and are unable to recollect without fear of overwhelming emotions. They also recollect when they are unprepared to do so. The purpose of recounting the trauma in therapy is 'to revisit the scene of the terror and horror and, in doing so remove the grip of the terror and horror'. Ochberg emphasizes the importance of the presence of the therapist which transforms the process from merely being cathartic to a partnership in survival. It is this partnership which enables the painful nature of the process to be endured.

Chung (1993) has suggested that the primary requirement of a treatment programme is the integration of one's understanding of the meaning of a trauma with current symptoms and life events. Krell (1985) used tape recordings of disclosure of traumatic experiences to do this in sessions to help child survivors of the Holocaust to integrate their experiences into a whole. Those who were unable to relate their stories often continued to suffer psychologically. This process of integration is more than simply abreaction. To integrate needs confrontation of the experience, in itself a painful process, and requires reprocessing of the emotions associated with it to allow reconstruction of a continuous narrative life story. This process of reconstruction has to continue until the client can withstand the experience.

An example of this process has been described by Mollica (1987) who discusses the central role of the 'trauma story' in treatment of PTSD among refugees from the war in Indochina. He suggests that once the patient is willing to tell the trauma story it opens up the possibility of changing previous interpretations of events. Previous feelings of helplessness and hopelessness can be reduced and a new story which is less rigid and fixed may be constructed which allows the possibility of connecting survivorship in the present with having overcome the events of the past. Bleich *et al.* (1986) have also discussed recounting of events as a corrective experience. They point to its dramatic impact but recognize that the process may be extremely distressing. Patients may feel that they are about to be overwhelmed by the experience but in talking they realize that they can undergo the experience without falling apart.

A number of authors such as Cienfuegos and Monelli (1983) and Agger and Jensen (1990) discuss the role of testimony in the treatment of torture survivors. In addition to recounting the trauma story their method allows for the channelling of rage and anger into some form of indictment. As a consequence of this they feel that their client develops a better understanding of what has happened to them through integration of fragmentary experiences into their life history. They also suggest that because the experience of suffering has been symbolized in a different form, in this case a written statement whose importance was recognized by the therapist, the need to express the suffering through somatization disappears.

THE PRESENT TREATMENT MODEL

The present approach to treatment of the effects of war trauma has been described by Robbins (1997). Its development was informed by the literature on helping Holocaust survivors or treating the results of more recent traumas and was inductively developed in the course of working with World War II veterans. It has subsequently been applied to survivors of more recent conflicts both military and civilian.

The extent of the distress and the nature of some of the traumatic memories have the power to be overwhelming for the therapist. It is possible to feel helpless in the face of such intensity of emotion. A simple model was needed to enable the therapist to cope with the level of emotion expressed by the client as well as their own responses. Without a framework within which to work it is difficult to keep a clear direction in working through some of the experiences. The model has as an overall aim the reduction of PTSD symptoms, especially intrusion, and the development of symbolic integration of the trauma experience into the overall life experience. It is based on principles embodied in cognitive behavioural methods and constructing a trauma story and is in keeping with the approach of Herman (1992) who has suggested that treatment has a number of stages:

- developing a sense of emotional safety
- remembrance and mourning

* reconnection to the world.

The model has a number of aims similar to those identified by Harvey (1996):

* to gain authority over the remembering process
* to integrate memory with affective states
* to build up tolerance for affective states
* to develop mastery over symptoms, especially hyperarousal
* to rebuild self-esteem and self-cohesion
* to give the trauma experience some meaning.

The current treatment model consists of five phases:

1. *Assessment of the nature of the problems* is made and the extent to which war experience has been a salient factor in the development of the current problems. Discussion of the treatment approach and the emotional 'costs' occurs. Full information is given before treatment outset to enable the client to make informed treatment choices and to retain a sense of control.

2. *Disclosure of events.* This is the beginning of the construction of the trauma story and is carried out in great detail occurring in two phases. Initially going through events to gain an overall picture of what happened followed by a more detailed review of events clarifying any confusion and identifying dysfunctional cognitions, such as irrational self blame, and the emotions associated with them.

3. *Exploration of cognitions and emotions associated with events.* This is carried out initially following a process of negotiation to identify specific issues for the individual which were referred to as themes for ease of working. The link between past events and current thoughts and feelings and their impact on behaviour is established.

4. *Change strategies.* Behaviours arising from the cognitions and emotions and the coping mechanisms used are examined and the potential for change in these areas is explored and implemented. This can involve anything from opening up communication with close relatives to anxiety management methods. Issues surrounding regaining control are central to this phase.

5. *Termination.* This phase is only partly about the ending of treatment and also involves the client assuming responsibility for planning for the future. Issues in ending treatment, including the sense of loss which this brings about, are explored and issues around future contact and follow-up are examined.

Case study

Mr B is a 74-year-old married man with four daughters. Three years prior to treatment he had been forced to retire as a consequence of the recession. Before his retirement he had a successful career as a self-employed chartered surveyor. In December 1941, while an NCO in the Royal Artillery, Mr B was sent to the beleaguered island of Singapore. In February 1942 the island fell and he was taken prisoner by the Japanese and imprisoned in Changi jail. The jail was grossly overcrowded, with poor sanitation and rife with disease. During his captivity he suffered from dysentery, beriberi, malaria, hepatitis and diphtheria and lost 53 per cent of his body weight. He also had his jaw broken with the butt of a rifle by a guard and needed surgery while in the camp. This was carried out in primitive conditions and resulted in septicaemia and osteomyelitis. He was liberated in 1945 and returned to the UK.

He presented for psychological help because he was plagued for many years by intrusive thoughts and images of life in the prison camp. He describes the intrusive thoughts and images as being qualitatively unlike memories in that they were present most of the time and he was experiencing them rather than recollecting them. The experiences in the camp had been compounded by the treatment which he and other Far East prisoners of war had received from the British government. There was a perception that the fall of Singapore had been an embarrassment to the government and consequently that period of history was simply being conveniently forgotten. The anger which this engendered contributed to nihilistic feelings which found their expression in thoughts of self harm. While he had experienced a high level of psychological problems throughout the post war period they had intensified since his retirement.

In approaching treatment the main motivation for Mr A was a desperation to be able to live his life more fully and to do more than merely exist tolerating the intrusive experiences. At the same time he was worried about his ability to cope with sharing the damaging experiences with a therapist without disintegration as well as the potential of his experiences to damage the therapist. Treatment which was carried out over a four-month period was based on the current model and focused on emotional processing of the prison camp experiences and understanding the post-war adaptation problems. On conclusion of the treatment he described the main benefit in terms of a change in the level of intrusion. The intrusive experiences were no longer present for much of the time. When they were present they were more like 'ordinary' memories and responded differently. At six-month and nine-month follow-ups he was still reporting improvement along with a reduction in the nihilism. He had also stopped thinking about harming himself. At more recent contact by telephone for the 50th anniversary of VJ day he confirmed that the treatment gains have remained.

Robbins (1997) discusses the use of this approach with a cohort of World War II veterans. A number of issues emerged as important during the course of therapy with this group:

1. *The fear of disintegration.* The clients seen felt that they had been holding themselves together, partly through refusing to talk about their experiences at all. There was a general reluctance to approach treatment because of a belief that if they started talking about their experiences they would fall apart completely and be unable to regain control again. Krystal (1975) has pointed to the importance of therapy in increasing clients' tolerance of their own emotions.

2. *Corrosive memories.* The fear of disintegration was partly fuelled by the feeling that the memories were so damaging that not only would talking about them damage the client, but it would also affect the therapist. Throughout the treatment process there was concern expressed about the therapist having to listen to the things being talked about. The memories were perceived as having a corrosive quality which could eat through attempts to block them out and it was this feeling which had eventually driven clients to seek help.

3. *The qualitative difference in the memories.* These are distinguished by the fact that they do not change but instead return in primary format each time and do not fade with the passing of time. These qualities of memories have been discussed by Horowitz (1986) in the context of diverse severe traumas.

4. *Inability to talk with family members and friends.* Most of the clients had been unable to talk with their immediate family about their war experiences. On the few occasions they did attempt it the result was usually in terms of platitudes rather than real discussion. Danielli (1985) has observed similar problems in Holocaust survivors being able to talk about their experiences with their own families.

5. *A sense of guilt about survival and the things done in the course of survival.* There was also intense guilt about the gratuitous killing and other actions which in the heat of battle seemed normal or were exciting but which in retrospect were seen to be immoral or criminal. This problem has also been observed by Elder and Clipp (1988) in the context of World War II veterans and Danielli (1988) with Holocaust survivors.

6. *The impact of ageing and loss of status* which had often led to a sense of helplessness. This was reinforced by increasing infirmity and for many who had been POWs had reawakened emotions associated with their captivity experience. This has also been observed by Elder and Clipp (1988) in the context of veterans of World War II.

7. *Anger.* There is often intense anger associated with events of the past and in particular the behaviour of the enemy. For many however the anger has become attached to the way in which the government has responded both to their needs and to the countries with which they were previously at war. Williams (1988) has discussed the way in

which soldiers' anger may be displaced from the enemy and onto governments. In many cases the feelings of worthlessness which have occurred with increasing age and frailty have evoked similar feelings brought about by war experience.

8. *It was the best of times and the worst of times.* For some the war contained some of their best experiences as well as the worst. They find that thinking about one will bring to mind the other. This gave a sense that the traumatic memories were contaminating both the memories of the past as well as their present existence.

9. *War traumas are not homogeneous.* It is important to recognize this heterogeneity both in terms of the original experience and subsequent adaptation.

Working with victims of more recent wars has found many of the same factors still to be salient. Similarly working as a therapist with war related problems raises a number of issues for the therapist. There is a need for experienced therapists, with multiple skills in areas such as cognitive behaviour therapy, anxiety management, working with older adults, working with interpreters, etc. who are happy to incorporate treatment methods into the model as client need dictates. Therapists need to be able to set limited and achievable goals for their therapy and should not try to address every problem that exists. While experience of being in the armed services or working in civil wars or refugee situations is useful it is not essential, although it is essential to have knowledge of the period of history and the events which the clients in which may have been involved. It is important that therapists are willing to learn from their clients about the nature of their experiences.

The intensity of the experience of conducting treatment is such that importance of debriefing and good supervision for therapists cannot be overemphasized. The intensity of emotional distress expressed can take therapists by surprise given expectations which may exist because of the age of the patients and the length of time since the trauma. It is extremely distressing to watch elderly men still being acutely tortured by events which occurred over half a century ago or to ask a refugee to relive a recent rape and torture or the loss of their families. Therapists need an awareness of transference and countertransference issues irrespective of their underlying therapeutic orientation. A number of clients raised the issue of therapist gender and stated that they felt they would not have been able to go through treatment with a female therapist. Equally many clients may have similar reservations about working with male therapists. Making it possible for the client to have choice in terms of therapist gender would seem to be more important than gender per se.

Discussion

The model of treatment described is at a stage of definition and description but even so has begun to demonstrate its effectiveness. The majority of those treated with this approach have shown a considerable reduction in symptoms and have felt themselves to have been helped. All of those who have experienced benefits from the treatment have discussed the qualitative changes in their memories. The experiences of those who have taken part in the treatment are qualitatively different. They distinguish between the 'normal memories' and the 'traumatic memories' in terms of their intensity and their ability to continue to damage. The damaging nature of these experiences and the belief in their ability to continue to damage are central to both the need for treatment and the reluctance to seek it. The intrusiveness and unchanging quality of some of these memories, which are experienced as distressing, are what defines them. The role of psychological factors such as intrusion and avoidance is important. Intrusive experiences of the war were strongly related to current psychopathology and levels of distress. Many of the clients had been practising active avoidance of war-related stimuli. This is in keeping with the work of McFarlane (1992) and Creamer, Burgess and Pattison (1992) who have pointed to the role of intrusion and avoidance in the development of trauma-related psychopathology. Their work was carried out fairly soon after traumatic incidents. What is surprising is the relatively enduring nature of intrusive memories.

The reticence of World War II veterans to seek help is very similar to Holocaust survivors (Danielli 1988; Ehrlich 1988) or to more recent refugees (Van der Veer 1992). It has been suggested by Zarit (1980) that when the offer of therapy is associated with other help such as physical treatments, pensions, housing, etc. survivors are more likely to avail themselves of the opportunity. In the UK the Holocaust Survivors Centre is associated with but separate from Shalvata a Jewish mental health facility. As a facility it offers far more than therapy, acting as a social centre and focus for survivors' lives. Increasingly survivors make use of therapy once they have been able to develop trust in the centre. Hassan (1995) feels that offering psychological therapy alone to this group would have a poor response. Many refugees are also reticent about seeking therapy. This may be in part because there is a stigma attached to mental illness, but may also relate to a lack of a tradition of formalized psychological therapy in their home country. A number however are reticent because they may have experienced torture during which health professionals played a part, a factor which traumatic stress services have to acknowledge in offering treatment.

Working with war trauma is painful for therapists. It involves exposure to aspects of human behaviour about which most people prefer not to know. It also involves being exposed to high levels of emotional pain in clients whose natural inclination is to want to try to bury the experience. Treatment approaches initially seem counter-intuitive and may cause clients feel worse to start with. The combination of these factors can make the whole process of working with this client group overwhelming. There is a lot of evidence that without help some survivors of warfare are unable to reconstruct their lives. The experience of the war can live on and affect their relationships with their families and communities. The true personal, social and economic consequences of warfare have not been fully realized but treatment at least offers the possibility of minimizing some of them.

REFERENCES

Abraham, P. (1984) 'Addendum to article by Price H.H. (1984) "The Falklands: the rate of British combat casualties compared to recent American wars".' *Journal of Royal Army Medical Corps 130*, 109–113.

Agger, I. and Jensen, S.B. (1990) 'Testimony as ritual and evidence in psychotherapy for political refugees.' *Journal of Traumatic Stress 3*, 115–130.

American Psychiatric Association (APA) (1987) Diagnostic and Statistical Manual of Mental Disorders. Third Edition. Washington: APA.

Anderson, R.S. (1966) *Neuropsychiatry in WWII. Vol 1*. Washington: Office of Surgeon General.

Archibald, H.C. and Tudenham, R.D. (1965) 'Persistent stress reactions after combat: a 20-year follow-up.' *Archives of General Psychiatry 12*, 475–481.

Aubrey, L. (1941) 'Incidence of neurosis in England under war conditions.' *Lancet 2*, 175–183.

Blake, D.D., Keane, T.M., Wine, P.R., Mora, C., Taylor, K.L. and Lyons, J.A. (1990) 'Prevalence of PTSD symptoms in combat veterans seeking medical treatment.' *Journal of Traumatic Stress 3*, 1, 15–27.

Bleich, A., Garb, M. and Kottler, M. (1986) 'Treatment of prolonged combat reactions.' *British Journal of Psychiatry 148*, 493–496.

Brill, N. and Beebe, G. (1955) *A Follow-up Study of War Neuroses*, Veterans Administration Medical Monograph no. 01571071. Washington DC: US Government Printing Office.

Chodoff, P. (1962) 'Late effects of the concentration camp syndrome.' *Archives of General Psychiatry 8*, 323–333.

Chung, M.C. (1993) 'Understanding post-traumatic stress. A biographical account.' *BPS Psychotherapy Section Newsletter 14*, 21–29.

Cienfuegos, A.J. and Monelli, C. (1983) 'The testimony of repression as a therapeutic instrument.' *American Journal of Orthopsychiatry 53*, 43–51.

Creamer, M., Burgess, P. and Pattison, P. (1992) 'Reaction to trauma: a cognitive processing model.' *Journal of Abnormal Psychology 101*, 3, 452–459.

Danielli, Y. (1985) 'The treatment and prevention of long term effects and inter-generational transmission of victimization.' In C.R. Figley (ed) *Trauma and Its Wake*. New York: Brunner-Mazel.

Danielli, Y. (1988) 'Confronting the unimaginable. Psychotherapists reactions to victims of the Nazi holocaust.' In J. Wilson, Z. Harel and B. Kahana (eds) *Human Adaptation to Severe Stress: From the Holocaust to Vietnam*. New York: Plenum.

Deahl, M.P., Gillham, A.B., Thomas, J., Searle, M.M. and Srinivasan, M. (1994) 'Psychological sequelae following the Gulf War: factors associated with subsequent morbidity and the effectiveness of psychological debriefing.' *British Journal of Psychiatry 165*, 1, 60–65.

DeFazio, V.J. (1978) 'Dynamic perspectives on the nature and effects of combat stress.' In C.R. Figley *Stress Disorders Amongst Vietnam Veterans: Theory, Research and Treatment*. New York: Brunner-Mazel.

Dejarlais, R., Eisenberg, L., Good, B. and Kleinman, A. (1995) *World Mental Health. Problems and Priorities in Low Income Countries*. New York: Oxford University Press.

Ehrlich, P. (1988) 'Treatment issues in the psychotherapy of Holocaust survivors.' In J. Wilson, Z. Harel and B. Kahana (eds) *Human Adaptation to Severe Stress: From the Holocaust to Vietnam*. New York: Plenum.

Eitinger, L. (1961) 'Pathology of the concentration camp syndrome.' *Archives of General Psychiatry 5*, 371–379.

Elder, G.H. and Clipp, E.C. (1988) 'Combat experience, comradeship and psychological health.' In J. Wilson, Z. Harel and BKahana (eds) *Human Adaptation to Severe Stress: From the Holocaust to Vietnam.* New York: Plenum.

Fairbank, J.A., Langley, K., Jarvie, G.J. and Keane, T.M. (1981) 'A selected bibliography on PTSD in Vietnam veterans.' *Professional Psychology 12,* 578–586.

Farhood, L., Zurayk, H., Chay, M., Saadeh, R., Meshefedjian, G. and Sidami, T. (1993) 'The impact of the war on the physical and mental health of the family: the Lebanese experience.' *Social Science and Medicine 36,* 12, 1155–1167.

Figley, C.R. (1978) *Stress Disorders Amongst Vietnam Veterans: Theory, Research and Treatment.* New York: Brunner-Mazel.

Futterman, S. and Pumpian-Mindlin, E. (1951) 'Traumatic war neurosis five years later.' *American Journal of Psychiatry 108,* 401–408.

Gillham, A.B. and Robbins, I. (1993) 'Brief therapy in a Battleshock Recovery Unit: three case studies.' *Journal of the Royal Army Medical Corps 139,* 58–60.

Hamilton, J.D. and Canteen, W. (1987) 'Post-traumatic stress disorder in World War II naval veterans.' *Hospital and Community Psychiatry 38,* 2, 197–199.

Harvey, M.R. (1996) 'An ecological view of psychological trauma and trauma recovery.' *Journal of Traumatic Stress 9,* 1, 3–24.

Hassan, J. (1985) 'Working with elderly survivors.' Paper presented to the European Colloquium on Therapeutic Work with Older People, University of Stirling.

Hausman, W. and Rioch, D. (1967) 'Military psychiatry.' *Archives of General Psychiatry 16,* 727–739.

Herman, J.L. (1992) *Trauma and Recovery.* New York: Basic Books.

Horowitz, M.J. (1986) 'Stress response syndromes: A review of post-traumatic and adjustment disorders.' *Hospital and Community Psychiatry 37,* 241–249.

Hovens, J.E., Falger, P.R.J., Op den velde, W., Meijer, P., de Groen, J.H.M. and van Dunn, H. (1994) 'A self-rating scale for the assessment of post traumatic stress disorder in Dutch resistance veterans of WWII.' *American Journal of Epidemiology 116,* 123–140.

Janis, I. (1951) *Air War and Emotional Stress: Psychological Studies of Bombing and Civilian Defence.* New York: McGraw-Hill.

Kalinowsky, L.B. (1950) 'Problems of war neuroses in light of experiences in other countries.' *American Journal of Psychiatry 107,* 340–346.

Krell, R. (1985) 'Therapeutic value of documenting child survivors.' *Journal of the American Academy of Child Psychiatry 24,* 4, 397–400.

Krystal, H. (1975) 'Affect tolerance.' *Annals of Psychoanalysis 3,* 241–249.

Kuch, K. and Cox, B.J. (1992) 'Symptoms of PTSD in 124 survivors of the holocaust.' *American Journal of Psychiatry 149,* 3, 337–340.

Lyons, H.A. (1979) 'Civil violence: the psychological aspects.' *Journal of Psychosomatic Research 23,* 373–393.

McCubbin, H.I., Dahl, B.B., Metres, P.J., Hunter, E.J. and Plag, J.A. (eds) (1974) Family separation and reunion: Families of prisoners of war and servicemen missing in action. Catalogue no: D-206.21.74-70. Washington DC: US Government Printing Office.

McCubbin, H. and Figley, C.R. (1983) *Stress and the Family.* New York: Brunner-Mazel.

McFarlane, A.C. (1992) 'Avoidance and intrusion in post-traumatic stress disorder.' *Journal of Nervous and Mental Diseases 180,* 7, 439–445.

Mazor, A., Gampel, Y., Enright, R.D. and Orenstein, R. (1990) 'Holocaust survivors: coping with post traumatic memories in childhood and 40 years later.' *Journal of Traumatic Stress 3,* 1, 1–14.

Mollica, R.M. (1987) 'The trauma story: the psychiatric care of refugee survivors of violence and torture.' In F.M. Ochberg (ed) *Post Traumatic Therapy and the Victims*. New York: Bruner-Mazel.

Moran, L. (1945) *The Anatomy of Courage*. London: Constable.

Murphy, J. (1977) 'War stress and civilian Vietnamese: a study of psychological effects.' *Acta Psychiatrica Scandanavia 56*, 92–108.

O'Brien, L.S. and Hughes, S.J. (1991) 'Symptoms of post-traumatic stress disorder in Falklands veterans five years after the conflict.' *British Journal of Psychiatry 159*, 135–141.

Ochberg, F.M. (1995) 'Post traumatic therapy.' In G.S. Everly and J.M. Lating (eds) *Psychotraumatology*. New York: Plenum.

Op den Velde, W., Falger, P.R.J., de Groen, J.H.M., van Duijn, H., Hovens, J.E., Meijer, P., Soons, M. and Schouten, E.G.W. (1990) 'Current psychiatric complaints of Dutch resistance veterans from WWII.' *Journal of Traumatic Stress 3*, 351–358.

Price, H.H. (1984) 'The Falklands: the rate of British combat casualties compared to recent American wars.' *Journal of the Royal Army Medical Corps 130*, 109–113.

Robbins, I. (1997) 'Treatment of war trauma in World War Two veterans.' In L. Hunt, M. Marshall and C. Rowlings (eds) *Past Trauma in Late Life: European Perspectives on Therapeutic Work with Older People*. London: Jessica Kingsley Publishers.

Rose, S. and Bisson, J. (1998) 'Brief early psychological interventions following trauma: a systematic review of the literature.' *Journal of Traumatic Stress 11*, 4, 697–710.

Salmon, T.W. (1919) 'The war neuroses and their lesson.' *New York State Journal of Medicine 59*, 993–994.

Shay, J. (1987) 'Learning about combat stress from Homer's Iliad.' *Journal of Traumatic Stress 4*, 4, 561–579.

Solomon, Z. and Benbenishty, R. (1986) 'The role of proximity, immediacy and expectancy in frontline treatment of combat stress reaction among Israelis in the Lebanon war.' *American Journal of Psychiatry 143*, 613–617.

Speed, N., Engdahl, B., Schwartz, J. and Eberly, R. (1989) 'Posttraumatic stress disorder as a consequence of the POW experience.' *The Journal of Nervous and Mental Disease 177*, 3, 147–153.

Sutker, P.B., Allain, A.N. and Winstead, D.K. (1993) 'Psychopathology and psychiatric diagnoses of World War II Pacific theatre prisoner of war survivors and combat veterans.' *American Journal of Psychiatry 150*, 2, 240–245.

UNICEF (1986) *Children in Situations of Armed Conflict*. E/ICEF.CRP.2. New York: UNICEF.

Van der Veer, G. (1992) *Counselling and Therapy with Refugees*. Chichester: Wiley.

Williams, T. (1988) 'The diagnosis of survivor guilt.' In J. Wilson, Z. Harel and B. Kahana (eds) *Human Adaptation to Severe Stress: From the Holocaust to Vietnam*. New York: Plenum.

Zeiss, R.A. and Dickman, H.R. (1989) 'PTSD 40 years later: incidence and person-situation correlates in former POWs.' *Journal of Clinical Psychology 45*, 1, 80–87.

Zarit, S. (1980) *Ageing and Mental Disorders*. New York: Free Press.

Zvi, A. and Ugalde, A. (1989) 'Towards an epidemiology of political violence in the third world.' *Social Science and Medicine 28*, 633–642.

CHAPTER 15

Working with the Aftermath of Violent Political Division

Marie Smyth

INTRODUCTION

This chapter is concerned with a particular form of violence, that of armed conflict and its aftermath. Northern Ireland has an ongoing recent experience of such conflict – locally referred to as the Troubles – since 1969. Since then, over 3600 people have been killed as a result, 117 of them since the ceasefires of 1994 (Fay, Morrissey and Smyth 1999a). Over 53 per cent of those killed have been civilians, British security forces account for over 16 per cent of the total, local security forces for almost 15 per cent, Republican paramilitaries for 10 per cent and Loyalist paramilitaries for just over 3 per cent (Fay, Morrissey and Smyth 1999a). Those killed were overwhelmingly male (91.1%) and disproportionately Catholic (43%), with Protestants accounting for 30 per cent of those killed and those from outside Northern Ireland accounting for 18 per cent (Fay, Morrissey and Smyth 1999a). This is in spite of the fact that Republican paramilitaries were responsible for 56 per cent of all deaths. Loyalist paramilitaries are responsible for 27 per cent and the security forces for 11 per cent (Fay, Morrissey and Smyth 1999a). The official figure (Northern Ireland Office 1999) of 40,000 injuries is likely to be an under-representation of the true picture since this figure does not include injuries that occurred outside Northern Ireland and not all injuries will have been reported.

These deaths and injuries are not evenly distributed across the population. Some of those killed have been citizens of Britain, the Republic of Ireland or other countries. Within Northern Ireland, the areas worst affected in terms of deaths lie within north and west Belfast, the border regions and Derry Londonderry City. The average death rate for Northern Ireland overall is 2.2 per thousand, but in some of these communities the death rate is five times that figure (Fay *et al.* 1999b) (See Figure 15.1).

1 Carrickfergus
2 Newtownabbey
3 Castlereagh
4 North Down

Figure 15.1 Outline map of Northern Ireland, district council areas

THE EFFECTS OF THE TROUBLES

The geographic concentration of Troubles-related violence in these areas has meant that people in these communities have had unprecedented levels of experience of the Troubles. *The Cost of the Troubles Study* conducted a survey in Northern Ireland of people's experiences of the Troubles and the effects on their lives (Smyth 1998). This survey found that 28 per cent of residents in the worst affected areas report having their homes attacked and 10 per cent report having their homes destroyed. One young woman interviewed in an earlier study (Smyth 1998) recounted how her family slept in one room because of fear of attack on her home, which is located on an interface. Perhaps the most notorious of such attacks was the petrol bombing of the Quinn family home in Ballymoney in 1998, which led to the deaths of three young children. Another such attack in Portadown in 1999 led to the death of Mrs O'Neill, when she tried to dispose of a blast-bomb thrown through the window of her home. Ongoing non-fatal attacks with stones, bricks and petrol bombs are common-place in areas that border on sectarian interfaces. Responses to a survey conducted across Northern Ireland in areas of 'high', 'medium' and 'low' concentrations of Troubles-related violence[1] suggest that there have been three key dimensions to life in the areas most affected by the Troubles:

1. There is much greater exposure to violence both from paramilitary or-ganisations and the security forces. The high intensity areas regularly reported experience of Troubles-related activity at twice the rate for medium intensity and four times the rate for low intensity areas.

2. People living in high intensity areas have insecurities and fears about being outside their own area and an acute wariness of outsiders, for example, reflected in efforts to conceal where they live under certain circumstances.

3. There is a strong overall pattern of segregation between Nationalist and Unionist communities which is particularly marked in areas where Troubles-related violence has been most intense (Fay et al. 1999b).

Multiple bereavement due to the Troubles, where two or more people within the same family have been killed, is, for example, a phenomenon largely limited to high intensity areas. There has also been heavy militarization of these communities, with high levels of security force and paramilitary activity and high levels of imprisonment for paramilitary activity. Furthermore, it is within these same communities that the worst levels of socio-economic deprivation in Northern Ireland can be found (Fay et al. 1999b).

The scale of the problem

That the violence of the current Troubles has been ongoing for almost thirty years has meant that its effects have been cumulative and the general effect on the population together with the attritional effect on the communities worst affected emerged in other findings of the same survey (Fay et al. 1999b). Whilst some people have been bereaved, others have been traumatized as eye witnesses to violence. Many others have been physically injured and some live with permanent physical disablement and all that this entails for families and carers. There are no reliable statistics on the number of people who have been permanently injured, lost limbs or live with the chronic pain of gunshot wounds.

Those in high intensity areas not only have more severe experiences, but in the survey reported more severe effects of the Troubles than those in the other two kinds of area. Those in the areas with the highest levels of violence also

---

1   'High' is taken to mean a death rate of over seven per thousand population, 'medium' is taken to mean a death rate of under seven per thousand and over one per thousand, and 'low' is taken to mean a death rate of under one per thousand.

reported more difficulties that could be related to psychological traumatization. Over a quarter of respondents in areas of highest intensity reported dreams and nightmares as a result of the Troubles compared to an eighth in the middle intensity areas (Fay *et al.* 1999b).

Preliminary research (Smyth, Hayes and Hayes 1994) has suggested that the emotional effects of violent bereavement do not necessarily disappear with time. Many psychological symptoms may appear, apparently for the first time, years after the trauma. If this is the case, in years to come symptoms related to the trauma of the Troubles may emerge for the first time.

How people cope

Coping mechanisms used in these communities and by individuals may present new sets of problems. Almost a quarter in areas of highest intensity had taken some form of medication for the effects of the Troubles compared to just under an eighth in middle intensity areas. Over 23 per cent had taken medication to help with the effects of the Troubles in high intensity areas compared to almost 12 per cent in medium areas and just over 9 per cent in low intensity areas. Of those who used medication, over 52 per cent of those in high intensity areas were on medication permanently, compared to 9 per cent in medium intensity and 35 per cent for low intensity areas. Those using medication in high intensity areas were likely to be using it for sleep disturbance, sedation or anti-depressive purposes, whereas those in low intensity areas used it for pain control. A further 22 per cent in areas of highest intensity reported an increase in alcohol consumption related to events in the Troubles compared to just over 4 per cent in middle intensity areas. Finally, those in high intensity areas also reported more health problems than respondents in the other two areas.

Availability and use of help

There have been a variety of approaches to the needs of those affected by the Troubles from various disciplines. Most immediate are the medical needs of those injured and from the outset the medical profession both implemented and documented their responses to the situation (see Hadden, Rutherford and Merrit 1978). Less tangible are the social, emotional and 'justice' needs of those affected, and it has been less obvious what the appropriate response to such needs might be. Relatively recently, since the ceasefires of 1994 when the level of violence decreased substantially, there has been a growing interest in the psychological and emotional needs of those affected. Arguably, this examination is only feasible in a situation of decreased violence. Since then, Northern Ireland has seen an increased tendency to apply psychiatric formulations to the situation of those with emotional or psychological distress. It might therefore be assumed that psychologists, psychiatrists and social workers have been the most commonly consulted by those seeking emotional or psychological help with distress or anxiety. In the *Cost of the Troubles Study* of Northern Ireland it was found, overwhelmingly, that those who had direct experience of the Troubles sought help within their own families – from spouses, parents and children (Fay *et al.* 1999b). Given that the Troubles have disproportionately affected certain geographical areas, this has meant that certain communities not only contain the highest level of need but have also had to provide support for their neighbours and kin in coping with Troubles-related crises.

The survey of Northern Ireland conducted by the *Cost of the Troubles Study* divided Northern Ireland into three kinds of areas: those with a Troubles-related death rate of less than 1 per thousand population (low intensity areas); those with a death rate of over 1 but less than 7 per thousand (medium intensity areas); and those with a death rate of more than 7 per thousand (high intensity areas). The survey examined how much Troubles-related stress was reported by respondents. Only 14 per cent of those who scored positively on the Troubles-related stress measure had seen a psychiatrist, 11 per cent had seen a social worker, yet general practitioners were consulted by 49 per cent of those reporting stress. This compared with 20 per cent who had consulted a minister or priest, 25 per cent who had consulted a community worker, and 20 per cent who had gone to some other voluntary organization (Fay *et al.* 1999b).

The survey also looked at two other sub-sets of respondents:

1. Those suffering 'severe impact' of the Troubles. (These reported two of the following experiences as a result of the Troubles: a great deal of distress; violence as part of their lives; feelings of helplessness; strong feelings of rage.)

2. Those suffering 'very severe impact'. (These reported one of the following experiences as a result of the Troubles: completely ruined life; damage to health; loss of loved ones through death; physical damage to self or family.)

The severe impact variable applied to just over 18 per cent of women compared to 16 per cent of men – over a fifth of Catholics, compared to less than a twelfth of Protestants – more than half of those with severe impact lived in areas which had had the highest intensity of violence. Over a quarter of respondents living in such wards met the criteria for 'severe impact', and over 80 per cent of these individuals scored positively on the measure of stress used in the survey. Almost 20 per cent of men and almost 18 per cent of women in the sample met the criteria for 'very severe impact' – just less than a quarter of Catholics in the sample and less than an eighth of Protestants – a third of the population of high intensity areas compared to less than a tenth of the population of least intensity areas.

Table 15.1 summarizes the forms of support received by each group, their respective assessment of that support and the sources from which they had the 'best' help.

It would appear that doctors are the primary source of support within the statutory system with professionals substantially less involved in delivering help. Priests and ministers of religion are also reported as a source of support, presumably because of their role in the rituals associated with death. The role of the family and the community sector emerges as the most important source of support for those affected by the Troubles.

The survey evidence (Fay *et al.* 1999b) also showed that those in high intensity areas sought help outside the family and neighbourhood more frequently than those in other areas. Those in high intensity areas were less likely to seek help from their minister or priest, solicitor, psychiatrist, counsellor or community nurse than those in the other two areas. Over 40 per cent of those who sought help in high intensity wards were unable to find satisfactory help, compared to 29 per cent in medium intensity and 29 per cent in low intensity areas. Over 83 per cent in high intensity wards believed that nothing could help them, compared to just over 4 per cent in medium intensity and just over 12 per cent in low intensity areas.

Smyth, Hayes and Hayes (1994) suggest that people who are living with the long-term effects of the troubles are often isolated, their needs are not explicitly addressed and 'normal' social services are not always appropriate to these needs. Many are unwilling to use existing psychiatric services because of stigma and are reluctant to be seen as mentally ill, given the manner in which they have acquired their difficulties.

Table 15.1 Summary of support for those with severe impact and very severe impact

	Severe impact %	Very severe impact %
Support received from:		
Psychiatrist	15.0	19.8
Clinical psychologist	4.0	4.0
GP/local doctor	50.3	62.2
Community nurse	22.0	24.6
Social worker	12.0	14.0
Minister/priest	19.2	26.1
Community worker	26.8	28.2
Voluntary organization	24.3	23.7
Support regarded as sympathetic and helpful	51.8	60.1
Source of best help:		
Spouse	24.6	24.8
Parents	17.9	16.2
Other close family	17.4	20.3
Close friends	7.2	9.9
Local doctor	2.1	4.1

Source: Fay et al. (1999b)

THE NATURE OF THE VIOLENCE

It is argued that armed conflict has specific and distinct characteristics and consequences and therefore calls for particular kinds of responses from human service workers involved with it. There has been a proliferation of ethnic conflicts globally and increased awareness of racial and ethnic conflicts within nations in the developed world. In many cases where armed conflict occurs, humanitarian assistance is provided by international non-governmental organizations (NGOs) operating and using staff from outside the area of conflict. Perhaps because of the 'low intensity' scale of the conflict, this has not been the pattern in Northern Ireland and those working – or not working – with the consequences of the conflict have largely been indigenous workers.

It is not feasible to view the violence in situations like Northern Ireland as simply a question of the breakdown of law and order, or of those acting out some personal pathology. Rather, the kind of violence seen in Northern Ireland, South Africa and the Middle East – to name three of the world's low intensity conflicts – has a clear political meaning. It is seen as a means of pursuing political ends and thus as justified by the various perpetrators.

Low intensity conflict has something in common with racist, sexist or homophobic violence. The violence of white supremacists, for example, within Britain and the USA, has an explicit political agenda and the violence emanating from them has clear political goals. The situation in Northern Ireland is distinct from that of racist violence in its actual scale. Nonetheless, the issues faced by victims of Northern Ireland's Troubles and the victims of white supremacists are similar in one important respect. Their victimizers are not only unrepentant, but they justify their actions in terms of political goals and are regarded by some as heroes. In Northern Ireland some of those who have served jail sentences have been publicly celebrated on their release from prison. White supremacists in Britain or the USA do not currently enjoy such widespread support, but are similarly celebrated among small extremist racist sub-cultures. This orientation towards the violence has implications for the healing of the victim and the treatment of the perpetrator, which we will explore later.

THE CHALLENGE TO PRACTITIONERS

This legitimization of violence for political ends – in Britain within a small fringe of the society and within Northern Ireland on a more widespread basis – constitutes a major challenge to the legal system, government and the human service practitioners working in the field. It also adds an important dimension to the suffering of victims of such violence and compounds the challenge of 'rehabilitating' the perpetrator. The identification and differentiation of this form of violence have three main implications for human service practitioners.

First, practitioners, as citizens, are part of the general population affected by this kind of violence. Practitioners are subject to traumatization, threat and victimization as citizens and, as such, use the general coping mechanisms applied by the rest of the population. They can also be exposed to risk as a result of carrying out their duties since they often work with those most in need.

Denial

Denial, for example, is widespread among populations living with armed conflict. People living in ongoing violent conflicts will typically say, for example, that things are not as bad as they appear, that everyone is learning to live with the situation, and so on.

Significantly, in both South Africa and Northern Ireland after ceasefires and peace accords were put in place, a sharp increase in numbers of people seeking help for difficulties as a result of the conflict was noted. While the conflict is ongoing, people cannot afford to 'feel' how difficult things are, so they employ denial and stoicism as coping mechanisms. Human service practitioners, as citizens themselves, can be part of this trend, and in their professional practice can overlook or minimize the impact of the conflict on their service users or patients. Recent work in Northern Ireland, for example, has suggested that there may have been under-diagnosing of post traumatic stress disorder (PTSD). The normalization of unduly high levels of anxiety makes this almost inevitable. Nonetheless, it can mean that human need is undetected, under-reported and unmet.

Neutrality

Populations living under conditions of armed conflict are usually highly polarized and divided and nothing (no one) is neutral. The desire to perform professionally in such polarized circumstances and to be seen to deliver services equitably in spite of personal or community loyalties is also a challenge. In the case of Northern Ireland, the issue of neutrality has given rise to a further set of problems in terms of service delivery. In Northern Ireland this 'neutrality' has led to a general lack of public policy in relation to service delivery to those affected by the Troubles and a specific lack of policy in relation to health and social provision to this population. The history of the public bodies in Northern Ireland dates from 1972, when agencies or 'boards' were established to deliver health and social services, housing and education independent of conflict-riven local councils. In the policy climate of the 1970s, this 'neutral' approach to service provision was an attempt to address the issue of equity in service provision. People were treated as if they were all the same and issues of difference were not explicitly addressed. This was compounded by the informal culture within these agencies, which was largely influenced by the denial prevalent in the wider society.

This 'neutrality' on the part of Health and Social Services Boards, the Northern Ireland Housing Executive and the Education and Library Boards was further compounded by the 'normalization' policy of the government. The 'special' nature of the Northern Ireland conflict was ignored in favour of an approach that regarded it as a crisis in criminal law enforcement. This meant that no special policies (beyond emergency law) were deemed necessary to deal with the conflict and the consequences of the Troubles. Policy silence on the Troubles was the result. Staff within public bodies were left without explicit policy or formal guidance and without an official language in which they could discuss or process the impact of the Troubles on their work. Since the ceasefires of 1994, a diminution of the pervasive societal denial about the effects of the Troubles has occurred and it has begun to be possible to re-evaluate the impact of the last 30 years and to begin to develop methods of identifying and dealing with that impact.

Identity management

The second major challenge emerging from situations of armed conflict for human service practitioners is the challenges it poses for the management of identity. Nothing or no one is neutral in the situations of extreme polarization that come with protracted violent conflict and societal division. Whether a worker is Catholic or Protestant in Northern Ireland may not matter so much if he or she is providing certain practical services to those whose lives have been relatively untouched by violence. However, if he or she is tending to the needs of a family bereaved by sectarian killing, then whether the worker is Catholic or Protestant can assume great significance.

The worker's identity cannot only influence their ability to engage the victim's family, but it can also affect the victim's family's ability to trust and engage with the worker. These are not simply matters of psychological identification, cultural sensitivity or competence, or countertransference issues, although these too may be involved. Issues of personal safety of the service user or the worker arise, male workers being particularly vulnerable in Northern Ireland. Talking to the 'other side', for example, can be dangerous if it entails being seen as a traitor in highly segregated and violent community settings.

In such circumstances, service users can sometimes request workers of a particular background. While this may be simply bigotry on the part of the service user, it may also be related to the service user's immediate practical and emotional needs. A person recently violently bereaved by a Republican paramilitary group may fear offending a Catholic worker with their anger, which may be generalized to begin with.

How such issues are managed in practice must be contextually defined and be capable of flexible adjustment to meet new circumstances. The establishment of standards of good practice in such circumstances can only be achieved through good open communication between staff teams on issues of sectarian division. This, in turn, depends on a sophisticated grasp on the part of individual workers of their own history, identity and role and the impact of these on others within and outside their own community.

Practice models

The nature and extent of need, which arises as a result of communal violence or armed conflict, and methods used by human service agencies to meet those needs, is relatively poorly documented. Therefore, practitioners are often in the position of never having been trained to deal with the scale of need facing them. Models of intervention that were developed to deal with, for example, bereavement, in contexts where bereavements usually happen one at a time, can prove inadequate to situations where multiple bereavements within families are a regular occurrence.

Models of intervention adopted by agencies and individual workers often rely on an individual approach to human suffering and need. Such approaches do not equip practitioners to move towards more collective approaches. This in turn can lead to practitioners being overwhelmed by a deluge of individual 'cases'. The development of practice wisdom and practice paradigms which adopt a more communal orientation will not only lessen the stigma associated with seeking and using help, but will lessen the burden on workers and better empower the service users. The 'normal' approaches to the provision of health and social services in peacetime or in times of consensus may not always be appropriate to the provision of such services in times of violent division. This calls for the development of community-based practice that emphasizes partnership with local communities and the provision of support to communities to foster and develop local community coping strategies such as social support networks and self-help initiatives. This approach is not only more empowering of local communities, but also more likely to deliver non-stigmatizing support to a wider section of the population. Furthermore, it allows for a more holistic approach to needs and services at the point of delivery.

The *Cost of the Troubles Study* found myriad problems facing those affected by the Troubles. Many reported isolation, even within their own families, where each family member was coping with his or her own difficulties and often there was an unspoken rule of silence surrounding the violent event. This meant that those interviewed in the study often reported speaking for the first time about certain aspects of their experiences – some over 20 years ago – to researchers. Some live with strong feelings of injustice and resultant anger at the failure of the justice system to apprehend the perpetrator, and in cases where the perpetrator is apprehended at the leniency of the punishment. For some who have been bereaved or injured by the security forces, these feelings are complicated by a lack of trust in the authorities to see their loss in the same light as other losses and treat it accordingly. Lack of trust of authority is found on a more widespread basis however. Faith in the authorities to deliver justice, practical or emotional services, with the possible exception of the medical emergency services, has been one of the casualties of the Troubles.

Some others who have been bereaved or injured, notably those who have not been included in public concern about victims, feel the lack of acknowledgement of their position. This can be particularly acute at times when public attention focuses on events with multiple casualties, such as the Omagh bomb of 1998. For those who perhaps lost a family member in an incident where their death was the only fatality, it can be hard to see the concentration of concern, attention and resources on certain victims while others have been substantially ignored. Anger at past neglect can also be a feature. Such anger can be seen among some of the victims organizations formed since the Good Friday Agreement, who have concentrated on campaigning on the political rather than on the humanitarian issues. Fear about further victimization and a corresponding lack of trust of 'outsiders' can be a consequence of violent attack in the Troubles, and has been a routine part of life for several decades for those in the security forces and for those living on interfaces and enclaves. More directly, many of those caught in bomb explosions or shooting incidents report phobias and anxiety-related conditions, particularly associated with places or events associated with the incident. Agoraphobia is not uncommon and avoidance of places or people associated with the event is a 'coping mechanism' employed by some people. Many of those bereaved or injured reported depression, and sleep disturbance was also commonly reported. Children and young people living in families affected by the Troubles often have to grow up quickly and perform adult functions in the family from an early age. For those injured, particularly those injured by gunshot wounds, the management of chronic pain and acquiring appropriate prostheses within the public health system can be difficult. Methods of stress management employed at an individual and community level can be a further cause of difficulty. Alcohol and drug use, including the use of prescribed medication, can lead to problems of misuse and dependence. Where disablement has resulted, problems associated with the loss of career or ability to work include those associated with reduced financial resources. Financial problems are also commonly experienced by families who lose a breadwinner through death or injury. The government operates a system of providing compensation for criminal injuries and criminal damages, but there have been manifest inequities and delays in operating this system, which was reviewed by the government in 1999. A further set of financial difficulties associated with loss of jobs and assets is faced by those owning or working for businesses that have been damaged or destroyed, and who may fail to qualify for compensation or have their compensation delayed. Many families, particularly those in the interface communities in north and west Belfast, experienced the loss of their homes and displacement has been an ongoing feature of the Troubles since the early 1970s, when Northern Ireland saw the largest movement of population in Europe since World War II. Finally, all of this has occurred in an atmosphere where the divided nature of the society has meant that these difficulties have not always been openly addressed or acknowledged.

Service providers

Whilst the statutory services have been involved in providing some of the more practical and medical services to those affected by the Troubles, it has been from within the voluntary sector that the bulk of services has been provided for those individuals and communities worst affected. Since 1993, there has been a steady growth in the number of organizations offering support and self-help facilities to those bereaved and injured in the Troubles. WAVE, an organization based in North Belfast but with branches throughout Northern Ireland, provides a range of services, significantly a home visiting service where volunteers who have direct personal experience of the Troubles will conduct home visits to those requesting them. WAVE (originally Widows Against Violence Empower, but reduced to WAVE after an expansion of membership) is perhaps the largest dedicated service offered to those affected by the Troubles. The Shankill Stress and Trauma Group offers a range of services to the Greater Shankill area. Smaller local groups such as Survivors of Trauma in the Ardoyne, Cunamh in Derry Londonderry, The Victims and Survivors Trust in West Belfast, The Cross Group across Northern Ireland, or Omagh Support and Self Help Group provide help and support of various kinds for members locally. Some groups, such as Relatives of the Disappeared, Justice for the Forgotten or the Bloody Sunday Trust have been campaigning for specific outcomes – the return of their relatives' bodies, a reopening of the investigation into the Dublin Monaghan bombs, or a public inquiry into Bloody Sunday, alongside offering support. Other groups take on an almost exclusive campaigning role, such as

FAIT (Families Against Intimidation and Terror, who campaign against punishment beatings). Other organizations offer services and support to particular occupational groups, such as the Disabled Police Officer's Association or the Prison Officer's Association.

There is also a plethora of organizations offering support and help to prisoners and ex-prisoners. From the Good Friday Agreement onwards a new wave of groups developed, mostly in the border regions, with rather narrower remits, such as Northern Ireland Terrorist Victims Together, or Families Acting for Innocent Relatives. These groups were born out of a frustration with the political developments of the time, the early release of paramilitary prisoners and the apparent lack of justice and concern for those bereaved or injured.

Some of the larger voluntary organizations such as Victim Support have shown an interest since the beginning of the peace process in developing services for those affected by the Troubles. Prior to this, many of the organizations in the voluntary sector followed the pattern set in the statutory sector of an absence of explicit acknowledgement of Troubles-related needs, undoubtedly related to their dependence on statutory funding. A survey of groups offering dedicated services in the voluntary sector to those affected by the Troubles showed large funding and resource discrepancies between them and other groups in the voluntary sector. Perhaps because of their relative newness, they were less well funded, and the average length of time for which they had secure funding was three to four months (Smyth and Kelly 1999). Within the statutory sector, a new Family Trauma Centre opened in Belfast in 1998, in the wake of the Good Friday Agreement. An earlier inspection of services provided by social workers to those affected by the Troubles concluded that the relationship between communities and social services were not conducive to communities seeking help from social services, because of the punitive manner in which the role of social services was perceived (Social Services Inspectorate 1997). Where social workers are involved with those affected by the Troubles, the effects of the Troubles may not be a focus for their work and, in many instances, resources dictate that only statutory involvements with clients are honoured. There has been no specific policy or provision beyond the compensation schemes for those affected by the Troubles. Earlier, it was pointed out that relatively few people sought help from mental health professionals. Of those who do, substantial numbers act in order to obtain forensic psychiatric reports in pursuance of a claim for compensation. The stigma of mental illness precludes all but those in the most desperate situations from availing of mental health services. There has been a growing counselling sector, some of which is in the voluntary sector and is heavily over-subscribed. Some of this provision is also in the private sector, which is largely beyond the reach of those in most need, who tend also to live in the most deprived areas.

Provision of services

This list of needs and the relative paucity of services can seem overwhelming and human service agencies and workers can experience powerlessness in the face of such a wide range of effects and needs. For the sake of policy generation, and division of responsibility, it is suggested that the list of services can be organised into three sub-divisions:

- provisions for issues of justice and human rights
- provisions for humanitarian needs
- provisions for public acknowledgement.

Even though any agency working in the field should be aware of range of issues, no one agency or profession can be responsible for all of them. The needs which are addressed by human service workers are the humanitarian needs. The work of providing humanitarian assistance is also impacted by the other two areas of need. However, it can be helpful formally to clarify where the primary responsibility for each set of needs lies. In Northern Ireland, issues relating to justice lie with the judiciary, police, courts, the legal profession and the human rights community. Issues of public acknowledgement lie with the government, politicians, the media, and the arts and culture sector. There is considerable overlap and awareness of other areas of concern and an ability to negotiate the thorny questions they pose is crucial in planning and delivering humanitarian services. However, the primary responsibility of the human service worker is in providing for the shelter, health, nutrition, education, and emotional well-being of those affected by armed conflict.

Differentiation and assessment of need

The provision of humanitarian assistance and support in times of violent community division has been the domain of health and social services and housing services. Yet these services can only serve a part of the need. The desire for acknowledgement and for justice exists alongside more practical and concrete requirements and can influence the way humanitarian needs are met. Felt needs for justice and acknowledgement can pose dilemmas; for example, in mental health services people may yearn for justice yet there may be little chance of achieving it, in the context of, say, the early release of prisoners or immunity from prosecution. Yet the desire for acknowledgement and justice co-exists alongside the need for shelter, food, medical attention, mental health provision, social support and so on. The need for justice involves feelings of perpetrators not being punished, deaths and injuries not being investigated, certain individuals and groups appearing to be above the law. The need for acknowledgement involves certain people feeling that their suffering has been forgotten in favour of the suffering of others. They may feel that their voices have not been heard or their stories told and that history has yet to be written in a way that includes their experience.

Emotional impact of the violence of division

The distinction between loss and injury due to wilful human agency (such as war, genocide) and so-called 'natural' disasters, accidents or other forms of violence can be significant in terms of how this affects the healing and recovery process of victims.

Victims of sectarian (or racial) violence are targeted because of their affiliations with a national or racial group, and there is no ostensible personal gain to the perpetrator. Sectarian or racial violence is the exercise of dominance, the 'proof' of superiority and the terrorizing of the rest of the national or racial group. Some victims struggle with the painful task of coming to terms with this aspect of their victimhood and awareness of the generalized hatred that is targeted at them by people who do not know them can be accentuated. Victims may struggle with strong feelings of anger and a desire for revenge, may find it difficult not to reciprocate hatred, and yet wish to avoid becoming embittered.

At this point, human service workers who can explicitly address these issues from a standpoint outside the victims' own community circumstances can offer some assistance with such struggles, in terms of emotional support and an observer's perspective.

Issues in work with perpetrators

The challenge of working with perpetrators of such violence is faced by many working in the justice system. Those who have been apprehended may require court reports and those convicted may require services while in custody. There are substantial ethical difficulties in 'rehabilitating' someone who espouses a set of political beliefs which, in their view, justifies their illegal actions. A difficult interface between therapeutic work and political re-education or indoctrination is manifest. For some of these reasons, the Probation Service in Northern Ireland decided at quite an early stage in the current Troubles not to work with politically motivated prisoners unless the prisoner specifically requested such work (Chapman and Pinkerton 1987). The issues of reconciliation, forgiveness, remorse and how responsibility for the suffering of others is managed also arise in work with this population. Currently in Northern Ireland, this field of work is highly emotionally loaded and some ex-paramilitaries and prisoners, for example, describe themselves as victims of the Troubles. At a broader societal level and at an individual level these claims often have legitimacy, in that many of those who have taken up arms in Northern Ireland have been bereaved or otherwise injured by the Troubles. While such experience entitles the sufferer to sympathy and services, when the sufferer is a former or current paramilitary such claims are often perceived as a strategy for avoiding responsibility for the harm they did to others in pursuit of their political goals. At historical moments when reconciliation and compromise are called for in order to achieve peace, it can be difficult to balance these considerations.

Impact on practitioners

Violence is always a difficult phenomenon with which to work, particularly as the level of threat to the worker increases. Working in environments in which violence is prevalent entails coping with violence on an ongoing basis, often in the context of altered expectations of life, lowered life expectancy and denial or silence about the risk and damage caused by violence. Working in environments in which violence is ongoing requires careful supervision of workers and regular debriefing. It could be argued that workers should also get regular professional exposure to less violent environments, in order to avoid the danger of habituation to the violent context. With habituation comes the danger of burn-out and erosion of professional and human rights standards. However, in the case of societal violence the removal of workers to less violent settings is not usually feasible on any significant scale. Nonetheless, workers ideally should not remain in certain high intensity environments for long periods, and certainly they should not remain in such environments without proper professional support, debriefing and in-service training on stress management and related issues. Critical incident debriefing should also be provided after such incidents occur on an ongoing basis.

THE DYNAMIC OF WORKING WITH VICTIMS

Very powerful almost primal emotions are elicited by contact with victims of violence, particularly those who have suffered terribly. When there is a political dimension to their victimhood, there may be many complicating factors associated with the status of victim.

The worker must struggle with his/her own feelings. They may feel powerful emotions of shame at what the victim has suffered at the hands of the worker's own community and guilt at the consequences for the victim. The worker in such circumstances can overcompensate in their practice in some way for these feelings, perhaps by 'smothering' the victim, or overworking the case. The worker, unless carefully and sensitively supervised in a way that allows identity issues to be explored, may become overinvolved or wrongly assess a case in such circumstances. In such situations, workers may begin to chronically overwork, fail to take their holidays or time off for extra hours worked. They may find their topics of conversation becoming more and more restricted to their work. They may find themselves experiencing rage at certain government policy, at certain politicians, at the ignorance of others of the plight of their clients. Some workers who are involved in intensive direct contact with victims may find themselves suffering from vicarious traumatization, involving sleep disturbance, heightened anxiety and other trauma-related symptoms.

Those working with perpetrators face other issues. The often powerful desire of the perpetrators to avoid facing the guilt of the consequences of their actions creates a force field in which workers may find themselves caught. Again, supervision, debriefing and 'time-out' in another setting can be useful strategies to manage these features of the work.

Victim identity

In addition to coping with the specific situation of their own victimization, the victim may become an icon of grievance for their entire community. The wrong done to them may come to symbolize the historic, multiple wrongs perpetrated against an entire religion, sexual orientation, race or nationality. The victim's identity can become bound up with the communal grievance. In such circumstances, some become well known and can be laden with expectations from their own community.

Sympathy and a certain latitude in terms of expectations of one's feelings, behaviour or responsibilities are concomitants of victimhood. Arguably, victim identity should ideally only be a temporary position and, with successful coping skills, the victim transforms him/herself into a survivor. However, in some cases, where for example disablement has resulted from the violence, living circumstances, health and identity are significantly and permanently altered. The intersection between the 'justice' paradigm and that of the 'humanitarian' can appear to be in direct conflict with one another. The victim, for example, says that he or she cannot rest easy until the perpetrator is brought to justice. The worker knows, perhaps, that this quite understandable desire for justice is unlikely to be fulfilled, given low detection rates or perhaps because of the power position of the perpetrator. Does the worker confront these issues in therapeutic work, and if s/he does, is s/he undermining the standards of justice that citizens are led to expect and uphold? How does the worker deal with the person whose son died at the hands of a paramilitary group, or in police custody, and who is suffering from symptoms of severe stress and yet is proposing to embark on the herculean task of seeking justice for the son's death? If the context is one where such a task faces little prospects of success, negotiating the interface between the therapeutic and other issues provides a range of dilemmas for the practitioner.

Media attention

Some people who have had no support or attention of any other kind to assist them in coming to terms with what has happened can experience media attention as positive and affirming. A media profile – however short lived – can impact on the identity of the victim in both positive and negative ways. Those who have no experience of the media can find themselves feeling exploited and abused by media representations of their circumstances. Others can use the media effectively to highlight concerns about justice or to redress a lack of public acknowledgement of their situation.

KEY POINTS FOR GOOD PRACTICE

- Workers should maintain a high level of consciousness of their own identity and history and maintain an awareness of their significance in terms of their meaning to and impact on colleagues and service users.

- Recognition of the needs and vulnerabilities of staff who may be at particular risk of violence is paramount, and issues of concern addressed openly and explicitly with the worker/s concerned.

- Staff who may be 'outnumbered' in particular contexts may require additional support and a validation by those in authority of their rights and position.

- The strong emotions aroused in workers within a climate of ongoing violence must be recognized and addressed in supervision, and vigilance should be maintained for evidence of such emotions 'contaminating' professional judgements.

- Everyone who has been affected by armed conflict should be treated equally in terms of their entitlement to concern and services; equivalent losses such as bereavement were equal to each other and there should be no hierarchy, nor should people be ranked into the more deserving and the less deserving.

- The delivery of services and the entitlement to services should be determined by an assessment of the impact of armed conflict on individuals, families or communities, and an assessment of need is the only viable way of allocating resources.

- Provision should be placed in the context of individual and agency responsibility for the impact of the Troubles, and our collective responsibility as citizens to contribute to the rebuilding of our lives together.

- Any provision must recognize and address the existence of sectarianism (or racism) as a pervasive influence in the society, and build in explicit ways of addressing it in any provision. All staff and workers are encouraged to acknowledge their own prejudices and the limitations of their own experience.
- Provision should be based on an understanding and respect for the needs for justice and acknowledgement, yet any provision must be based on a realistic appraisal of justice and its attainability.
- Any provision is centrally concerned with the prevalence and acceptability of violence in the present and the danger this poses for the future, and that work to undermine the acceptability of violence is engaged in. The de-legitimizing of violence and the restoration of a culture of compassion is a priority.
- Any provision should recognize priority sub-groups in the population, such as children, interfaces or communities where the impact of the Troubles has been severe.
- The depletion of the resources of communities particularly affected is acknowledged – that some communities have had to provide a lot more social support than others and have had to endure quantum amounts of intense suffering in comparison to other communities.
- The danger of raising unrealistic expectations must be acknowledged and any strategy must avoid further disappointing or hurting people who have already been hurt and disappointed enough.
- Staff require good information from research about the impact of armed conflict, in order to know what to look for and to begin to reassess their work.
- Existing experience of staff of handling Troubles-related issues should be harvested, documented and evaluated and, where appropriate, used to formalize practice standards and value existing practice wisdom.
- Addressing the impact of the Troubles has implications for basic professional training, for post-qualifying and in-service training for all staff, including ancillary staff.

METHODS OF PROVISION

- The principles of community development and the acknowledgement of the key role played by families and communities in providing social support to those affected by armed conflict should underpin all provision.
- Any provision must become more future oriented and concentrate on the implications for the future and work shifting the emphasis to a concern for the future rather than concentrating on the past.
- All provision has to be stay practical and feasible in the light of resource limitations.

- Existing practice in this field could be characterized as 'firefighting' and it is necessary to move away from that approach in post-conflict situations into one which recognizes the long term work to be done and makes provision for this work.

- One of the most powerful ways that this work can be done is by listening to people's experiences and encouraging people to articulate their experiences (but we must be able to bear what we hear with patience and compassion).

RECOMMENDATIONS

- Supervision and regular individual and group debriefing for staff working in environments in which violence has become normalized are essential to the maintenance of standards of practice and the exercise of due care for staff welfare.

- In situations of continued risk, care must be taken to ensure that human service practitioners are not under-reporting or skewing their assessments of need as a result of being part of a widespread use of denial as a 'coping mechanism'.

- Clear differentiation between the humanitarian needs of victims, their desire for justice and the quest of some for public recognition must be explicitly addressed and differentiated in policy and practice, and the roles of staff clarified in relation to these three areas of need.

REFERENCES

Chapman, T. and Pinkerton, J. (1987) 'Contradiction in the Community.' *Probation Journal*, 13–16.

Fay, M.T., Morrissey, M. and Smyth, M. (1999a) *Northern Ireland's Troubles: The Human Costs.* London: Pluto.

Fay, M.T., Morrissey, M., Smyth, M. and Wong, T. (1999b) *Report on the Northern Ireland Survey: The Cost of the Troubles Study.* Derry: INCORE/United Nations University/University of Ulster.

Hadden, W.A., Rutherford, W.H. and Merrit, J.D. (1978) 'The injuries of terrorist bombing: a study of 1532 consecutive patients.' *British Journal of Surgery 65*, 525–531.

Northern Ireland Office (1999)

Smyth, M. (1998) *Half the Battle: Understanding the Impact of the Troubles on Children and Young People.* Derry: INCORE/University of Ulster.

Smyth, M., Hayes, E. and Hayes, P. (1994) 'Post traumatic stress and victims of violence in Northern Ireland: the case of the families of the Bloody Sunday victims.' Paper presented at the Centre for the Study of Conflict/NI Association for Mental Health Conference on Violence and Mental Health, Queen's University, September.

Smyth, M. and Kelly, G. (1999) *A Survey of Voluntary Groups Providing Service to Those Bereaved and Injured in the Troubles.* Belfast: HMSO.

Social Services Inspectorate (1997) *A Developmental Project to Assess the Services Provided to those Affected by the Troubles in Northern Ireland.* Belfast: SSI/HMSO.

The Contributors

Ann Cattanach is a Dramatherapist and Play Therapist. She is Course Director for the Play Therapy programmes at Roehampton Institute, London. The programmes include a Graduate diploma/MA, PhD research programme and a Diploma in Supervision in Play Therapy. She works as a therapist with children for the Community NHS Trust in Harrow and as a consultant/therapist for a number of social services departments.

Cary L. Cooper is currently BUPA Professor of Organizational Psychology and Health in the Manchester School of Management and Pro-Vice-Chancellor (External Activities) of the University of Manchester Institute of Science and Technology (UMIST). He is the author of over 80 books (on occupational stress, women at work and industrial psychology), has written over 300 scholarly articles for academic journals and is a frequent contributor to national newspapers, TV and radio. He is currently founding editor of the *Journal of Organizational Behaviours*, co-editor of the medical journal *Stress Medicine*, Co-editor of the *International Journal of Management Review* and President of the British Academy of Management.

Kim Etherington is a BAC accredited counsellor, an accredited supervisor, a trainer and researcher. She works part-time at the University of Bristol where she co-ordinates and tutors on the post-graduate Diploma in Counselling in Primary Care/Health Settings; she also co-ordinates and tutors the MSc in Counselling (Research Methods and Dissertation). Kim undertook a study of adult male survivors of childhood sexual abuse for which she was awarded a PhD in 1995. She is the author of *Adult Male Survivors of Childhood Sexual Abuse* (Pavilion Pubs, UK) and has just completed *Narrative Approaches to Working With Adult Male Survivors: The Clients', the Counsellor's and The Researcher's Story* (Jessica Kingsley Publishers 2000). She is also a proud grandmother.

Brenda Fearns is Detective Inspector, Knowsley Family Support Unit, Merseyside Police. Prior to taking up this post she worked as a police trainer within a Home Office CID Training School and most notably was part of a small team of police officers who wrote the first Home Office Investigative Interviewing Training Package. Brenda is Treasurer for the national organization PAVA (Practitioner Alliance Against Abuse of Vulnerable Adults) and Chair of the Merseyside network.

Helge Hoel is a Research Associate at the Manchester School of Management (UMIST). He is currently working with Professor Cary Cooper on the first nationwide survey of workplace bullying across industrial sectors to be undertaken in the UK. After leaving the position of training manager at the SAS Scandinavia Hotel, Oslo, he came to Britain in 1991 to study Human Resource Management and Industrial Relations. Following the completion of his Master degree, he held consecutive posts at the University of Salford, where he was involved with research and teaching in the field of occupational health and safety. He also lectured on a part-time basis at the Manchester Metropolitan University in Human Resource Management.

Robert Johnson successfully de-toxed after becoming heavily dependent on tranquillizers and sleeping pills for over 14 years. The trauma of withdrawal from these drugs encouraged his decision to work in the field of addiction. After studying for five years at various college and university settings, he eventually set up a successful community drug project with his work being nationally recognized. The project encourages a holistic approach of complementary therapy and support to drug users whose lives have often been affected by abuse. The impact of historic abuse and its close links with adult drug dependency is of special interest to Robert, who is also active in research into the topic.

Hazel Kemshall is currently Senior Research Fellow at the Department of Social and Community Studies at DeMontfort University. She was previously a senior lecturer at Birmingham University and has practice and management experience with the Probation Service. She has written extensively on risk assessment and risk management and has recently completed research for the Economic and Social Research Council.

Andrew Mellor is a teacher with 25 years classroom experience. He conducted the first government sponsored research on bullying in Scotland and has written widely on the topics of anti-bullying, discipline and child protection. As Scottish Anti-Bullying Development Officer from 1993 to 1995, he encouraged and helped schools to develop anti-bullying policies. In April 1999 he left his post as Principal Teacher of Guidance at Dalry School in Galloway to become Manager of the Anti-Bullying Network, which is a Scottish Executive funded service based at the University of Edinburgh.

John O'Connor is presently serving a life sentence. He is currently seeking to have his conviction reduced to manslaughter.

Jonathan Parker BA (Hons), MA, CQSW is a Lecturer in Social Work and Director of the Family Assessment and Support Unit at the University of Hull. He is a social worker and cognitive-behavioural psychotherapist by profession and has worked with adults on an Employee Assistance Programme. His main areas of interest and research concern older adults with dementia and interpersonal violence.

Jacki Pritchard is a qualified social worker who has worked as a practitioner and manager in both fieldwork and hospital settings. She is currently working as a trainer, consultant and researcher focusing on abuse, risk and violence. She is also Co-Chair of the national organization PAVA (Practitioner Alliance Against Abuse of Vulnerable Adults).

Peter Randall, BSc, MSc, PhD, MAE, ABPsS, Cpsychol is a psychologist in private practice, often engaged in legal proceedings concerning harassment in the workplace. He is also a Senior Research Fellow at the University of Hull where he has been researching inter-personal aggression since his first degree there 30 years ago. His study of adult bullying began five years ago and was assisted by involvement in Employee Assistance Programmes. Bullying is one of the most frequent causes of self-referrals to such programmes and often leads to reviews of workplace culture and personal harassment policies. He is the author of *Adult Bullying: Perpetrators and Victims* (Routledge 1997), which has since been translated into Japanese. A further book on the psycho-legal assessment of bully–victim dyads is at the planning stage.

Ian Robbins is currently a Consultant Clinical Psychologist and Co-Director of the Traumatic Stress Service at St George's Hospital, London. This is a specialist centre which works primarily but not exclusively with victims of violence. Within this centre he has a specialist interest in war trauma. Prior to this he has held a number of clinical and academic psychology posts. During the Gulf War he served as a Royal Army Medical Corps Officer. He has also worked in a number of refugee health programmes in East Africa and continues to offer consultancy to aid agencies.

Marie Smyth is a Research Fellow at INCORE (University of Ulster and The United Nations University) and also teaches at Smith College in Massachusetts. She has researched and written on issues such as the social, economic and political effects of violence and low intensity conflict, segregation, mixed marriage, women's roles, and life in enclaves. She is also licensed to practice individual, couples and family therapy in Massachusetts, and holds a CQSW in the UK. She initiated and directed a two-and-a-half-year research project on the effect of political violence in Northern Ireland on the general population – *The Cost of the Troubles Study* – which provided the baseline data for Sir Kenneth Bloomfield's report to government on the situation of those bereaved and injured by the Troubles in Northern Ireland. She also contributed to the equivalent report produced by the Irish Government's Victim's Commission.

Barbara Tudor was appointed as Mediator in the Coventry division of West Midlands Probation Service in one of the 1985 Home Office Reparation Scheme Pilots and became Manager of that unit in 1987 and Manager of the Coventry Unit for Community Safety (incorporating Mediation/Reparation Services) in 1993. She moved to Birmingham in 1996 as the County Victim/Offender Development Officer with a remit to develop, train, monitor and evaluate the whole of the work undertaken with victims within WMPS. She has personal experience of some 3,500 mediation (victim/offender) cases, mostly within the Criminal Justice System from the stage of caution through Youth, Magistrates, Crown and Civil courts to the rehabilitation into the community of offenders released from custody, and some community mediation cases undertaken for crime prevention/community safety purposes.

Paul Tyrer is a research associate in the department of sociology at the University of Manchester. He is currently working four days a week for the Violence, Sexuality and Space project, part of the ESRC's Violence Research Programme, which is considering the relationship between safety, sexual identity and space in cities. On his day off he has been working for the Institute of Education at the University of London, preparing the groundwork for the launch of the National Healthy Schools Scheme. More recently, he has been a research consultant on Urbis, Manchester's millennial exhibition space about the modern city. Although Paul's career has been mainly focused around health, education and sexual politics, he was lucky enough to take three years out in the mid-1990s to do a PhD in literature and film at the University of Sheffield.

Sandra Walklate is Professor of Sociology at Manchester Metropolitan University. She is author of *Victimology: The Victim and the Criminal Justice Process* (Unwin Hyman 1989), *Gender and Crime* (Harvester Wheatsheaf 1995), *Understanding Criminology* (Open University 1998), co-author with R. Mawby of *Critical Victimology* (Sage 1994), and *Zero Tolerance or Community Tolerance? Managing Crime in High Crime Areas* (Ashgate 1999) with K. Evans. As well as being an academic, she has worked extensively in the training and development of victim support workers and police officers on victim-related issues.

David Webb is a probation officer who works with male lifers in the early years of their sentence. He has previously worked in a community supervision team and in a through-care team, and took up his current post in January 1998. His MA dissertation on Prison Writing Programmes was published as a Probation Monograph in 1995.

Brian Williams is Senior Research Fellow in the Community and Criminal Justice Studies Unit at De Montfort University, Leicester, having previously worked as a probation officer. His previous publications include *Working with Victims of Crime* (Jessica Kingsley Publishers 1999) and *Counselling in Criminal Justice* (Open University 1996).

Judy Woodfield has more than 22 years service with the West Midlands Police Force. She has done all sorts of jobs in the force (e.g. been the local beat person, been involved in accident investigation inquiries), both in the inner city, rural areas and even the airport. In 1987 she became involved in Child Protection and since 1997 she has worked in the Domestic Violence Unit which includes work with vulnerable adults. She has been involved in the working group which has been further developing and promoting The Vulnerable Adults Policy in the Solihull area. She is also an executive committee member of PAVA (Practitioner Alliance Against Abuse of Vulnerable Adults).

Subject Index

Author index